D0115815

WARTIME BASKETBALL

WARTIME BASKETBALL

The Emergence of a National Sport during World War II

DOUGLAS STARK

UNIVERSITY OF NEBRASKA PRESS

Lincoln and London

© 2016 by Douglas Stark

All rights reserved
Manufactured in the United States of America

∞

Library of Congress Cataloging-in-Publication Data
Names: Stark, Douglas (Douglas Andrew), 1972–
Title: Wartime basketball: the emergence of a national
sport during World War II / Douglas Stark.
Description: Lincoln: University of Nebraska Press,
[2016] | Includes bibliographical references and index.
Identifiers: LCCN 2015033878
ISBN 9780803245280 (cloth: alk. paper)
ISBN 9780803286917 (epub)
ISBN 9780803286924 (mobi)
ISBN 9780803286931 (pdf)
Subjects: LCSH: Basketball—United States—History—
20th century. | Basketball and war—United States.
World War, 1939–1945—United States.
Classification: LCC GV885.7 .S77 2016 | DDC
796.323097309044—dc23 LC record available at
http://lccn.loc.gov/2015033878

Designed and set in Cambria by Rachel Gould.

For Bennett and Alexis
Two big basketball fans

Rally to our nation's colors
For the glory of our land
To ensure our peace and freedom
Hearken to our chief's command

Never shirk and never weary
To defend our hearth and home
We hold dear each hill and valley
Lakes and oceans white with foam

Never will we knuckle under
Any tyrant's bold demand
We'll defend our country's honor
Every inch of our land

Woe to him who courts the favor
Of that small minority
Who would sell us down the river
Threaten our security

There are some, I know not wherefore
They are men who would destroy
Our democracy and freedom
Which we cherish and enjoy

We must stand at once united
Against this foe wherever he be
Ensure our everlasting freedom
For us and our posterity

—JULIUS STARK, OCTOBER 1941

CONTENTS

ILLUSTRATIONS

PROLOGUE

While I was writing my first book, *The SPHAS: The Life and Times of Basketball's Greatest Jewish Team*, I devoted a chapter to basketball and war. The chapter focused on how World War II impacted basketball: leagues were forced to contract, players had to split their time between military service and basketball, and service basketball emerged on bases across the country. It was a short chapter, brief in its content, and only hinting at a larger story waiting to be told. It did not even mention the integration of professional basketball, which occurred during the war years. As I came to learn, nothing substantial had been written about this period of basketball history during World War II. It was largely undocumented.

In contrast, much has been written about baseball and football during World War II. Recent books have captured this period in baseball and football history, showing the sacrifices these sports made to support the war effort and how the war impacted those sports. Movie reels contain footage of baseball stars Hank Greenberg and Joe DiMaggio enlisting in the military. But basketball was a much different sport. Although a distinctly American game founded in 1891 in Springfield, Massachusetts, basketball was still regional on the eve of World War II, its popularity confined to certain parts of the country. Its coverage in newspapers was not nearly as comprehensive or extensive as those other sports. Sometimes away games for professional teams were not covered in the newspapers at all. Sometimes only a box score survived. In some instances, only a score made its way into the sports pages.

Basketball did not have the same advocates as baseball. President Franklin D. Roosevelt wrote his famous "Green Light" letter saying baseball should be played during the war, but he did not advocate for basketball. Baseball writers Wendell Smith and Sam Lacy used their positions as influential African American writers to urge Major League Baseball to integrate, something the sport finally did in 1947 with Jackie Robinson. Basketball had no journalist—black or white—championing for the game's integration. Basketball was on its own.

Yet World War II greatly impacted basketball. The style of play changed. It became more up-tempo, which increased scoring. It also acquired a more national character. In the 1930s with college basketball doubleheaders, teams from different parts of the country faced each other in highly anticipated match-ups in New York, Philadelphia, and Chicago, but military basketball forced players from different parts of the country to play *with* each other. As this happened, a more national game emerged, eliminating the regional differences in the game and creating a game everyone could recognize. Finally, professional basketball integrated five years before Jackie Robinson broke the color barrier in baseball. Unlike baseball, basketball integrated with less fanfare and problems. It just happened. The success of basketball during World War II also led to the formation of the Basketball Association of America (BAA) and the ensuing success of basketball in the post–World War II era.

Basketball today is a global sport, played in all countries by people of all abilities. Its success today can be traced to World War II and how the game changed for the better during that time. This is a story that deserves to be told alongside the chronicles of other professional sports.

ACKNOWLEDGMENTS

World War II is a period in our history that continues to fascinate us more than seventy-five years later. This has been particularly true regarding sports during the war years. For me, this interest in basketball's place in World War II developed while I was working on my first book, *The SPHAS: The Life and Times of Basketball's Greatest Jewish Team*. I became intrigued with the role that service basketball played and how many of the players and coaches in the postwar years had their start during the war. As I researched this book, I came to appreciate not only the sacrifices everyone made but also how the game was still developing and the impact these players had on the game's growth and development. Today's game is a direct descendent of the game during the war years. My research shed light on an important time in the game's history, one that is largely ignored. It was a wonderful journey of discovery.

This journey could not have been completed without the help of Bill Himmelman, one of the most generous people I have met, always willing to share his time and knowledge. As I came to learn, it is never too late to call Bill with a question. His knowledge of the game's early history and his research into the players and their playing statistics are unmatched and a tremendous resource for those researching basketball prior to the founding of the NBA. I owe him thanks for all his assistance and most importantly his patience.

Additional individuals were especially helpful. David Smith, former librarian at the New York Public Library, continued tracking down footnotes and sources. Matt Zeysing, historian at the Naismith Memorial Basketball Hall of Fame, opened the Hall of Fame's archives on many a Saturday morning for me to pull items for researching. Robin Deutsch spent countless hours helping to revamp my Web site. Seymour Smith, former sportswriter and editor at the *Baltimore Sun*, who read many drafts of the manuscript, also offered his recollections of knowing those players, including Buddy Jeannette. Josh Kantor and Suanna Crowley were unstinting in their moral support throughout the long journey. To all of them, many thanks.

Many repositories proved helpful in my research, including the Great Lakes Naval Museum, the National Archives and Record Administration, the University of Notre Dame Library, the Wisconsin Veterans Museum, and the Worcester Historical Society. Special thanks to the staff of the Interlibrary Loan Department at the Widener Library at Harvard University for their assistance in locating microfilm, and to Walt Wilson, an independent researcher who confirmed many citations from the *Chicago Herald American* at the Chicago History Museum. I greatly appreciate the help in scanning images that Scott Glowa and Troy Gowen offered.

Photographs for this book were generously provided by Bill Himmelman, the Naismith Memorial Basketball Hall of Fame, and New York University.

I am indebted to Rob Taylor, my editor at the University of Nebraska Press, who championed this book from our first conversation and carefully guided it to its finished product.

As always, family plays an important role—Mom, Dad, Jim, Sunday, Nick, and Rachel—deserve my heartfelt thanks for their continued support.

Although too young now to appreciate this book, Bennett and Alexis have certainly been in my thoughts during its creation. I hope they will grow up to love basketball and appreciate a good story.

WARTIME BASKETBALL

INTRODUCTION

A New Game

You fellows have put me in a class with Abner Doubleday, who invented baseball. If basketball filled a need in the winter sports picture, I am glad, but I had nothing to do with making it grow. Honestly, I never believed that it ever would be played outside of that gymnasium in Springfield. —JAMES NAISMITH

The year 1941 was a milestone for the game of basketball. It marked the fiftieth anniversary of the game. Celebrations were scheduled around the country with the proceeds raised to benefit a memorial to be built in Springfield, Massachusetts, the game's birthplace. Proponents of the game felt strongly about basketball's place in the country's sporting landscape. "Take basketball out of the sport picture today and you would have an empty spot that nothing could fill. It is part and parcel of American life. It exudes the wholesome, healthy, free and fair competitive spirit that is one of the features of the American way of life. And it helps definitely and immeasurably in building better men and women."[1] The goal of the Golden Jubilee of Basketball was to raise funds to support a "Temple of Basketball" that "will bear the same relationship to the court game as baseball's Hall of Fame at Cooperstown, New York, bears to the diamond pastime. And it will have the same commemorative significance in regard to the founder of the game as the Walter Camp Memorial at New Haven has for the father of American football."[2]

The "Temple of Basketball," as it was known, was to include a Hall of Fame, a historical museum, and a basketball court. The Naismith Memorial Committee envisioned "a permanent monument to Dr. Naismith, but in its archives will be perpetuated the names and accomplishments of the game's foremost players, past, present and future. Deposited and safeguarded in the Temple of Basketball will be documents, curios, souvenirs and records of the sport. And enshrined each year in a suitable manner will be the names of the annual All-American basketball teams."[3]

As Grantland Rice, America's preeminent sportswriter, wrote, "No better time could exist than right now to pay homage to one who brought so much joy into the hearts of Americans without worldly benefit to himself, while elsewhere about us other men are exploiting humanity for their own selfish gains. Dr. James Naismith has taken his place among the Immortals of Sports and the idea of perpetuating his memory and his vital contributions to the American scene in the Naismith Memorial at Springfield should receive the wholehearted support of every red-blooded player and fan in the country."[4]

The joy Grantland Rice associated with James Naismith and the game of basketball, however, almost did not happen.

As December 1891 approached, students and faculty at the International Young Men's Christian Association (YMCA) Training School in Springfield, Massachusetts, were preparing for end-of-term examinations and making arrangements to travel home for the holiday season. Another semester was coming to a close as a typical New England winter descended on the region. Most campus-wide activities were winding down. Students and faculty alike were preparing for some time away from the demands of an academic semester.

One room above the gymnasium, however, was bright with activity. James Naismith, a thirty-year-old faculty member, who the previous year was a student, was obsessed with finishing an assignment for his boss, Luther Gulick, head of the school's physical education department.

The task before him was to create a new indoor game "that would be interesting, easy to learn, and easy to play in the winter and by artificial light."[5]

This assignment had formed the basis of a new course in psychology that Gulick offered for the first time in the fall of 1891. This seminar on psychology discussed a number of topics related to physical education. The class was composed of faculty members who also taught the regular student body, including the class of YMCA secretaries that was the subject of Naismith's assignment. Of particular importance was the need to find a new game that these students could engage in during the winter months. Winter sports in the 1880s were largely confined to gymnastics. The Swedish, German, and French variations of gymnastics had all been tried but more often had left the students bored and unsatisfied. The monotony of gymnastic work could not compare to the high energy of football, lacrosse, and baseball, all of which the students played with great enthusiasm the rest of the year. Gulick's class began tackling the problem of finding a new game to be played by the students in the winter. This particular issue engaged everyone and quickly became the central focus of the class. Midway through the semester, one class period centered on the theme of inventions, and Gulick challenged his class when he said, "There is nothing new under the sun. All so-called things are recombinations of factors of things that are now in existence."[6]

The comment piqued the interest of the students, particularly Naismith, who replied, "Doctor, if that is so, we can invent a new game that will meet our needs. All that we have to do is to take the factors of our known game and recombine them, and we will have the game we are looking for."[7] Naismith's response spurred Gulick's thinking, and he asked his students, all of whom were on the faculty—F. N. Seerley, Robert A. Clark, A. T. Halstead, Amos Alonzo Stagg, and Naismith—to each come up with an idea for a new game by the next class.

When the class reconvened the following week, however, not one new idea was forthcoming. Busy with their teaching assignments, none of the faculty members had any time to think of a new game. With the winter sports season soon approaching, Gulick realized that this problem needed to be addressed quickly so he assigned Halstead to the class of secretaries, the one class that had expressed its dislike for the current makeup of the winter sports activities. An expert in marching and calisthenics, Halstead focused on these activities with the class. After one week, he was completely discouraged by the students' response and requested a new class.

Gulick then assigned Clark to the task, hoping that he could find a more successful way to inspire the students with some form of physical activity. A gymnast by training and according to Naismith the best athlete on the faculty, Clark discarded the marching and calisthenics championed by Halstead and focused on apparatus work, his specialty. Again, the class was less than enthused. In reporting back to his colleagues the next week, he observed, "The difficulty is, with that particular group of men what we want is recreative work; something that will please them and something they will want to do."[8] Reflecting on this many years later, Naismith wrote, "Try as hard as he could, he [Clark] could arouse little enthusiasm for this kind of work."[9]

In class the following week, a despondent group of faculty members sat trying to figure out a solution. Looking again to spur discussion, Naismith said, "The trouble is not with the men but with the system we are using. The kind of work for this particular class should be of a recreative nature, something that would appeal to their play instincts."[10]

Naismith's comments challenged his colleagues, who sat quietly until Gulick broke the silence. Quickly, he turned and said, "Naismith, I want you to take that class and see what you can do with it."[11] Naismith was speechless. His comments were meant to encourage his classmates to find a solution, not to be an invitation for a new assignment. Naismith was disheartened by the turn of events, and in a speech given in 1932 at Springfield College, he vividly recalled that fateful day when the responsibility of that class fell to him.

"If I ever tried to back out of anything, I did then. I did not want to do it. I had charge of a group interested in boxing, wrestling, fencing, and swimming and I was perfectly satisfied with my work. Dr. Gulick said he wanted me to do it. I had to do it or get out and I felt pretty sore about it. I thought Dr. Gulick had imposed on me by giving me something I did not want to do and compelling me to do it. As we walked down along the hall, talking about it, he said, 'Naismith, this would be a good time for you to invent that new game you said you could.' I closed my fist, and looked at Dr. Gulick's face for a spot to plant my fist, but I saw a peculiar twinkle in his eye which seemed to say 'put up or shut up.'"[12]

Faced with this new challenge and two weeks to solve the problem, Naismith retreated to his office above the gymnasium. He reflected back on his childhood in Canada, and the games he played as a youth.

A common misconception has developed over the years that an American invented basketball. To the contrary, Naismith was Canadian, born in Almonte, Ontario, on November 6, 1861. The second of three children, he lived with his family on Grand Calumet Island on the banks of the Ottawa River, where his father owned a sawmill. Tragedy struck in 1870 as a typhoid epidemic claimed the lives of his parents. His father died first, and three weeks later his mother passed away on his ninth birthday. Orphaned, Naismith; his sister, Annie; and their brother, Robert, moved into the home of their grandmother and their uncle Pete in a farm area between Bennie's Corner and Almonte.

Growing up, Naismith was known for his strength and spent much of his time outdoors, working in the wilderness, shocking grain, and riding horses. As his grandson Stuart recalled in a 2000 interview, "One time the Mississippi River was frozen over and he thought the ice was strong enough to cross. It was not and the horse foundered and went through the ice. He worked and finally got the horse out of the water. When he was finished, he saw his Uncle Pete watching, who said, 'He got himself into that pickle and he will have to get himself out.' And he did. That was the type of childhood my grandfather had."[13]

Midway through high school, Naismith dropped out to help support his uncle and siblings. He worked for several years but eventually returned to school to complete his education. After high school Naismith enrolled at McGill University in Montreal, where he studied for the ministry. Studious about his professional pursuit, he spent all his time studying until one day a fellow classmate approached him to comment, "Naismith, we have been watching you for some time, and we see that you never take part in any of the activities. You spend too much time with your books."[14]

Soon enough Naismith was in the gymnasium, playing tumbling, soccer, lacrosse, and fencing. He also joined the football team. One day during practice the guard next to Naismith encountered a difficult situation and started swearing. Recognizing that Naismith was next to him, he stopped and said, "I beg your pardon, Jim; I forgot you were there."[15] Startled, Naismith continued practicing, but the exchange was not far from his mind. As his grandson Stuart noted, "He realized that sportsmanship was not isolated from a Godly life and decided that he was going to do both."[16] This incident, as Naismith correctly noted, changed his "career from the profession of the ministry to that of athletics."[17] It was this duality of academics and athletics, sports and clean living that eventually became the primary intellectual pursuit in his life. For the next fifty years, physical education became the central tenet of his life's work.

Naismith graduated from McGill in 1887 but elected to stay on as a physical instructor. He began studying theology at nearby Presbyterian College, where he received his degree in 1890. Although he enjoyed studying religion, Naismith was becoming more interested in finding a way to merge physical education and Christianity, convinced that the two could coexist.

At the time the only school in North America to offer a program that trained physical education instructors was the International YMCA Training School in Springfield, Massachusetts. In the fall of 1890 Naismith traveled to Springfield to begin his studies. Upon his arrival, he met his professor, Luther Halsey Gulick, a man who would have a profound impact on his life as well as on the emerging physical education movement in this country.

Born to Congregationalist missionaries in Honolulu, Hawaii, on December 4, 1865, a few months after the conclusion of the Civil War, Luther was the fifth of seven children. For the first fifteen years of his life, he and his siblings lived in Hawaii, Spain, Italy, and Japan. His life on the move would come to characterize his own professional development and the rapidly changing fabric of the country.

After returning to the United States with his family in 1880, Gulick began his formal education. For the next two years, he was enrolled in the preparatory department at Oberlin College in Ohio. He later attended Hanover High School in Hanover, New Hampshire, and then returned to Oberlin, where he entered college to study physical education, a subject that he would have an immense influence on in the years to come. He left school a little more than a year later due to illness and eventually matriculated at the Sargent School of Physical Education in Cambridge, Massachusetts. After a brief stay there, he was again on the move and left to pursue a medical degree at the City College of New York, where he graduated in 1889.

Since he first studied physical education as a college student, the subject, though still in its infancy, had continued to fascinate him. As a medical student, he took a job as the director of physical education of the YMCA in Jackson, Michigan. He joined the Young Men's Christian Association Training School in 1887 as head of the gymnastics department.

When Gulick arrived at Springfield, the School for Christian Workers, as it was known then, was in its second year. Prior to opening in 1885, the school had issued a statement declaring its purpose, which said in part, "There has been developed a pressing and growing demand for men qualified to enter the various fields of Christian work now open to laymen. The demand is especially pressing for men fitted to be secretaries of Young Men's Christian Associations, superintendents of Sunday-schools, and helpers of pastors in mission work and in the general work of the church."[18]

With this charge of training future YMCA secretaries, the faculty developed a course of study designed to meet this challenge. Among the courses offered were The Bible, The Outlines of Evangelical Theology, The History of Evangelical Christianity, Christian Ethics, and The Lives of Eminent Christians.[19] The YMCA became the primary vehicle for training men to uphold and pass along these values.

The YMCA was founded in England in 1844 and eventually was transplanted to the United States in the years prior to the Civil War. Its original purpose rested in providing spiritual guidance and physical help to the burgeoning group of young men who relocated to the industrial cities in the Northeast and the Midwest. After the Civil War a fundamental shift occurred in the YMCA. Rather than providing a haven for newly arrived young men, it began offering programs in physical activity such as gymnastics and calisthenics. Young men who worked in business or clerical positions joined their local YMCA and during lunch breaks or after work took classes in "physical culture." The not-so-subtle message was to encourage a more "muscular Christianity."

In the post–Civil War era American Protestants believed that society was becoming too feminine, steeped in Victorian values of humility and weakness. In its place this group of evangelical Protestants advocated a form of Christianity that viewed Jesus as an athlete and a fighter. The "strenuous life," later championed by Theodore Roosevelt, was promoted by these Christians, who believed in a new Christianity that stressed physical activity, character building, and a new manliness. The concept that sports can build a good Christian character became a central premise of muscular Christianity.

By the 1890s the YMCA had become the foremost proponent of muscular Christianity in America. The Progressive Era, which lasted from 1880 to 1920, witnessed one of the largest upsurges in recreation and emphasis on physical activity that the country had ever witnessed. Due to the increasingly sedentary nature of work, Americans sought more physical activities. Gymnastics, bicycling, and other forms of outdoor activity became hugely popular.

With Gulick at the helm, the YMCA Training School in Springfield was at the forefront of responding to this change. Believing that a person's spiritual life develops equally from the mind and the body, Gulick invented the YMCA emblem, the inverted triangle, still in use today, that symbolizes the spiritual supported by the mental and the physical. In an article Gulick wrote about physical education at the YMCA, he made a strong case for the importance of activity to other aspects of a healthy life. "The object of our organization is to develop perfect men and we hold that the perfect man is one with his physical nature, healthy, strong, evenly developed and well disciplined; his spiritual nature strong, well balanced and trained. Either quality absent in either nature renders the individual less of a man. Each nature is an essential part of the man himself. Thus we believe that physical education is important not merely because it is necessary in order to perfect intellectual and spiritual manhood, but because the physical is in itself a part of the essential 'ego.'" He later concluded, "Our endeavor is for true symmetry, not merely symmetry of body, symmetry of mind, symmetry of soul, but symmetry of these symmetries, a symmetry of body with mind with soul."[20]

Gulick introduced sports into the YMCA, and his focus on play and activities ushered in the largest boys' sports movement the country had ever seen. His pioneering course on the psychology of play that challenged his faculty to invent new games to be played indoors reinforced this effort. The first faculty member to understand and successfully respond to this challenge was James Naismith.

With two weeks before him, Naismith set out to solve the problem of this "class of incorrigibles," as this group of YMCA secretary students was deemed by the faculty. The class was tough, and though they had already been through two instructors, Naismith certainly sympathized with them. "I felt that if I were in their place, I would probably have done all I could to get rid of the obnoxious requirements." "No problems arose so long as we could get out of doors for exercise, but when Winter came, my worries began."[21] As he recalled in January 1939, "Those boys simply would not play drop the handkerchief."[22] Putting aside any reservations he may have had, Naismith forged ahead with his task.

Immediately, he laid aside the heavy gymnastic equipment and tried popular games of the era such as Three Deep and Sailor's Tag. Both games he soon discovered appealed for ten to fifteen minutes but could not sustain interest for an entire class period. He then turned to some recently introduced games including Battle-Ball and two games developed by Gulick, "one a modification of ante-over with a medicine ball and the other a modification of cricket."[23] These, too, proved unsuccessful.

Modifying a few of the popular outdoor games became his next course of action. He started with football and attempted to eliminate as much of the roughness as possible. He asked his students to alter the tackling style from below to above the hips. From the outset, this proved a disaster; as Naismith noted years later, "To ask these men to handle their opponents gently was to make their favorite sport a laughing stock, and they would have nothing of it."[24] Next up for Naismith was soccer. He thought that playing soccer indoors with soft-soled shoes would force the students to "use caution in kicking the ball."[25] Nothing was further from the truth, for students were accustomed to hitting the ball as hard as they could. Naismith recalled, "As a result of this, many of them went limping off the floor; instead of an indoor soccer game, we had a practical lesson in first aid. I had pinned my hopes on these two games, and when they failed me, there seemed little chance of success. Each attempt was becoming more difficult."[26]

Finally, Naismith considered lacrosse, another popular game of the day and one in which he starred for the semiprofessional Montreal Shamrocks while a student at McGill. His hope was to modify the lacrosse stick, but as he wrote years later, this too was an abject failure. "In the group there were seven Canadians; and when these men put into practice some of the tricks they had been taught in the outdoor game, football and soccer appeared tame in comparison. No bones were broken in the game, but faces were scarred and hands were hacked. Those who had never played the game were unfortunate, for it was these men to whom the flying crosses did the most damage. The beginners were injured and the experts were disgusted; another game went into the discard."[27]

After trying all he could to engage the class in some form of athletic activity, Naismith was left without any answers. No new ideas. No popular game that he could modify. Nothing. Instead of trying something new, he left the students to their own devices, letting them do whatever they wanted. He stood off to the side, discouraged that none of his ideas and good intentions had worked. As the class period ended, Naismith watched as the class went to change in the locker room. He felt as if he had failed.

He later described the aftermath of that class: "With weary footsteps I mounted the flight of narrow stairs that led to my office directly over the locker room. I slumped down in my chair, my head in my hands and my elbows on the desk. I was a thoroughly disheartened and discouraged young instructor. Below me, I could hear the boys in the locker room having a good time; they were giving expression to the very spirit that I had tried so hard to evoke."[28]

Despite this discouragement, Naismith was willing to give it one more try. That night he sat at his desk and methodically analyzed each game. He thought back to the comment he had made in the seminar months earlier: "All that we have to do is to take the factors of our known game and recombine them, and we will have the game we are looking for."[29] Slowly tapping his pencil to the paper, Naismith let his mind wonder back through all the games played and tested over the past two weeks. "As I sat there at my desk, I began to study games from the philosophical side. I had been taking one game at a time and had failed to find what I was looking for. This time I would take games as a whole and study them."[30]

Using a holistic approach, Naismith soon found the answers he was looking for. First, he asked himself, what do all team sports have? He realized that all of them incorporated a ball, either a small one or a large one. Small balls used in games like baseball, lacrosse, and hockey needed some form of an implement such as a bat or stick. He thought this would be too much of an obstacle for indoor play, so instead he thought of games that used a large ball.

American rugby, the most popular game of the Gilded Age, was one that Naismith was quite familiar with. He asked himself why this game was not played indoors. The answer: it was too rough. The only way to stop a player running with the ball was to tackle him. "If he can't run with the ball, we don't have to tackle; and if we don't have to tackle, the roughness will be eliminated," Naismith mused. "I can still recall how I snapped my fingers and shouted I've got it!"[31]

Eliminating the tackling was Naismith's first big revelation. He had the outlines of the first part of the game: "In my mind, I was still sticking to the traditions of the older games, especially football. In this new game, however, the player with the ball could not advance. So far, I had a game that was played with a large light ball; the players could not run with the ball, but must pass it or bat it with the hands; and the pass could be in any direction."[32]

His final task was to create an objective. For this, he harkened back to his youth in Bennie's Corner and a game, Duck on the Rock, that he played there. As Naismith described it, "We found a rock two feet high and two feet across. Each one took a stone about the size of his fist. One put his stone on the rock and the rest of us got behind a line and tried to knock it off. We would throw stones as hard as we could at his and if we happened to hit it, it was all right, but if we missed it, we went way down. Once in a while we threw the ball in such a way that it would knock [the other player's] off and come back again and we would walk up and get it."[33] Naismith, in remembering his childhood game, had found the answer: a game in which players tossed a ball at a vertical goal, based on accuracy and not roughness.

The next day Naismith, hoping that this new game would be the answer, entered the gym several hours before the class arrived. He carried with him a soccer ball but realized that he still needed two goals for the students to toss the ball at.

"As I walked down the hall, I met Mr. Stebbins the superintendent of buildings," Naismith wrote years later in *Basketball: Its Origin and Development*. "I asked him if he had two boxes about eighteen inches square. Stebbins thought a minute, and then said: "'No, I haven't any boxes, but I'll tell you what I do have. I have two old peach baskets down in the store room, if they will do you any good.'"

Naismith took him up on the offer. "I told him to bring them up, and a few minutes later he appeared with the two baskets tucked under his arm. They were round and somewhat larger at the top than at the bottom. I found a hammer and some nails and tacked the baskets to the lower rail of the balcony, one at either end of the gym."[34]

Once this task was completed, Naismith retreated briefly to his office to write the rules. After about an hour, he came back downstairs and handed them to Mrs. Lyons, the secretary, to type up and post outside for the students. The original thirteen rules state:

1. The ball may be thrown in any direction with one or both hands.
2. The ball may be batted in any direction with one or both hands (never with a fist).
3. A player cannot run with the ball. The player must throw it from the spot on which he catches it, allowance to be made for a man who catches the ball when running if he tries to stop it.
4. The ball must be held by the hands. The arms or the body must not be used for holding it.
5. No shouldering, holding, pushing, tripping, or striking in any way the person of an opponent shall be allowed; the first infringement of this rule by any player shall count as a foul, the second shall disqualify him until the next goal is made, or, if there was evident intent to injure the person, for the whole of the game, no substitute allowed.
6. A foul is striking at the ball with the fist, violation of Rules 3, 4, and such as described in Rule 5.
7. If either side makes three consecutive fouls it shall count as a goal for the opponents (consecutive means without the opponents in the meantime making a foul).
8. A goal shall be made when the ball is thrown or batted from the grounds into the basket and stays there, providing those defending the goal do not touch or disturb the goal. If the ball rests on the edges and the opponent moves the basket, it shall count as a goal.
9. When the ball goes out of bounds, it shall be thrown into the field of play by the person first touching it. He has a right to hold it unmolested for five seconds. In case of a dispute the umpire shall throw it straight into the field. The thrower-in is allowed five seconds; if he holds it longer it shall go to the opponent. If any side persists in delaying the game the umpire shall call a foul on that side.

10. The umpire shall be the judge of the men and shall note the fouls and notify the referee when three consecutive fouls have been made. He shall have the power to disqualify men according to Rule 5.

11. The referee shall be the judge of the ball and shall decide when the ball is in play, in bounds, to which side it belongs, and shall keep the time. He shall decide when a goal has been made and keep accounts of the goals, with any other duties that are usually performed by a referee.

12. The time shall be two fifteen-minute halves, with five minutes rest between.

13. The side making the most goals in that time shall be declared the winner. In the case of a draw the game may, by agreement of the captains, be continued until another goal is made.

Once the rules were posted and the two peach baskets affixed on the top of the balcony of the running track, Naismith took the soccer ball and went inside the gym. He nervously awaited the students' arrival and hoped that this game would finally end the trouble with this class. This was his last idea. If the class did not take to this game, he would be forced to tell Gulick that his ideas had not worked.

At 11:30 that morning, shortly before the lunch hour, the class arrived wearing the standard gray pants and matching sweatshirts typical of physical education classes at the time. As they viewed the two baskets and read the rules, grumbles passed among the students. "Huh! Another new game!"[35] "Just try this one game," Naismith pleaded. "If you don't like it, I promise I won't try to invent another one." Without any further delays, the first game began.

"There were 18 in the class," Naismith wrote years later. "I selected two captains and had them choose sides. I placed the men on the floor. There were three forwards, three centers, and three backs on each team. I chose two of the center men to jump, then threw the ball

FIG. 1. James Naismith and the first team played the first game of basketball in December 1891 at the International YMCA Training School in Springfield, Massachusetts. Naismith Memorial Basketball Hall of Fame.

between them. It was the start of the first basketball game and the finish of trouble with that class."[36]

The class played the entire period, and by all accounts everyone enjoyed the new activity. William R. Chase, of New Bedford, Massachusetts, made the first and only basket. The final score was 1–0.

That first game was a crude predecessor of the game as it is played today. Rough and awkward, it more resembled a game of keep away than it did basketball. Ernest Hildner was a member of that first class. In December 1966, nearly seventy-five years after that first game, Hildner gave the most complete and possibly only interview that has survived regarding that historic game. The interview, which was taped on cassette, has been stored in a box at the Naismith Memorial Basketball Hall of Fame, in Springfield, undisturbed for more than twenty years until I listened to it. Although the years may have dimmed his memory, Hildner's recollections offer insight into the primitive nature of the game and a testament to the appeal generated by this new activity.

"Jimmy picked the sides, and he said there are so many people and we'll divide the class in half," Hildner recalled in the interview.

> He said the object of the game is to pass the ball and get it in the other fellow's basket. We began playing basketball, and there were about fourteen fellows on each side, and the gym was so small it would not hold them all. So he threw out the ball and said go to it fellows. And that was it.
>
> There was no time in the game. Nothing. If you could just understand how absolutely everything was gathered around how one side was shoving the ball one way and the other side was shoving the ball the other way. There was so many men that they could not operate. The gym was too small. They couldn't find a place to land.
>
> We passed the ball back and forth. That is all there was for a while. We played this game of one side throwing the other side and the other side throwing the other side. It wasn't very pleasant.
>
> It was just one side against the other side and smash in to the other guy. The other guy would try to pass it, and he would get caught and someone would grab him. It was just a game of throwing that ball so as to get it in the other fellow's basket.[37]

One of Hildner's classmates that first day was Ray Kaighn, a Philadelphia native, who sixty-eight years after that first game, also recalled some of the details in an article in the *Philadelphia Inquirer*. "We used a soccer ball. Just as the players of today, the players then all wanted to shoot. We were all tired of Swedish calisthenics. We wanted a winter sport with the excitement of football but without its danger."[38] It appeared that they had found what they were looking for.

After the invention of basketball, Naismith and Gulick worked together for a few more years before Naismith moved to Colorado. Gulick, meanwhile, stayed at Springfield until 1903. During those years, he continued as the head of the gymnastics department, while also serving as an international secretary for the physical training department at the YMCA. He also acted as the secretary for the American Association for the Advancement of Physical Education.

When he departed Springfield in 1903, Gulick entered a period of his life that contributed greatly to his legacy, one in which he further developed his ideas of play and physical education. He moved to New York City, where he became the first director of physical education for the city public schools. He became involved in many related issues, including chairing the Physical Education Training Lecture Committee of the St. Louis Exposition in 1904 and serving as a member of the U.S. Olympic Committee for 1906 (Athens) and 1908 (London). He taught, lectured, consulted, and wrote a number of books, many of which became required reading for students of physical education and hygiene.

Gulick was a founding member of the Boys Scouts of America and, together with his wife, founded the Campfire Girls. In the later years of his life, he was quite active and founded a number of other organizations, including the American Folk Dance Society and the Playground Association. In 1918, toward the end of World War I, he served as chairman of the YMCA's International Committee on Physical Recreation of the War Work Council. In that capacity he traveled to France and interviewed serviceman about sex hygiene and their moral and physical well-being. He died later that year at the age of fifty-three.

From the moment Naismith threw up the first ball, basketball's newness earned it an expanding group of admirers. Its popularity spread so fast that within weeks the game was played in YMCAs across the country. Naismith's first game, the one he introduced to his students, is often credited with being on December 21, 1891, days before the

Christmas break. Armed with this new indoor game and a growing sense of curiosity, the "eighteen incorrigibles" brought it with them to their hometown YMCAs. Writing an article in *The Rotarian* in January 1939, less than a year before his death, Naismith noted, "The prospective leaders of youth, in schools at Springfield, found this game interesting, and they took it with them as they spread their tasks as YMCA secretaries through the United States, or became missionaries in other lands."[39]

The first official game occurred in March 1892, between "the teachers of the International Young Men's Christian Association training school and the students." More than two hundred spectators watched that game. They included Naismith, Gulick, and Stagg among others. "The teachers worked hard and performed wonders of agility and strength, but were not 'in it' with the students, who had the advantage in science, and the score at the end was 5–1 in favor of the latter."[40] The most noteworthy figure was Amos Alonzo Stagg. "The most conspicuous figure on the floor was Stagg, in the blue Yale uniform, who managed to have a hand in every scrimmage. His football training hampered him, and he was perpetually making fouls by shoving his opponents. He managed, however, to score the only goal that the instructors made."[41]

By April 1892, this new game of basketball had made its way into the *New York Times*. On April 26, 1892, the *Times* wrote a four-paragraph article under the header "A New Game of Ball: A Substitute for Football without Its Rough Features." The articles notes, "The game is played with an ordinary association football, and the object of each team is to get the ball into its opponent's goal. The top of the basket is about nine feet above the ground, and a ladder is necessary to take the ball out after a goal has been made. When a player gets the ball he is not allowed to run with it, but must stand and pass it to some other member of his own team within fifteen seconds after he touches it."[42] The *Times* observed that "a match was played between the Twenty-third Street Branch of the Young Men's Christian Association and a team composed of members of the Students' Club. The students won by a score of 1 to 0."[43]

In October 1892, ten months after the game's inauspicious beginnings, a friend of Naismith's wrote, "It is doubtful whether a gymnastic game has ever spread so rapidly over the continent as has 'basketball.' It is played from New York to San Francisco and from Maine to Texas, by hundreds of teams in associations, athletic clubs, and schools."[44] Indeed, the game's instant popularity has been unmatched in the history of sport.

Within a few years many colleges across the country supported basketball teams that competed against YMCAs and other college squads. Naismith's fellow instructor and friend, Amos Alonzo Stagg, left the International YMCA Training School in 1892 to become the first athletic director at the University of Chicago. Naturally, he brought the game with him, and shortly thereafter basketball was added to the athletic schedule.

Charles O. Bemies, a student at Springfield, was captivated by the game. In 1892 he left Springfield and became the athletic director and football coach at Geneva College, in Beaver Falls, Pennsylvania. When he arrived in western Pennsylvania, so too did the game of basketball. In April 1893 Geneva played its first game against the New Brighton YMCA. In the team's only game that year, it defeated New Brighton 3–0.

In 1893, less than two years after Naismith invented the game, YMCAs across the country had formed basketball leagues. Colleges started introducing the game at roughly the same time as the YMCA. The University of Iowa began playing in 1893, and Hamline University in St. Paul, Minnesota, played its first game against the Minneapolis YMCA that same year. Played in the basement of the Science Building at Hamline with nine-foot ceilings, the local YMCA defeated Hamline 13–12. Also that year Vanderbilt University defeated a team from the Nashville YMCA 9–6. As the middle of the decade approached, the game was becoming more widespread in the collegiate ranks. On February

9, 1895, the Minneapolis State College of Agriculture defeated Hamline 9–3 in what is believed to be the first intercollegiate game.

By the end of the nineteenth century, basketball was being played in fifteen different countries. YMCA students who were sent to foreign YMCAs introduced the game, helping to introduce basketball to China, Japan, and India as well as to Canada and other countries. What started as a class assignment was now a popular new game spreading to all parts of the globe.

While the game was being introduced to all parts of the globe, it was gaining popularity in the states. A mere seven years after the game was invented, a professional basketball league was founded that paid players to play the game. The National Basketball League debuted in 1898–99, and although the moniker suggests it encompassed teams nationwide, that was hardly the case. Early professional basketball had its strongest roots in the Trenton-Philadelphia corridor. Many of the early professional leagues were based in that general vicinity, and the National Basketball League of 1898–99 was no different. That first league had six teams—three based in Trenton, Millville, and Camden, New Jersey, and three in Philadelphia and Germantown. The Philadelphia Clover Wheelman, the Germantown Nationals, and the Hancock AA all dropped out, leaving the first official professional title to be contested among the three New Jersey teams. The Trenton Nationals claimed the inaugural championship, sporting an 18-2-1 record.

Despite the uncertainty of the three teams dropping out, the National Basketball League returned for its sophomore season and continued play for five seasons until the 1902–3 season concluded. In Philadelphia the Philadelphia Basketball League replaced the National Basketball League and lasted for six seasons, from 1902–3 to 1908–9. After that the Eastern League became the most successful of the early professional basketball leagues, enjoying the longest tenure among them. From 1909–10 to 1932–33 the Eastern League became the most stable league of the game's early years.

Professional basketball, though, was not confined to the Trenton-Philadelphia corridor. Soon the game spread through New England and New York State. Leagues such as the New England Basketball League, the Western Massachusetts Basketball League, the New England Basketball Association, the Western Pennsylvania Basketball League, the Central Basketball League, the New York State League, the Pennsylvania State League, the Interstate League, the Metropolitan Basketball League, and the Connecticut State League all came and went, helping to spread the game's emerging popularity. Many of the early pioneers of the game and future members of the Naismith Memorial Basketball Hall of Fame, including Ed Watcher, Barney Sedran, and Max Friedman, all made a name for themselves in these early leagues.

It was not until 1925–26, though, that the first major attempt to create a national basketball league was attempted. The American Basketball League (ABL) lasted six seasons from 1925–26 to 1930–31 before the effects of the Great Depression caused the commissioner, John J. O'Brien, to suspend operations. Prior to that, however, the league was successful, and franchises stretched from the East Coast to Chicago. Teams were located in Philadelphia, Chicago, Rochester, Brooklyn, Washington DC, Cleveland, Detroit, Fort Wayne, and Toledo. The league made an impact, including forcing all players to sign exclusive contracts. As Robert Peterson, author of *Cages to Jump Shots: Pro Basketball's Early Years,* notes, "The advent of the American Basketball League spelled doom for the old professional basketball game because the new league adopted AAU rules almost in toto. Cages and the double dribble were outlawed in the ABL. Henceforth the professional game would gradually become faster and depend less on bulk and strength and more on speed, agility, and cleverness."[45] The league enjoyed success, including the participation of the Original Celtics, the game's first great professional team. The league, however, could not withstand the effects of the Great Depression, and after the conclusion of the 1930–31 season, it suspended operation.

When the league resumed in 1933–34, it was no longer national in scope but rather a regional league concentrated in the New York, New Jersey, and Pennsylvania area. Teams that first season were located in Trenton, Brooklyn, Philadelphia, Newark, Hoboken, and New Britain. During the 1930s the ABL was the premier professional basketball league in the country. The Philadelphia SPHAS, an all-Jewish squad, dominated league play and captured seven titles in thirteen seasons. Soon the ABL would have competition from the National Basketball League (NBL), which began as the Midwest Basketball Conference in 1935–36. By 1937–38, the NBL was poised as a strong midwestern circuit, with teams in Akron, Buffalo, Oshkosh, Fort Wayne, Indianapolis, and Dayton. The NBL eventually overtook the ABL in prestige and popularity, but until then basketball had two professional circuits as the 1930s came to a close.

At the start of the 1939–40 basketball season, the game lost its founder. On November 28, 1939, with the Thanksgiving holiday past and the 1939–40 season just under way, newspapers and radios across the country reported that James Naismith, the game's founder, had died of a cerebral hemorrhage. He was seventy-eight years old. The *New York Times*, in its obituary, noted that more than twenty million people were now playing the game worldwide. "The fast, sprightly, colorful basketball of today, enjoyed in many lands by the young of both sexes in college, school, club, association and society gymnasiums and on professional courts, bears at least the same resemblance to the early game as that of a modern airliner to the Wright brothers' first 'flying machine.' The father of basketball had the distinction of originating the only major sport created in the United States."[46]

After inventing the game of basketball in December 1891, Naismith had continued to teach at the International YMCA Training School in Springfield until 1895. Initially, he stayed involved with the game, printing its rules, first in 1892 with *Rules for Basket Ball*. Gulick joined Naismith, and the two collaborated on printing the rules for two years before Naismith left Springfield. After he left, he had virtually no contact with the game, its development, or advancing the rules and regulations. His sole interest was in collecting foreign editions of the printed rules of the game.

Seeking to tackle another challenge in his life, Naismith, his wife, Maude, and their young family left Western Massachusetts and headed for Denver, where he enrolled at Gross Medical College. While earning his medical degree, the father of basketball continued his association with the YMCA movement, serving as physical education director at the Denver YMCA. "While in Denver, he experienced a terrible tragedy," his grandson Stuart Naismith recounted. "He was spotting a young lad in gymnastics, and the child fell and broke his neck and later died. My grandfather was heartbroken. It was one of the great tragedies of his life."[47]

In 1898 Naismith joined the faculty at the University of Kansas in Lawrence as a professor of physical education and university chaplain, but he never practiced medicine. He would remain there until his death in 1939. As one would expect, Naismith became the school's first basketball coach. He compiled a 55-60 career record, the only coach in school history to have a losing record. As the game spread and grew in popularity in the ensuing decades after it was invented, Naismith seemed to have little interest in the game. He played it twice, once in 1892 shortly after inventing it and then in 1898 after arriving at Kansas. By his own admission, he "just didn't get around to playing."[48] The two times he did play, he remembered committing a number of fouls. "I guess my early training in wrestling, boxing and football was too much for me," he later reflected. "My reflexes made me hold my opponents. Once I even used a grapevine wrestling clamp on a man who was too big for me to handle."[49]

He was humble about the recognition he received and often remarked that he did not deserve all the attention that had been bestowed on him. "You fellows have put me in a class with Abner

Doubleday, who invented baseball. If basketball filled a need in the winter sports picture, I am glad, but I had nothing to do with making it grow. Honestly, I never believed that it ever would be played outside of that gymnasium in Springfield."[50]

Basketball to him was just one episode in a long series of career choices designed to improve how people lived their lives, physically and socially. His sole interest lay in counseling students. When one of his students, Forrest "Phog" Allen, told Naismith he was going to accept a job coaching basketball at Baker University, also in Kansas, Naismith quipped, "Why, you can't coach basketball, you just play it."[51] Allen later became one of the most successful coaches in college basketball history.

As Naismith's grandson, Stuart, recalled, "He looked upon basketball as a game to play, get physical exercise and to gain skills."[52] During his long-tenured career in Lawrence, Naismith counseled many students on life lessons and never strayed far from his Springfield teachings of "a sound mind is a sound body." John McLendon, one his students at Kansas and later a pioneer African American Naismith Memorial Basketball Hall of Fame coach, summed up Naismith's philosophy: "Naismith believed you can do as much toward helping people become better people, teaching them the lessons of life through athletics than you can through preaching."[53]

Despite the passing of Naismith, the game was healthy as it embarked on its next fifty years. The American Basketball League and the National Basketball League both vied for the game's best collegiate talent. Basketball was played in the 1936 Olympics, and the United States was victorious. In a span of two years (1938–39), the National Invitation Tournament (NIT), the National Collegiate Athletic Association (NCAA) tournament, and the World Professional Basketball Tournament in Chicago were all founded. These three tournaments brought together teams from across the country and soon spread the game's popularity. As the 1941–42 season loomed on the horizon, basketball had much to look forward to.

1

AMERICA GOES TO WAR, 1941–1942

These boys cavorting on the basketball court tonight who are being cheered to the echo by all of us in the stands, in some way reflect our boys in the armed forces, being supported by those of us behind the lines. —EDWARD COCHRANE, SPORTS EDITOR, *CHICAGO HERALD AMERICAN*, 1942

Ralph Kaplowitz had high hopes for his senior year. As a sophomore in 1939–40, Kaplowitz was an important player on the New York University Violets, scoring 183 points as the Violets won eighteen games that season. He was named to the second-team All-Metropolitan. Kaplowitz improved as a junior, scoring 193 points and leading the team to a 13-6 record in 1940–41. In the process he had finally earned his role as the team's best player and centerpiece. As he recalled, "Bobby Lewis, who was an excellent ballplayer the previous season, graduated, and so did some of the other players. So I was left as the fulcrum of the new NYU team."[1] As the team's star he was named to the first-team All-Metropolitan. With steady improvement individually and a good team returning, the Violets, under future Naismith Memorial Basketball Hall of Fame coach Howard Cann, were seeking a postseason invitation for the 1941–42 season. High hopes followed the team throughout the summer of 1941.

Weeks before students returned to school in late August, Kaplowitz received his draft notice. The Army Air Corps, the forerunner to the air

FIG. 2 Ralph Kaplowitz served five years in the Army Air Corps and flew thirteen missions in the Pacific theater before resuming his basketball career in January 1946. Courtesy of New York University Archives, Photographic Collection.

force, drafted him. He immediately reported, which ended his college career and any hopes the Violets had of being a top team on the East Coast. As Kaplowitz recalled, "I was drafted August 13, 1941. I went to Camp Upton, New York, as a draftee. I immediately applied for the flying school. At the time a draftee was in the service for one year because there was no war at that stage. I wanted to get into flying so they sent me to Jefferson Barracks, Missouri, where I would take an examination to get into the cadets. I took the examination, and I passed so they sent me to Chanute Field, Illinois, where I went to Air Mechanics School. I was waiting for them to accept me into flying school."[2] While waiting to be accepted into flying school, Kaplowitz stayed in shape by playing basketball at Chanute Field.

"I was in Chicago on a weekend when the announcement on the radio said that we were attacked at Pearl Harbor," he recounted. "Therefore, all the soldiers—I was a private at the time—had to report back to the barracks. I went to the barracks, and I found out more about Pearl Harbor. Meanwhile, we went about our normal duties."[3]

Part of his regular duties included playing basketball for the Chanute Field team. Kaplowitz recalled, "I played basketball at Chanute Field with a bunch of all-American ballplayers like Bill Hapac from the University of Illinois, Ted Skrodsky, Osborne, Menke from DePaul and a few others. We were undefeated in the six games that I played with them before I got called to go to Cadet School to take up flying."[4] Prior to reporting to Cadet School, "we had a game with Chanute Field against Scott Field, another team in the Air Corps."[5] His teammates made him captain of the team. On that occasion, Kaplowitz remembered, "I scored 37 points and I did not miss a shot. That was my going-away present. Then, I got on the train and went to Kelly Field, Texas, where I had six weeks of preliminary training."[6] Over the next five years, Kaplowitz crisscrossed the country for training before being sent to the Pacific theater, where he flew thirteen missions as a fighter pilot and nearly lost his life several times. He spent five years in the military, his basketball career interrupted by war.

Kaplowitz, like millions of Americans, saw his life irrevocably altered on that fateful December day. In the quiet hours of December 7, 1941, the Japanese had sailed undetected across the Pacific Ocean with sixty ships, and the intent to inflict devastating damage on the U.S. Navy. That is exactly what they did as the U.S. Navy suffered horrific losses. It was an attack that shattered the nation's confidence and awoke it from its isolationist sensibility. The following day, newspapers across the country decried the devastation that the Japanese had unleashed. The headline of the *New York Daily News* declared "JAPS BOMB HAWAII DECLARE WAR ON U.S. AND BRITAIN." In large block letters on the front page, the *Boston Herald* announced, "JAPS OPEN WAR ON U.S. BOMB HAWAII, KILL 350." The *New York Times* reported, "JAPAN WARS ON U.S. AND BRITAIN, MAKES SUDDEN ATTACK ON HAWAII, HEAVY FIGHTING AT SEAS REPORTED." Later that day, President Franklin Roosevelt addressed Congress and gave his soon-to-be famous "day that will live in infamy" speech. Soon thereafter, the country was headed to war for the second time in a generation.

In the days preceding the attack on Pearl Harbor, however, another basketball season loomed, and teams across the country readied for another season of basketball. In St. Louis, the Washington University Bears prepared for the start of their season with a warm-up game against McKendree College, while crosstown rival St. Louis University, coming off a terrible loss, 51–22, to the University of Notre Dame the week before, sought to redeem itself against the University of Missouri and answer the question of "whether the Tigers of the University of Missouri rate[d] as high in basketball as they [did] in football."[7] In New York future Naismith Memorial Basketball Hall of Fame coach Clair Bee was contemplating making a change to his Long Island University starting five for the preseason finale against Lawrence Tech of Detroit.

FIG. 3. The *Converse Yearbook* was an annual guide that chronicled the previous season in basketball. The 1941–42 edition captured the mood of the country with an image of a basketball player and the silhouette of a soldier. Naismith Memorial Basketball Hall of Fame.

He was thinking of replacing Dick Holub in the starting lineup with Irv Rothenberg, a six-foot-seven, two-hundred-pound sophomore whom Bee felt would "be of greater help to the varsity in securing control of the ball."[8] Excitement surrounded George Washington University as the basketball team geared up for its first season in the Southern Conference with a game against Wake Forest University. Throughout the country a new season of basketball was set to begin in the shadow of the looming war.

In Indianapolis the Indianapolis Kautskys and the Toledo Jim White Chevies, both teams in the National Basketball League (NBL), returned to the court after the halftime intermission. The teams were loosening up and going through the lay-up drills before heading to the benches for a final review of the second-half strategy. But before the teams could start the second half, the public address announcer broke through the noise of the crowd to make an announcement. Indianapolis's Frank Baird recalled, "Suddenly, the announcer said, 'we have an important announcement. Japan has bombed Pearl Harbor.' We stopped warm-ups and started talking to each other at midcourt. I remember so well that when we got together, we got into a bit of an argument, so to speak. We didn't know whether Pearl Harbor was in the Philippines or in Hawaii. Just goes to show how few of us had even heard of Pearl Harbor to that point. Most of us thought there was surely no way the Japanese could come all the way over to bomb Hawaii. Well, of course we were wrong, unfortunately."[9] Bob Deitz, one of the Kautskys' players remembered the announcement and the shock that it caused.

> At halftime they didn't know whether to continue with the game or not. But they did decide to finish. I honestly can't tell you whether we won or lost that day. All the way back we had the radio on with all the news about what happened. It got progressively worse the more we listened. I had already been sworn into the Navy. I knew my date to report was January 29. I was coaching at Brownsburg

High School at the time, and the school board kept saying, "'We'll get you a deferment. Don't worry about a thing." Well, after I heard that [announcement], I knew the deferment was long gone. We knew that once war was declared, we were on our way.[10]

Indianapolis finished out its season with a first-round loss to the Oshkosh All-Stars in the NBL playoffs. The war, however, loomed in the minds of everyone, and the team made a conscious decision to cease operations for the upcoming season. As Baird recalled, "After the playoffs many of the fellas on the ball club enlisted or were drafted. There was a real shortage of players. And Frank Kautsky thought that this just wasn't the time to keep an NBL franchise going."[11] In an interview after the conclusion of the season, Kautsky declared, "I felt as though I'd be doing something wrong."[12] It would be a decision that every team would face in the coming years.

In those early days of U.S. involvement in the war, nobody could foresee the changes that the war would have on the game of basketball. Basketball in the 1930s underwent a transformation that after World War II propelled the game to a more exciting level of play and greater financial success. For its first thirty years, basketball was a rough, slow, and deliberate game, played mostly by working-class kids who had little formal education. Scores were low, and teams with the lead late in games would stall the ball. The only requirement was to possess the ball after each center jump. This feat placed a premium on having one tall center whose only objective was to win the center jump after each basket and obtain the ball for his team.

In 1937 the center jump after each basket was eliminated, and the game slowly lost the last vestiges of its formative years. As Robert Peterson noted in his book *Cages to Jump Shots*, "Elimination of the center jump was the most radical change in basketball's early evolution. It speeded up play considerably because the ball did not have to be brought to center court for a tip-off after each score. It also contributed to the development of the skills of tall players because teams could no longer afford to carry a big center whose only value was to get the tip-off. The consensus of coaches was that ending the center jump would help small players most, but in fact the day of the dominating big man was still in the future."[13]

The game was opening up, and big men were required to do more than just gain possession of the ball. If a center could not run or score or defend, he was a liability and less useful to his teammates. The game was becoming faster, and the call was out for players with more ability. That ability soon would be found on campuses across the country. The emergence of college basketball on a national level was the other significant change during the thirties. Colleges had fielded teams since shortly after the game was invented, but college ball was local and played mostly on campuses in small gymnasiums or reconfigured spaces.

All of that began to change in the 1930s, and the man responsible was Ned Irish. Although he did not invent the idea of the doubleheader, he, better than most, understood how to sell it to the public. It was Irish's success at promoting doubleheaders at Madison Square Garden that propelled basketball to its status as a national sport. Joe Lapchick, one of the game's great players during the 1920s, understood the impact Irish had on the game: "He was a tough man, but he took basketball out of the dance halls. He gave it the respectability it deserved. No one ever did more for the game."[14]

A newspaperman by training, Irish was a temperamental man, who at heart was a businessman who saw an opportunity. He covered college basketball games for the *New York World Telegram*, focusing mostly on local schools. College basketball drew huge enthusiastic crowds on campuses in New York. These small on-campus arenas often could not hold all these fans and soon turned away many unhappy customers.

One night in 1934, on assignment to cover a game at Manhattan College, Irish was barred from entering due to one of these overflow and boisterous crowds. Legend has it that he tore his pants as he tried to crawl through a window to see the game. Upset but not discouraged, he decided to schedule college basketball doubleheaders at Madison Square Garden to capitalize on this interest. His lone experience in this venture was promoting two triple headers in the early 1930s for the mayor's Unemployment Relief Fund.

Seizing on his idea, Irish met with General John Reed Kilpatrick, Madison Square Garden president, and Tim Mara, owner of the New York Giants football team. Together, they decided that college basketball would operate as a concession to the Garden, guaranteeing Kilpatrick $4,000 a night. Within days everyone agreed, and Irish set his sights on arranging and promoting college basketball's first doubleheader.

Thanks to Irish's newspaper background and understanding of how to generate press, the local media immediately seized on the novelty of a college basketball doubleheader at the Garden. On December 29, 1934, the New York dailies were hyping Saturday's main event featuring Westminster College facing St. John's University and New York University hosting the University of Notre Dame. The *New York Times* wrote, "College basketball will move into a definite niche on the Madison Square Garden program tonight with the staging of six double-headers."[15] Everett B. Morris, writing for the *New York Herald Tribune*, opened his preview by stating, "Metropolitan college basketball will step out of its cramped gymnasiums and gloomy armories tonight into the bright lights and spaciousness of Madison Square Garden for the first of a series of six double-headers arranged in the hope of proving this winter that the sport deserves and will thrive in a major league setting."[16]

Not to be outdone, noted sportswriter Jimmy Powers, wrote in his lead article for the *New York Daily News*, "Using Notre Dame as a bait, basketball makes its big time debut at Madison Square Garden tonight before an expected attendance of collegiate rah-rahs and their sweeties numbering 12,000 and a gate totaling $16,000. This is the first time aside from a hasty charity affair—that the famed sport of sinking a leather ball in a basket of twine has attempted to crash the big leagues."[17]

Aside from marking college basketball's first doubleheader, the evening was equally important for introducing an intersectional (East versus Midwest) basketball game on a national level. In his *New York Post* article, Stanley Frank remarked, "Intersectional games are a distinct novelty in New York, which is pretty snooty in the belief that the best basketball in the country is played here. That burning issue will be decided, more or less, tonight. N.Y.U., one of the few major teams in the nation without a slip, appears to be just as good as it was in 1933–34. Notre Dame is plugged as a team capable of carrying the torch for the Middle West."[18]

With an anticipated full house and four nationally known teams, General Kilpatrick and Madison Square Garden were sure to pull out all the stops. The canvas floor was replaced by "a new board floor that [would] afford all the security of a college gymnasium. The backboards [would] be of glass in order to provide an uninterrupted view."[19] All that remained was for basketball to be played. Both games lived up to the evening's expectations as more than sixteen thousand paying customers went through the turnstiles and "received with intense enthusiasm and partisanship college basketball's debut on a big-time basis."[20]

In the first game Westminster gave St. John's its first loss in six games as "little Westminster overpower[ed] St John's in a hair-raising thriller in which the score was tied seven times before the Titans put on the pressure to triumph."[21] Wes Bennett, the high scorer in the country a year ago, "put on a demonstration of individual prowess that was awesome in its effectiveness."[22] He paced Westminster with twenty-one points on seven field goals and seven foul shots as they defeated local favorite St. John's, 37–33.

The evening's second and final game attracted the most attention. Notre Dame was a national power in football. Its basketball program was slowly building a tradition and under future Naismith Memorial Basketball Hall of Fame coach George Keogan was making its first basketball visit to New York City. The Ramblers, its nickname then, coming off a 20-4 record the previous season, sported a 3-1 record entering their contest against the Violets. "Using a style of play more familiar to metropolitan courts than the zone defense and deliberate set-play attack of Westminster," Notre Dame built a 12–10 halftime lead "with a fast-passing attack built around the pivot play with the huge Marty Peters and the even huger Don Elser in the bucket" observed the *New York Herald Tribune* the following day.[23]

Trailing at the half, New York University, behind Sid Gross, Willie Rubenstein, Milt Shulman, and Len Maiden, opened the second half with an 8–4 run to build a 20–14 lead. The "South Benders" answered and cut the deficit to 20–18 before NYU scored the game's final five points. Balanced scoring led the Violets as four players tallied five or more points. NYU's two big men, Irving Tergesen and Irwin Klein, fouled out trying to guard Peters and Elser, but Notre Dame was its own worst enemy, missing twelve of eighteen foul shots. New York University held Notre Dame to six second-half points.

The evening was deemed a major success, and before long every college team sought the opportunity to play a doubleheader under the bright lights of Madison Square Garden. Eight doubleheaders were scheduled that first season, and national teams such as Kentucky, Temple, Purdue, Notre Dame, Westminster, Duquesne, and Pittsburgh faced the best college teams in New York. More than one hundred thousand spectators paid to watch eight doubleheaders. Two years later "the unqualified success of college basketball in large arenas such as Madison Square Garden" propelled basketball onto the national level.[24] By 1936 Chicago and Philadelphia had organized their own college games, and "capacity houses at every program . . . served to open up the game. An interchange of ideas on the part of coaches . . . resulted from his [Ned Irish's] innovation of bringing teams from every section together. Never [had] the college campuses discussed basketball with such fervor and never [had] the newspapers devoted as much space to the game."[25]

A date at the Garden signified that your team had arrived. It offered more exposure to the national press and potential recruits than an entire season of games on campus. The games provided an opportunity for the spectators and fans to see teams from different parts of the country employing different styles of play. Over the next several years, newspapers carried stories and photographs extolling the great performances at arenas across the country. College basketball was growing, and the need for an end-of-the-season tournament soon followed.

In 1938 the Metropolitan Basketball Writers Association, consisting of New York City sportswriters, decided that the college game needed a national champion. The sportswriters, already covering doubleheaders at Madison Square Garden and chronicling the great city programs like Manhattan College, Long Island University, City College of New York, New York University, and St. John's University, recognized the sport's growing popularity and decided a national championship tournament was needed. Immediately, their idea was met with success, and with that the National Invitation Tournament, the nation's oldest postseason collegiate basketball tournament, was founded.

A year later the NCAA Tournament was established as a response to the success of the NIT. Ohio State coach and future Naismith Memorial Basketball Hall of Fame member Harold Olsen proposed that the colleges sponsor a postseason tournament. While the NIT invited the best teams that college basketball had to offer, the NCAA tournament structured its brackets geographically, giving its tournament a regional flavor. The NCAA held its tournament in the Midwest, while the NIT preferred Madison Square Garden as the host site. In March 1939 the NCAA Tournament began, and William B. Owens, the NCAA president noted, "It is entirely fitting that the 'prestige' of college basketball should be supported, and demonstrated to the nation, by the colleges themselves, rather than that this be left to private promotion and enterprise."[26] Eight teams competed that first year, and the Oregon Ducks emerged victorious. Despite a strong start, however, it would be more than ten years before the NCAA supplanted the NIT in prestige and popular opinion.

The college doubleheaders and the intersectional games helped popularize the game. One of the key figures during the late 1930s was an unassuming gentleman from California. Angelo "Hank" Luisetti, the son of Italian immigrants, played the game as a child and later played during his high school years at Galileo High in San Francisco. He once scored seventy-one points in a high school game. After graduation, he matriculated at Stanford University. A star at Stanford, Luisetti was a three-time All-America and led Stanford to three consecutive Pacific Coast titles from 1936 to 1938. As a sophomore, he averaged 14 points a game and then upped it to 15 points per game as a junior. As a senior Luisetti was setting records and making headlines while averaging 19.4 points per game. He was a two-time College Player of the Year and a three-time Helms Foundation All American. His team's success and his popularity benefited from the newly created college basketball doubleheaders that were popular in large eastern cities.

In 1937 Luisetti's Stanford team traveled east to face Long Island University, which was sporting a forty-three-game winning streak. In that highly anticipated match-up, Stanford defeated LIU before a sellout crowd in Madison Square Garden. Luisetti played 39.5 of the 40 minutes, scoring fifteen points. Larry Burton, writing the next day in the *New York American*, said, "Owing largely to the depredations of Angelo Luisetti, a dark, lean, agile San Francisco youth, the longest winning streak in modern intercollegiate basketball came to an abrupt end at Madison Square Garden last night. Behind the impetus provided by Luisetti, Stanford snuffed out Long Island University's 43-game string with a thorough beating, 45–31. He played 39½ minutes and when his coach, John Bunn, thoughtfully removed him with 30 seconds to go,

FIG. 4. A star at Stanford University in the late 1930s, Angelo "Hank" Luisetti helped popularize the jump shot, which revolutionized the game. Courtesy of Bill Himmelman.

the place broke into a noisy celebration as the Garden ever heard for a basketballer."[27]

The following season in 1938, Luisetti's Stanford team again came east. In a game against Duquesne, he scored fifty points, at that time a record for most points scored in a single game. Luisetti became known for popularizing the one-handed shot. He explained,

I started shooting one handed when I was a kid. I would play basketball with the other kids around, and I just couldn't reach the way they shot. So I threw it kind of like a baseball.

I was lucky later on. I had coaches that left me alone and let me develop my own style. I could play any position on the court, and so I just naturally moved around. I guess I started something. The Eastern teams practically ignored anyone west of the Mississippi. Then, we (Stanford) went on a road trip back east and won all our games. That put them on notice that, "hey, we are here and we're ready to play."[28]

As Moe Goldman, a standout center for the City College of New York in the early 1930s, said, "Hank Luisetti changed the whole game of basketball with his one-handed shot."[29]

Luisetti's play left a lasting impression on young players who would eventually make a mark for themselves in the NBA. Max Zaslofsky, a guard in the Basketball Association of America (BAA) after the war, remembered seeing Luisetti: "I watched this man handle himself. I saw how fluid and acrobatic he was in everything he did. . . . He was uncanny the way he moved and everything. I was deeply impressed with him. You could call him something of an idol."[30] Jim Pollard was a youngster growing up in Oakland and used to watch Luisetti play his college ball at Stanford. Pollard would eventually play at Stanford and in the NBA before earning a spot in the Naismith Memorial Basketball Hall of Fame. As he recalled years later, "He had great style. He was a great guy to watch. He had that charisma about him that everybody liked. . . . He was my hero when I was a kid."[31]

After graduation Luisetti followed his basketball career to the Olympic Club, the Phillips 66 Oilers, and during World War II with St. Mary's Preflight. In 1943 he joined the navy as an officer and trained cadets in physical fitness. He was later sent to Annapolis to help coach the navy basketball team as an assistant coach. "Then, in 1944 I contracted spinal meningitis," he recalled. "I was scheduled to report aboard an aircraft carrier for sea duty, and I was out celebrating with my friends. We had started out for home, when I felt awful all of a sudden. I was taken to sick bay, and the diagnosis was made."[32] Despite his career ending prematurely, Luisetti was an important transitional figure for the game of basketball during the 1930s.

With these changes—college basketball doubleheaders, elimination of the center jump, and Hank Luisetti's one-handed shot—the game was slowly coming of age, loosening the grips from its formative years, and introducing a style that was more popular and exciting on the eve of World War II.

The 1941–42 American Basketball League (ABL) season held high hopes for the Philadelphia SPHAS (South Philadelphia Hebrew Association team). As two-time defending league champions, the SPHAS looked to continue their dominant ways. In beginning their ninth season in the ABL, the SPHAS were clearly the league's most accomplished team. In the first eight years, the SPHAS had captured five championships, including the 1940–41 season with a 3–1 series victory over the Brooklyn Celtics. The SPHAS had now won back-to-back titles twice, the first time in 1935–36 and again in 1936–37. The team, behind owner, coach, and promoter Eddie Gottlieb, looked poised to continue its winning ways and to become the first team in league history to win three consecutive titles. After opening the season with a 34–31 victory at home at the Broadwood Hotel against the New York Jewels, the SPHAS traveled to Delaware to face the Wilmington Blue Bombers. A resounding 40–24 defeat was a bad omen for the SPHAS for the remainder of the season.

A dominant team in the 1930s and 1940s, the SPHAS had its origins early in the twentieth century. At the turn of the twentieth century, basketball was still in its infancy, but the game quickly became a favorite of the children of Jewish immigrants who were flocking to urban areas in the Northeast as they emigrated from Eastern Europe. As opposed to football and baseball, this new game of basketball was easier to play, required less space—important in the tenements of the cities—and was less expensive to play. Harry Litwack, who played for the SPHAS and later became a Naismith Memorial Basketball Hall of Fame coach for Temple University, recalled, "The Jews never got much into football or baseball. They were too crowded then."[33] Playing basketball required far less space and equipment than football or baseball. One needed only a hoop and a ball. The ball could be made of rags rolled together or newspapers held together by string. The hoop could be a basket hung from a pole or a ladder behind an apartment. Jerry Fleishman, who came of age as a youngster in the 1930s, remembers how he and his neighborhood friends improvised playing the game as a child. "When we were growing up, we were poor kids. We did not have basketballs. We rolled up newspapers and tied it together with a cord. There were fire escapes on the building, and the lower rung had a hole there, and we threw it through the lower rung. If it went through, it was either a basket or touchdown. That was our football and basketball."[34]

Much space was not a requirement as the game revolved around passing, ball possession, and tossing the ball toward the goal. As Sam "Leaden" Bernstein, who grew up playing basketball in South Philadelphia and later attended the SPHAS games as a fan, remarked, "Basketball was a slower game. It was a mental game. If you were a dumb ballplayer, you could not play in the game. If you were slow or could not concentrate or were not capable of playing, then you did not play. You had to be the best to play. There was a lot of competition."[35] Soon enough, basketball became a Jewish game and a certain style emerged. As Litwack noted, "It was a quick-passing running game as opposed to the bullying and fighting way which was popular other places."[36] Ossie Schectman, who would one day become known for scoring the first basket in the Basketball Association of America (BAA), grew up playing ball in New York. "Playing basketball in those days was confined to smaller areas," he explained. "The physical setup was not too much. The ceilings were low, and there were ten men on the court. You played in a figure-eight and there was lots of movement. It was devoid of long set shots."[37]

Philadelphia quickly emerged as a hotbed of basketball on the high school, college, and nascent professional circuit. After a successful run as city champions, some members of the Southern High School basketball team desired to keep playing after graduation. Three of them, Eddie Gottlieb, Edwin (Hughie) Black, and Harry Passon, joined forces and with the support of the Young Men's Hebrew Association (YMHA) formed a team. In exchange for uniforms, the team played as the YMHA in the American League of Philadelphia. After one season the YMHA discontinued its sponsorship, and Gottlieb, Black, and Passon sought a new organization to support its basketball endeavor. They did not have to look very far. The South Philadelphia Hebrew Association (SPHA) at Fourth and Reed Streets in South Philadelphia was the perfect organization. In exchange for uniforms the team played as the SPHAS. The SPHAS continued to play well and improve, but soon the association followed in the footsteps of the YMHA and discontinued its sponsorship. This time around the threesome of Gottlieb, Black, and Passon did not need to search for a new sponsor. Instead, they opened their own sporting goods store, Passon, Gottlieb, and Black, (P.G.B), made their own uniforms, and continued to call themselves the SPHAS, always, as they later acknowledged, to remember their origins.

By the mid-1920s the SPHAS had started to win local championships and even joined the American Basketball League for two seasons, where they acquitted themselves quite well. As the late 1920s rolled around, the SPHAS were a dominant team in the Eastern Basketball League and in the greater Philadelphia vicinity. Due to the Depression the American Basketball League shut down for two seasons before resuming in 1933–34. Eddie Gottlieb quickly joined the reconstituted ABL, and the SPHAS soon became the league's marquee team. Beginning with that first season in 1933–34, the SPHAS were not only one of the best professional teams in the country but also the greatest Jewish team

FIG. 5. Eddie Gottlieb coached, promoted, and managed the Philadelphia SPHAS for more than thirty years and helped make the SPHAS one of the best teams during the 1930s. Courtesy of Bill Himmelman.

ever assembled. Although the SPHAS' history spanned forty years, the team of the mid-1930s is the one that has endured in folklore and the memory of fans. At a time of great economic struggle and the rise of anti-Semitism, the SPHAS became a symbol for the Jewish community. Comprised of players from Philadelphia and New York, the two dominant cities for basketball, the SPHAS were all Jewish. The team traveled the Eastern Seaboard and the Midwest promoting professional baskctball while fighting off racial stereotypes of inferiority and weakness. Many difficult instances abounded, and the players stuck together as Gil Fitch recounted, "Gotty said the best way to answer them was to be the best team in basketball. When people in the crowd said 'get those Jews' or 'kill those Jews' we played extra hard."[38] As Harry Litwack later summed it up: "We had to stick together, and we had to fight to defend our people."[39]

The SPHAS not only persevered; they succeeded by winning three championships in four years from 1933–34 to 1936–37. Gottlieb, always one to find new ways to improve, remade the team as it approached the late 1930s. Stalwarts Gil Fitch and Harry Litwack retired to pursue other interests, while local star Alexander "Petey" Rosenberg joined the club. With a slightly retooled roster, the SPHAS again found their winning ways, capturing two more titles in 1939–40 and 1940–41.

As the 1941–42 American Basketball League campaign was set to begin, the SPHAS were considered the team to beat. The complexion of the league was slightly altered as the Brooklyn Celtics and the Baltimore Clippers ceased operation. The City of Brooklyn would eventually field another team in 1942–43, while Baltimore would again host a team in 1944–45. But for the 1941–42 season, neither city played professional ball. The Trenton Tigers and the Wilmington Blue Bombers represented the two new teams to replace Baltimore and Brooklyn. For Trenton this was the first time since the end of the 1935–36 season that the city had a professional team. Wilmington's entry was the first in a professional league, and its brief stay would prove to be quite successful. The league campaign would feature a first half and a second half, and the winners of each half would meet to crown a champion. After only seven games and sporting a dismal 1-6 record, the New York Jewels withdrew for the remainder of the season. Thus it would be Philadelphia, Trenton, Wilmington, and Washington to play out the campaign.

Their loss to Wilmington in the season's second game proved to be a bad sign for the SPHAS. Wilmington soon became one of the league's better teams and set its sights on challenging the SPHAS' supremacy. While Wilmington raced out to a 10-3 record in the first half, Philadelphia struggled and finished in second place with an 8-6 mark. It lost four times in the first half to Wilmington, but managed to win the final three games to finish with a respectable 8-6 record. Wilmington proved to be a tough opponent. In three of those four losses to the Blue Bombers, Wilmington won by a double-digit margin. Wilmington's defense proved to be too much of an obstacle for the SPHAS to overcome. In the first game on December 3, a smothering defense set the tone early. "From the time the Bombers deadlocked the count at 3–3 on a field toss by Moe Frankel, until six minutes of the second period had elapsed, the SPHAS failed to garner a point, while the Bombers stormed the nets from all angles to assume a 20–3 advantage."[40] The teams met a week later, and the result was much the same. The SPHAS scored the game's first two points for their only lead. After that "the Bombers flashed brilliant speed and a fine passing game in their rout of the defending champions at the Broadwood."[41] It was their defense that established the tone and set the key for their offense. New acquisition Ed Sadowski proved the game's key player: "Big Ed Sadowski was at center for the Bombers and this six-foot-six player was a power on defense. Ed intercepted numerous passes and deflected many well directed passes that hurt the SPHAS' scoring chances on many scoring occasions."[42] A much stronger front line proved the key difference for Wilmington that season.

Bernie Fliegel, a one-time SPHA, joined Wilmington for its inaugural season in 1941–42. He was accompanied that season by two newcomers, Jerry Bush and Ed Sadowski, both of whom had a tremendous impact on Wilmington's fortunes. As Fliegel recalled in a 2007 interview,

> The Detroit team had won the World Professional Basketball Tournament the previous spring, and we were able to sign a few of their players. We signed Jerry Bush, who was six three, and Ed Sadowski,

who was six five or six six. For the first time, I did not have to play center. We had a great team because of our height. The SPHAS at that time always had two or three big guys in Mike Bloom, Irv Torgoff, and Moe Goldman. In our first game against the SPHAS, Bloom outplayed Sadowski. We won, but Sadowski played poorly. Afterward I said, "Ed, we got you because you are a big, strong guy. You let Bloom push you around." He was steamed. The next time we played the SPHAS, he just killed Bloom. We beat everybody that year. We won both the first and second halves of the regular season, so we won the championship.[43]

Fliegel was right. The Blue Bombers beat all comers that season. After topping the league in the first half with a 10-3 record, the team won the second half with an 8–4 mark. Philadelphia slipped to a 5-7 record, never able to gain any consistency. By winning both halves Wilmington was crowned the champion; no championship series was needed. It was the only time in league history that this feat occurred. As a Wilmington Blue Bombers game program proudly touted, "Barney [Sedran] guided the Blue Bombers—the name given the Wilmington team—to a clean sweep of both halves of the circuit. This shattered the dynasty of the Philadelphia SPHAS, rulers of the Eastern and American Leagues for so long that the celebrated hirelings of Eddie Gottlieb had come to be regarded as the invincible monarchs of all they surveyed in the basketball world."[44] Fliegel recognized the SPHAS as a great team but also pointed out why Wilmington had the SPHAS number all season. "The SPHAS were a smart team. They had good shooters who passed the ball well, did give and goes, and were good underneath the boards. They were a great team and one of the best teams in the ABL for many years. After I went to Wilmington, we got Jerry Bush and Ed Sadowski and beat the SPHAS nine out of ten times one year."[45] In fact, it was seven of eight times, but nonetheless, their dominance was duly noted.

The improvement of the front line proved to be the key difference for Wilmington. A bigger, stronger, and more athletic front line proved troublesome for the SPHAS. Wilmington, though, had a more-than-capable offense, one that proved highly effective in keeping the SPHAS off balance. As Fliegel recalled, "On our team, we had one standard play. Chick Reiser would block for Charlie Hoefer, who would shoot it. Three of us would get under the boards and bat the ball back and forth. He would shoot, and we had three big guys who would bat the ball around if he missed, and finally one of us would tip it in. That was our sure point play. It was a great year. Years later the *New York Times* ran an article that said we were the best professional basketball team prior to the Los Angeles Lakers with Wilt Chamberlain and Elgin Baylor."[46]

Eddie Glennon, the publicity person in charge of publishing the official program for the Wilmington Blue Bombers, wrote a poem after the team's championship season, capturing the team effort it took to win.

> Barney, you're the man who taught your trick
> To Bernie, Moe, Ed and Nick,
> Also Charlie, Jerry, Sam and Chick—
> And we can't forget Moe and Mac,
> Here's hoping they'll be back![47]

Looking back in 1944–45, Glennon noted, "Barney Sedran came to Wilmington in '41 with the 'Bombers' who made history by winning both halves of the schedule. Captain Bernie Fliegel, former City College of New York luminary, had as his teammates Chick Reiser, Jerry Bush, now with Fort Wayne, a member of the National League, Sam Kaplan, now in the Army, Charley Hoefer, who is in the Coast Guard, somewhere in the South Pacific, Moe Spahn, now assistant coach of CCNY, also Ed Sadowski, Mac Kinsbrunner and our present Captain, Moe Frankel."[48] Wilmington's impressive campaign in 1941–42 altered the balance of power in the American Basketball League and gave the league's reigning power, the SPHAS, much to contemplate at the beginning of World War II.

While Wilmington was an upstart team looking to shock the balance of power in the American Basketball League, Oshkosh was an established team, finally reaching its prime.

The National Basketball League (NBL), founded in 1935 as the Midwest Basketball Conference, later became the NBL in 1937. Until its merger in 1949 with the Basketball Association of America to form the National Basketball Association, the NBL was the Midwest's answer to professional basketball in the East. The NBL provided a sense of order, professionalism, and stability to basketball in the Midwest. The Midwest's answer to professional basketball consisted of barnstorming, independent, and company-sponsored teams. In 1935–36 the Midwest Basketball Conference was founded behind the efforts of Frank Kautsky, a grocery-story owner in Indianapolis, and Paul Sheeks, an employee of the Firestone Tire and Rubber Company in Akron, Ohio. Over the next two years, the Midwest Basketball Conference was loosely organized. Each team was responsible for arranging its own games, ten of which were required to be league games and four of those had to be played on the road. In 1937 three company teams—General Electric, Goodyear, and Firestone—founded the National Basketball League, a league that all three hoped would finally supplant the industrial league teams that had dominated Midwest basketball for decades. Companies seeking to expand their community goodwill and athletic success sponsored teams in the newly formed league. The Akron Firestone Non-Skids, the Akron Goodyear Wingfoots, and the Fort Wayne General Electrics all hired men to work in the factories during the day and play basketball at nights and on the weekends.

In the league's first three years, the teams from Akron, the former industrial teams, dominated the National Basketball League. The Akron Goodyear Wingfoots won the title the first year, while their crosstown rival, the Akron Firestone Non-Skids, captured the next two championships. Losing in the finals all three years was Oshkosh. Each year Oshkosh took the series to the final game, only to fall short. Finally in

1940–41, Oshkosh put it all together and handily defeated its in-state Wisconsin rival, Sheboygan, to win its first championship. The team was led by Leroy "Cowboy" Edwards, a big, bruising center who dominated the interior. As the 1941–42 season was set to begin, the consensus was that Oshkosh was the team to beat.

The National Basketball League was changing as the industrial teams that defined the league in the early years were slowly being replaced by teams based in larger Midwest cities. The Akron Firestone Non-Skids ceased participating in the league at the conclusion of the 1940–41 season, and the upcoming season would mark the last go-round for the Goodyear Wingfoots. The Sheboygan Red Skins and the Chicago Bruins joined Oshkosh for another season, while the Detroit Eagles, winners of the 1941 World Professional Basketball Tournament dropped out of the league to become an independent team. For most of the season, Detroit was a road team as it "lost [its] home floor, the Armory, to a much more important need—Uncle Sam's forces."[49] The Indianapolis Kautskys returned after a one-year hiatus. The Kautskys were led by Jewell Young, a scoring machine, who in the upcoming season would tally 263 points. Two new teams, the Toledo Jim White Chevrolets and the Fort Wayne Zollner Pistons, entered the fray. Toledo had its own scoring ace, Chuck Chuckovits, a former standout at the University of Toledo. His performance during the 1941–42 league schedule would be nothing short of spectacular. "Chuckovits broke the National league basketball scoring record of Leroy Edwards by establishing a new record of 406 points for this season. This in spite of the fact that he missed two of the league's 24 regular scheduled games, establishing a record in 22 games that exceeded 'Cowboy' Edwards' record which was made in 28 games."[50]

It was the introduction of the Fort Wayne Zollner Pistons that would have the most lasting effect from that season: the team continues to play today in the National Basketball Association as the Detroit Pistons. The Piston company worked on defense contracts for the United

States government, and the players were employed at the company during the week and played games in the evenings and on weekends. The Zollner plant turned out "thousands of heavy-duty pistons for the maritime, airplane, tank, tractor, and truck engines being produced for war equipment."[51] Prior to joining the league, the team mostly played independent ball and traveled around the Indiana area. The North Side High School served as the team's home court. As Buddy Jeannette once noted, "At that time, North Side was a nice place to play. A nice floor."[52] However, the company's owner, Fred Zollner, who had grown up a huge sports fan, had grander aspirations. A native of Minnesota, he graduated from the University of Minnesota with a degree in metallurgical engineering. Upon graduation Fred followed his father into the family business, but his father was looking to grow the business so he relocated the company to Fort Wayne, Indiana, to be closer to Detroit and better serve the automobile industry with the company's truck pistons. The company also sponsored athletic teams for the workers, and Fred soon became a strong backer and ever bigger fan of the teams. Fred was a reserved gentleman, "a soft-voiced, curly-headed manufacturer, a friendly man with a taste for expensive, striped suits, and the engaging knack of making them look as if [he'd] worn them to bed."[53]

With basketball in particular he believed the team could compete with the best, so he sent his manager, Carl Bennett, on a trip to Chicago to find better competition. "Mr. Zollner, after our first year, wanted to play stronger teams, so I went into Chicago on a train, at that time, and saw Mr. Fischer, who was president of the league and asked him to book some exhibition games with us, so we'd have better competition," Bennett recalled. "And, of course, they were struggling and he said, 'why don't you fellows join the league?' And, by golly, he went back to Fort Wayne with me and we talked to Mr. Zollner, and of course it didn't take long to say, 'let's do it.'"[54] "In no time we became the NBL's newest franchise. Fred appointed me the coach, manager, recruiter, scorekeeper, equipment manager, and the head of ticket sales. I did

FIG. 6. A member of Indiana University's 1940 NCAA championship team, Herm Schaefer was a key player for the Fort Wayne Zollner Pistons before losing time for military service. Courtesy of Bill Himmelman.

it all."[55] Within two years after joining the league, the Pistons would come to dominate the competition.

The Fort Wayne club for 1941–42 included Paul "Curly" Armstrong and Herm Schaefer, two former Indiana University players who had led the team to the 1940 NCAA championship. Schaefer served as the team's player-coach. Also on that squad making his NBL debut was

Carlisle "Blackie" Towery, who was considered the "greatest player in Western Kentucky history" according to his coach Ed Diddle, who later earned a spot in the Naismith Memorial Basketball Hall of Fame.[56] At six feet five Towery was a big, imposing man who gave the Zollner Pistons a large, strong man to counter Oshkosh's Cowboy Edwards. Towery learned the game on a farm in a small town in Kentucky. He later said, "We never had an indoor gymnasium until my senior year in high school. I remember during the high school season we'd play all our home games on an outdoor court—that is, until the court froze over or got too muddy. Heck, there were only two indoor gyms in the entire county. When it got too cold, we'd try to schedule most of our games away from home, especially if our opponents had an indoor gym. But we had no set schedule at the time. We just played games whenever we could."[57] After graduating from Western Kentucky, Towery began exploring options for a professional career: "At the time, I had offers from Firestone, Goodyear, and Phillips 66 to play ball and work in the plant. Those firms offered me a good job in the plant but only promised that I could play just two years of basketball. I really wanted to play more than that. So when Herm [Schaefer] and I went to Fort Wayne, Fred [Zollner] offered me more [playing time]. Just sitting down and talking with Fred was like talking to one of your old school buddies. We really hit it off. I realized then and there that Fort Wayne was where I wanted to be."[58] With Towery joining Schaefer and Armstrong, Fort Wayne played well in its freshman season in the league.

While Fort Wayne was the league's future, its present was Oshkosh. The Oshkosh All-Stars were the brainchild of Arthur Heywood, the long-time sports editor of the *Oshkosh Daily Northwestern*. Heywood approached Lon Darling, who founded and assembled the first team for the 1929–30 season. Darling became synonymous with the All-Stars and operated the team until it disbanded in 1948. The All-Stars eventually played all twelve years in the NBL from 1937 to 1949 and won six

FIG. 7. Carlisle "Blackie" Towery starred at Western Kentucky University before joining the Fort Wayne Zollner Pistons, where he became an integral player in two National Basketball League championships. Courtesy of Bill Himmelman.

divisional titles and two league championships during that span. The All-Stars came to symbolize the city, and Oshkosh took great pride in the team. Scott Armstrong, a former player, remembered,

> Playing in Oshkosh was a horse of a different color. I'll tell you, you were king of the hill up there. The people held you in high esteem.

You'd get invitations to this and that and meals here and there. People would speak to you on the street and ask for your autograph.

The fans in Oshkosh were really rabid. Sheboygan was the big rival, of course. We were playing the Redskins at home one night and a Sheboygan player named Paul Sokody and I got our hands on a rebound near the sidelines. I knew the whistle was coming so I let go of it and Sokody fell backwards. He came up with his hands up as if he was going to hit me, and I pushed him and he went into the first row of seats.

Well, you'd think I had just made the greatest stunt in the world! Of course, the crowd didn't like him in the first place because he played for Sheboygan. Some fellow in Oshkosh even offered to buy me a hat.[59]

Wisconsin was still a very rural state at that time, and the All-Stars toured throughout, playing in rural towns and spreading the game's popularity. As Armstrong noted, "We went out on what we called the kerosene circuit. We'd go up north in Wisconsin and play colleges and little town teams maybe a couple of times a week. The gyms had electric lights, but a lot of the homes were still lit by kerosene. Things were still rural in those areas."[60] By the early 1940s, however, these trips were paying off.

As defending champions Oshkosh sought to become the second team since the Akron Firestone Non-Skids to repeat as champion. Riding high on a good showing in its preseason schedule, Oshkosh jumped out to an 11-0 record before finally losing. The only question was, who would finish second? Well balanced and playing with much confidence, Oshkosh finished the regular season with a 20-4 record, the first team to win more than twenty games since the Akron Firestone Non-Skids won twenty-four games in 1938–39. Only the top four teams qualified for the playoffs, and Oshkosh faced fourth-seed Indianapolis, while Fort Wayne battled Akron. Oshkosh quickly dispatched Indianapolis in two games, while Fort Wayne advanced in three games. The finals matched the present versus the future of the National Basketball League.

The finals were scheduled to be played on three consecutive days. The first game was played in Fort Wayne, while the next two would be contested in Oshkosh. The teams played evenly during the season, and that figured to be the case during the championship round. The teams faced each other four times during the regular season and one exhibition game, and Oshkosh won three of those regular season games. However, the scores were close as noted by the *Oshkosh Daily Northwestern*: "Fans can expect high-scoring and thrilling contests in the playoffs if the games follow the pattern set by competition between the two teams in the five games in which they have met previously this season. Oshkosh scored 244 points for an average of nearly 49 a game in those tilts while Fort Wayne totaled 213 or about 43 a game."[61]

In the first game Fort Wayne avenged its regular-season troubles by besting Oshkosh 61–43. Fort Wayne was led by Bobby McDermott, who tallied nine field goals and two foul shots for twenty points on "long shots [that] were little short of phenomenal."[62] McDermott was a new addition to the team this year. As the *Chicago Herald American* noted, "the Pistons added considerable strength to their cause midway in the season by the acquisition of Bobby McDermott, brilliant star of the New York Celtics. McDermott, a great point-getter, has forged almost to the top in National League individual standings."[63] A top player for many years, McDermott excelled with the Original Celtics and was known for his accurate outside shooting. As a kid growing up in Philadelphia, Jerry Rullo would often see McDermott play the hometown SPHAS. It was an impression that never left him: "I saw the greatest exhibition by a guy named Bobby McDermott. He shot the ball from the foul line set shot. The next time he would move back and shoot. He did this seven different times until he was at the opposite foul line, where he took a shot and missed. The crowd went nuts and gave him a big hand."[64]

On December 13, 1941, four games into the season, Fort Wayne signed legendary player Bobby McDermott. The following day the *Fort Wayne Journal Gazette* hailed the recent signing of McDermott and what he would mean for the team:

> McDermott, late star of the New York Celtics and often referred to as the greatest player in the country today, was signed by the Pistons yesterday and worked out with the club last night for the first time. It was possible to secure McDermott because of the fact that the team was able to offer him regular employment in the Zollner plant in addition to his playing and will be on the same basis as the rest of the squad in that respect. While Herman Schaefer will remain player/coach, McDermott's long experience in the professional game will be utilized to the greatest possible extent in an advisory capacity in matter of strategy. McDermott will move his wife and two children here within a few weeks and plans to make Fort Wayne his permanent home.[65]

According to Carl Bennett, signing McDermott made sense not only for the team but also for the player.

> Bob McDermott was our biggest coup. I watched him play in exhibition games, and he was amazing. He was making shots from at least 40–45 feet away from the basket. It was incredible. It certainly didn't take long to realize what a talent he was. It really wasn't difficult to convince him to come to Fort Wayne, because all of Fred's basketball players worked in the plant. So we guaranteed him a job during the week and plenty of basketball games on the weekend. When you have a family and you're looking for a good-paying job, it not hard to convince someone like McDermott that Fort Wayne was the place to be.[66]

Joining McDermott on the team was Paul Birch, a former New York Celtics player, who added toughness and a veteran presence to the squad. As Towery recalled, "McDermott and Birch played so well together. Paul could really read the defense and set Bobby up like nobody's business. Birch would set picks for him, dish off the ball, then Mac could get off one of those long, two-handed set shots. They were really a tough two-man team."[67]

While the newcomer McDermott propelled Fort Wayne to a series-opening win, it was old stalwart Cowboy Edwards who righted the ship for Oshkosh in their Game Two 68–60 win. He tallied thirty-five points in a performance described as "one of the best the great cager has turned in in a long and brilliant career. He played the full 40 minutes of the game, the only one of the 20 players who saw action to go the entire route and kept 'pitching' throughout with five points in the first quarter, 11 in the second, 11 in the third and eight in the fourth."[68]

The third and final game saw the largest crowd ever in Oshkosh, 2,083 fans, watch the All-Stars repeat as league champions with a 52–46 win. McDermott and Edwards, the stars of the first two games, were nonfactors as Oshkosh's Lou Barle led the charge. Oshkosh had now repeated as NBL champions and made its city proud. As one newspaper report proudly declared, "It's the Oshkosh All-Stars—the quintet which has made that Wisconsin city as famous in the tossing pastime as the Packers have made Green Bay on the football field. And like Green Bay, it's a community affair sponsored and promoted by Oshkosh citizens as a civic enterprise."[69] The Packers provided the model for the organization of the All-Stars; according to author Todd Gould, "The success of Wisconsin's other city-owned sports attraction, pro football's Green Bay Packers, had inspired [Lon] Darling to sell stock in his club, and more than 100 businessmen, industrialists, and fans had purchased shares in the franchise, guaranteeing good salaries for the players and bolstering community support for the team."[70]

Fresh off its triumph as National Basketball League champion, Oshkosh prepared itself for the fourth annual World Professional Basketball Tournament held in Chicago. As the 1930s were drawing to a close, the concept of single-elimination basketball tournaments was gaining

FIG. 8. The Oshkosh All-Stars won their only National Basketball League championship in 1941–42 by defeating the Fort Wayne Zollner Pistons in three games. Courtesy of Bill Himmelman.

greater currency among the public and astute promoters. The National Invitation Tournament (NIT) and the National Collegiate Athletic Association (NCAA) founded their annual postseason tournaments in 1938 and 1939 respectively. Though still young both tournaments were gaining a foothold and in the decades to come would attain tremendous success in terms of popularity and at the gate. By 1939 the time seemed right to have a comparable tournament for professional basketball. The task of realizing this idea fell to two Chicago entrepreneurs. The first was Harry Hannin, a successful businessman in the clothing industry, and the second was Harry Wilson, who had gained attention as a local sports promoter. Together the two Harrys approached the *Chicago Herald American* (a merger between the *American* and the *Herald-Examiner*), a newspaper owned by William Randolph Hearst, for support. The newspaper soon agreed, and on March 26–28, 1939, the first World Professional Basketball Tournament was held.

As John Schleppi, the author of *Chicago's Showcase of Basketball: The World Tournament of Professional Basketball and the College All Star Game*, notes, "During the Great Depression many organizations and events, as well as several college football bowls (the Sugar, Cotton, and Sun), the National Collegiate Athletic Association basketball tournament, the National Invitational Tournament, the National Association of Intercollegiate Basketball (present NAIA) tournament, and Amateur Softball Association tournament, were all promotions born out of financial necessity to put backsides in arena seats. The developing World Tournament of Professional Basketball was to become another of these events."[71]

That first tournament was played over three days at the Madison Street Armory at the end of March 1939. The tournament came together quickly, in some instances, haphazardly, as the organizers rushed to assemble a representative field of teams. The field that first year consisted of eleven squads ranging in locations from New York to Indiana to Wisconsin to West Virginia to Michigan and to Illinois. Those teams included the Clarksburg Oilers, the New York Yankees, the New York Renaissance (Rens), the New York Celtics, the Harlem Globetrotters, the Chicago Harmons, the Illinois Grads, the Fort Wayne Harvesters, the Oshkosh All-Stars, the Sheboygan Red Skins, and the Benton Harbor House of David. Some of the teams were added mere days before the tournament commenced. Despite the "seat-of-the-pants" approach, the tournament not only attracted quality teams; it was also able to raise $10,000 in prize money. It was billed as the "World Series" of professional basketball in what was proclaimed as "the greatest array of cage talent ever assembled in one place."[72] The tournament did not disappoint as the New York Renaissance defeated the Oshkosh All-Stars, thus earning the title of world basketball champion.

From 1939 to 1948 the World Professional Basketball Tournament played a significant role in promoting the game, establishing the professional game on a national level, drawing teams from across the country, and providing a forum for quality professional basketball during World War II. Held in Chicago, the country's second largest city, the tournament was operated and sponsored by the *Chicago Herald American*. Four individuals were most responsible for the successful promotion and management of the tournament. Harry Wilson was the tournament secretary, while Harry Hannin served as director of arrangements. The publicity fell to Leo Fischer, who wrote articles about the team, published the annual program, and later served as commissioner of the National Basketball League. His affiliation with the National Basketball League provided the tournament with a decidedly midwestern flavor as many of the teams who competed over the years hailed from the Midwest or were affiliated at some point with the National Basketball League. Many eastern-based teams chose not to participate. Finally, Edward Cochrane, as sports editor of the newspaper, rounded out the group of the four men in charge of operating the tournament. Due to the great support of the *Chicago Herald American*, the tournament always received great coverage in the newspaper and attracted record crowds. It was during those days in March from 1939 to 1948 that the Original March Madness was born.

That attention was needed, because, as Schleppi notes, "Professional basketball was in disarray in the late 1930s due to poor financial backing, quixotic leadership, and the effects of the Depression. Against this background entrepreneur Harry Hannin and Leo Fischer of the *Chicago Herald American* promoted the World Tournament of Professional Basketball, which began in March 1939. Attracting the best available teams, they included the leading black and integrated teams. This was the first time blacks competed with whites on an even footing for a professional team championship. Using major facilities, including the Amphitheatre and the Stadium, attention was drawn to the game during the war years."[73]

The fact that the tournament served as the first venue for all-black and integrated teams to play for a professional championship was the World Professional Basketball Tournament's most important and lasting legacy. From its very first year in 1939 until it concluded in 1948, the World Professional Basketball Tournament invited the best black teams to participate. The New York Renaissance (Rens) won the inaugural tournament in 1939 and earned the unique distinction of being the only team to participate all ten years. One of the Rens best players, William "Pop" Gates, was the only player to compete all ten years, although not all with the Rens. The following year, the Harlem Globetrotters won the title. Thus, in the first two years, the two best black teams captured the title as basketball champions of the world.

As black teams won, recognition fell to their players. A strong array of black players competed in the tournament, including Robert "Sonny" Wood, Nat "Sweetwater" Clifton, George Crowe, William "Pop" Gates, Zack Clayton, Bernie Price, William "Dolly" King, Johnny Isaacs, Clarence "Puggy" Bell, Louis "Babe" Pressley, and Wyatt "Sonny" Boswell, and all garnered recognition. Except for the 1946 and 1947 tournaments, at least one black player was named to the all-tournament first or second teams every year. Other players such as Al Price, Tarzan "Chuck" Cooper, and Willie Smith all made contributions to integrating the game.

The fourth year looked to be the year of the Oshkosh All-Stars. The tournament, set to begin play on March 7 with first-round matches, was a mere three months to the day after Pearl Harbor. The country was mobilizing for war, and even though most of the players had yet to be drafted, war permeated the air around the tournament. Edward Cochrane, the sports editor of the *Chicago Herald American* (who was also a boxing referee and an NFL official) and one of the organizers of the tournament, wrote a piece in the tournament program reflecting the new realities faced by the country and how the upcoming basketball matches epitomized the struggle that the country now faced. In part, he stated:

FIG. 9. Pop Gates is the only player to play all ten years in the World Professional Basketball Tournament, and he did so with the New York Renaissance, the Washington Bears, and the Long Island Grummans. Courtesy of Bill Himmelman.

True to the American tradition, our international relations have always reflected our attitude in sport, with the Americans always displaying towards their vanquished enemies the great soul of magnanimity which has too often allowed our generosity to blind our good judgment, enabling some despotic rulers to rise and take

FIG. 10. A star player for the Harlem Globetrotters, Louis "Babe" Pressley played in the World Professional Basketball Tournament. Courtesy of Bill Himmelman.

advantage of this American attitude, and mistake it as a sign of weakness.

The great struggle going on in the world today will be carried to a successful conclusion by all of us. These boys cavorting on the basketball court tonight who are being cheered to the echo by all of us in the stands, in some way reflect our boys in the armed forces, being supported by those of us behind the lines. Let us do more than cheer. Let us get behind our great national leaders and our great American boys at the present time defending not only our freedom, but the freedom of all liberty loving people of the world.[74]

Excitement surrounded the 1942 World Professional Basketball Tournament as preview articles generated hype and anticipation more than one month before the start of the tournament. The games would be broken up into six sessions over a five-day period, March 7–11. Since this tournament was an invitational, the organizers made it a point to mention that teams apply for the right to be selected and play in the tournament: "The entire country from coast to coast is being combed for the best representatives of the cage sport. Records and personnel will determine the admission of a team to the meet, thus insuring the continuation of the hysteria-producing thrillers which have made the event the outstanding basketball tournament of the year."[75] When the organizers said they were searching coast to coast, they certainly did not leave any stone unturned even if in 1942 "coast-to-coast" generally meant East, Midwest, and Southeast. Teams that submitted applications and were being considered represented the following towns: Kenosha, Wisconsin; Akron, Ohio; Philadelphia, Pennsylvania; Washington DC; Rochester, New York; Newark, New Jersey; Memphis, Tennessee; Minneapolis, Minnesota; Bismarck, North Dakota; Buffalo, New York; Cleveland, Ohio; Steubenville, Ohio; East Liverpool, Ohio; and Atlanta, Georgia.

Sixteen teams entered the field, and there were many holdovers from the year before, including the three previous champions, the New York Renaissance (Rens) (1939), the Harlem Globetrotters (1940), and the Detroit Eagles (1941). Each sought to become the first repeat champion. A strong contingent of National Basketball League teams, including six of the seven in the circuit—the Oshkosh All-Stars, the Chicago Bruins, the Sheboygan Red Skins, the Toledo Jim White Chevrolets, the Fort

Wayne Zollner Pistons, and the Indianapolis Kautskys—all joined the field. Toledo was led by star Chuck Chuckovits, who had set a record in last year's tournament with eighty-eight points in four games. In its initial season in the NBL, Fort Wayne acquitted itself well. The team was also making the necessary sacrifices due to the war. As the tournament program noted, "The feature of the team that is especially appealing is that the boys, on account of being engaged in defense work, have voluntarily worked overtime in order to make up for any lost hours that they may have taken away for the playing of any basketball games during the current season."[76] Chicago, Sheboygan, Toledo, Fort Wayne, and Indianapolis all looked to advance and stay on the other side of the bracket from Oshkosh, a team that had given everyone problems during the NBL season. So important was the participation of these six teams fighting for the tournament championship that "the loop speeded up its own championship playoffs to permit its quintets to take part."[77]

Other Midwest squads such as the Detroit AAA, the Columbus Bobb Chevrolets, the Northern Indiana Steelers, and the Davenport Central Turner Rockets threw their hats in the ring. The city of Detroit was represented by two teams, while the Steelers of Northern Indiana represented the smallest city in the tournament, Michigan City, Indiana. Davenport was an independent team, while Columbus was making its first appearance in the tournament. The state of Maryland was represented by the Hagerstown Conoco Oilers. Hagerstown was led by Fred Crum, who in 1934 set a record in the national YMCA tournament with 125 points in five games, a mark that still stood on the eve of the 1942 tournament. Crum also had the distinction of playing on the first American Olympic basketball team, which earned a gold medal at the 1936 Berlin Olympics with a win over Canada in a game played outdoors in the rain. This roster made fourteen of the sixteen teams.

For the first time in tournament play, two teams with military ties entered. One was the Aberdeen Army Ordnance Training Center in Aberdeen, Maryland. The other was the Long Island Grumman Flyers from Bethpage, New York. In previewing the Grumman Flyers in the *Chicago Herald American*, Leo Fischer provided the reader with an enticing capsule of the team, and for many of the paper's readers it would be their only knowledge of them: "The team averages better than six feet two and one-half inches in height with [Ossie] Schectman—an All-American guard—as the smallest member. He's an even six feet. It has played a schedule of ten games—all of them victories—and has scored 510 points against the best clubs in the East. It is a short-passing team with an attack reminiscent of the New York Celtics in their palmiest days, and the sharp-shooters won't be far off, if they make this club one of the pre-tournament favorites."[78]

Indeed, the Grumman Flyers were a team to watch not only for its play but also for the fact that the team was integrated. Three black players, Pop Gates, Tarzan Cooper, and Dolly King, all former New York Renaissance players, were integral members of the team. What is interesting to note is that this fact did not garner much attention in the newspapers and appears not to have been an issue with opposing players and fans. The *Chicago Defender* wrote about the Grumman team: "The easterners had three Negro players on their squad and all three got into the game. Talk about a real All-American democratic outfit—this was one. There were Tarzan Cooper and Pop Gates, two ex-New York Ren players, and Dolly King, who gained fame at Long Island university and later played one year with the Rens."[79] Gates, a key member of the squad, remembered his time with the Flyers and their trip to Chicago:

> There was a time during the war when the Rens weren't traveling all that much, and myself and several others went to Grumman Aircraft. I was working at Grumman for a weekly salary, and we weren't getting paid for the ball games. We didn't play every day of the week; we played whenever we were able to play. I played with the Washington Bears also.

At Grumman Aircraft, I worked first in a stock room. Then I became what they called a pre-flight mechanic. We played mostly at Freeport High School—probably one game per week. We went out to Chicago for the World Tournament once, maybe twice. We had some of the best players in the East—Ed Sadowski, Nat Frankel, all the big-name ballplayers. We went out there and got our ass whipped right away by a team we never heard of. Because we didn't have our show together—we had the ballplayers, but we didn't know how to run the race. I was playing with the Washington Bears at the same time, going down there on weekends.[80]

Gates's recollection, although many decades after his playing career ended, was partially correct. Grumman did field a team called the Hellcats that played in the 1945 tournament. Their asses were whipped in the first round by the Dayton Acmes, 43–27, most likely the team they had never heard of. However, in 1942 the Grumman Flyers were a very good team, consisting of former New York Renaissance players such as Dolly King, Pop Gates, and Tarzan Cooper, along with former Long Island University and Philadelphia SPHAS players such as Ossie Schectman, Irv Torgoff, Butch Schwartz, and Si Lobello. They were a sound, all-around team, looking to make their mark on the tournament. The Grumman Flyers played as an integrated team. The other interesting side note from the tournament was that the Davenport Rockets center, Bob Karstens, would one day become the only white player to suit up for the Harlem Globetrotters.

The Grumman company was actively involved in the war effort. The tournament program offered a profile of the company's effort:

Every man on the team is employed in the Grumman Aircraft Engineering Corporation, busily engaged in making flying ships for our boys engaged in the more serious business of polishing off Hitler, Hirohito, Mussolini & Co. The historical and dramatic defense of Wake Island, a feat which has gone down in history as one of the most memorable in the long annals of the United States Marine courage, was aided with 16 Grumman built airplanes which constituted the only air support for the small handful of Marines that so successfully warded off for nearly two weeks a horde of over 10,000 Japanese troops supported by naval and air forces ten times the size of the small United States garrison.[81]

The Grumman Flyers were not the only team with military ties to acquit itself well in the tournament. The Aberdeen Army Ordnance squad pulled an early upset by defeating the heavily favored Fort Wayne Zollner Pistons. The team, an army team, was composed of players from around the country, mostly recent college graduates including Duquesne's Moe Becker, Santa Clara's Marty Passaglia, and Lou Romano, from little Glenville Teachers of West Virginia. Previewing his own team, Aberdeen's Moe Becker declared, "Although this is the first venture of a service team into tournament play, they'll have to beat us before we concede anything to any one."[82] Playing with only five players, Aberdeen had an easy time with Fort Wayne, winning comfortably, 56–42. Fort Wayne was playing its sixth game in seven nights, including losing to Oshkosh in the NBL finals the previous week, and simply ran out of steam. In the following game Aberdeen met the defending champions, the Detroit Eagles, and lost a close 40–34 contest. In its first appearance in the World Professional Basketball Tournament, Aberdeen acquitted itself well and figured to be a competitive military team in the coming years.

Having a military-based team and an independent-aircraft-plant-sponsored team in the tournament was a huge coup for the organizers, who sought to capitalize on the patriotic fervor engulfing the nation. In their preview of the Aberdeen squad, the organizers hoped that the crowd would respond with appropriate support for these soldiers and players: "It goes without saying that when these boys in the service of our country walk out on to the basketball court for their first game in this meet, the International Amphitheatre will hear an ovation that will virtually raise the roof and will undoubtedly be the most spontaneous and noisiest reception ever given an athletic group in Chicago, that is famous for its treatment accorded visiting athletes. Let's go, soldiers, the best of luck in this tournament and in your military careers."[83]

The war was not yet in full swing, and only a few players had been drafted. The military had yet to take a heavy toll on basketball, and the flexibility of the military early in the war was of great benefit to the tournament. As a sportswriter observed, "Even the call made by Uncle Sam on caging talent has failed to keep the tournament from exceeding all previous records for the brilliance of its personnel. As a matter of fact, the military phase is well represented. Half a dozen athletes have secured furloughs to play for the teams which they represented before joining the colors, while one of the contesting clubs is made up of entirely of men from the U.S. Army Ordnance Proving Ground at Aberdeen, Md. Another represents one of our most vital defense industries, an airplane manufacturing concern."[84]

One of the selling points for the tournament organizers was promoting the players, a concept that would define sports marketing in the decades to come. With the rise of the college game, the increase of doubleheaders around the country, and the early success of the NIT and NCAA tournaments, the organizers made a point of mentioning the players and highlighting their respective colleges. Players were recognized for the colleges they attended. Among the standout players participating in that year's tournament were Ossie Schectman of Long Island University, Herm Schaefer of Indiana University, Gene Englund from the University of Wisconsin, Jack Garfinkel of St. John's University in New York, Eddie Riska of Notre Dame, Moe Becker of Duquesne, and Bob Dietz of Butler University.

In contrast to the players of the 1930s who had attended college, in the game's infancy "most professional rosters were still filled by alumni of the school of hard knocks in regional leagues, YMCAs, high schools, and settlement house teams."[85] This shift toward college players started in the 1930s; as Robert Peterson explains, "Two factors were at work. First, with the onset of the Depression, it was hard for even a college graduate to find a job—any job—and professional basketball offered a good living in season and sometimes a job for the off-season. And for a lucky player who *did* have another job, pro basketball was a pleasant way to supplement his income. The second factor was the game itself. Players who had benefitted from good coaching in college and had played the game with a high level of skill welcomed the chance to continue playing. It was pure love of the game that sent them into the professional ranks."[86]

With new teams complementing the old guard, the promoters readied themselves for what they hoped would be an outstanding tournament. Tickets were available and could be purchased at Bond's Clothes, the Stockyards Inn, and the tournament headquarters at 326 West Madison Avenue. Mail and phone orders were also accepted. Improvements were the order of the day as recounted in the *Chicago Herald American*.

> Seating arrangements, parking, and every other facility for the comfort of the spectators is being handled so that no detail will be overlooked. Fans who marveled at the manner in which these things were provided for last year will find improvement all along the line.
>
> That gleaming new floor, built at a cost of $5,000 for last year's tournament, again will be much in evidence. It has been widened several feet, however, to provide more room for the dazzling and intricate team play and passing which features the performances of the contesting teams. Baskets with transparent backboards again will be used so that every seat in the place commands a view of all that transpires on the court—and you can bet that it will be plenty.
>
> Most important of all is the free parking space. Every sports fan who has suffered from the "'watch your car" pest will appreciate that.

Particularly so, in view of the fact that tires and parts are so valuable these days. More than 4,000 automobiles can be accommodated in the brightly-lighted, well guarded parking lot.[87]

As the tournament continued to grow, so too did its coverage. "The amount of national interest being shown in the meet is evidenced by the fact that in addition to the International News, Associated Press and United Press, scores of newspapers are sending staff men to report the event. These include publications in Cleveland, Indianapolis, Oshkosh, Sheboygan, Milwaukee, Fort Wayne, Toledo, Memphis, Des Moines, Cumberland, Md., Long Island, N.Y., Akron, Kenosha, Atlanta and other points. Besides these, the newsreels will be out in force to record the action, while arrangements have already been made for two play-by-play broadcasts, with others pending."[88]

In addition to the news coverage, the organizers spent considerable attention on live entertainers to perform either before or during halftimes of the games. As recounted in the *Chicago Herald American*,

> The talent includes Willie Shore, ace comedian for the Chez Paree; Danny Thomas, side splitter, who has been packing 'em in at the 5100 Club for almost two years; Dolly Kay, one of the nation's top blues singers now top-starring at Colosimos; Jackie Green, mimic de luxe, the master of ceremonies at Harry's New Yorker; Wallie Vernon, former screen star, now emcee at Colosimo's, and the famous San Souci Dancers from the same famous night spot in their internationally famous Rhumba and Hawaiian Dancers. In addition to this array of all-American entertainment, a familiar musical group will return in the persons of Floyd Campbell and his Harlem Swingsters, whose hot licks have been a feature of each of the previous world's championship tournament.[89]

The entertainment figured to be one of the highlights of the tournament. Ample attention was also given to the referees. "Then, of course, there's Pat Kennedy, who is also a thespian of no little ability when he gets out on the floor and starts tooting that whistle. Pat heads a list of top notch officials who include Nat Messenger [sic], Jim Enright, Frank Kriznecky, Art Mansfield, Al Cervi, Christy Harrold, Elmer Hooker, Dick Kuzma [sic], H. C. Warren and Sam Pecoraro [sic]."[90] With improved amenities, star entertainers booked, and the nation's best referees signed on, all that was left was for the games to begin.

From the outset the posturing started among the head coaches. Dutch Dehnert, the coach of the defending champions, the Detroit Eagles, proclaimed, "Even though we've lost Jimmy Brown and Bob Calihan to the navy and Ed Sadowski to the army, we're going to be right in there once more, and trying our hardest to keep our championship as a tribute to the three boys who helped us so much last year. Bud Jeannette, Jack Ahearn and Ed Parry are back from last year, and we have added Paul Widowitz and Lou Kasperik from Duquesne, along with 'Dutch' Garfinkel of St. John's. He and Moe Becker were the stars of last November's all-star game. We also expect Jerry Bush to rejoin us in time for the tournament."[91] In their run to the title the previous year, Detroit had defeated the Indianapolis Kautskys, the Harlem Globetrotters, the New York Renaissance (Rens), and the Oshkosh All-Stars on four consecutive days to earn the title of "Cinderella team" of the tournament. The team's feat was even more impressive because the Eagles had played with only six players after two were injured in the opening minutes of the first contest. With their experience, battle-tested Detroit hoped for a repeat performance.

The Harlem Globetrotters' Abe Saperstein stated, "If my boys show any semblance of the form they displayed while winning games all over the United States, Canada, and Mexico, you can put them down as the first repeater in the history of the meet. I think we have the best club in fifteen seasons."[92] In the fourteen previous seasons, the Globetrotters won more than two thousand games, and Saperstein had incorporated two young players, Tony Peyton and Roosie Hudson, to complement the core group of Ted Strong, Inman Jackson, Babe Pressley, Bernie Price, and Bill Ford.

Meanwhile, Bob Douglas of the New York Renaissance countered, "Our boys felt that we should and could have won the title last year except for a little carelessness. They're determined not to make the same mistakes. The Rens are represented by the youngest and best team in their history."[93] Douglas was looking to keep pace and also signed the best black talent available. For the 1941–42 season, he added Sonny Boswell, Hillery Brown, and Sonny Wood. These three new stars joined a formidable lineup including Willie Smith, Puggy Bell, Zack Clayton, Charlie Isles, and Johnny Isaacs. Both the Renaissance and the Globetrotters looked to make a deep run in the tournament.

The host team was the Chicago Bruins, owned by Chicago Bears football coach George Halas. "Two years ago we came so close to winning the championship that we still can't understand how we lost," noted Arch Wolfe of the Chicago Bruins. "We're adding four new players for the tournament, and with a nucleus of the best from our season's squad we'll put up a real fight."[94] The loss in 1940 still haunted the Bruins as they let an eight-point lead with four minutes remaining evaporate as the Globetrotters took home the title. Even the newcomer Hagerstown Conoco Oilers sounded optimistic as Bill Young stated, "Keep your eyes on our Blue Ridge boys. We've lost only one game this year and have beaten the best of them."[95]

A strong regular season finish to the NBL campaign offset a disappointing start for the Sheboygan Red Skins. A key regular-season win over Toledo, in which the team scored sixty-seven points and Ed Dancker connected on twelve field goals, seemed to propel the Red Skins to a strong finish. The team hoped that the momentum would carry over to the tournament. "We have lacked that certain something all season," manager Carl Roth declared. "We came close several times, but when we were about ready to make a harvest something always turned against us. After that great showing against Toledo, I really

FIG. 11. Abe Saperstein managed the Harlem Globetrotters for decades and made them one of the most entertaining teams in basketball history. Courtesy of Bill Himmelman.

think we are strong enough to win not only the league playoffs, but the world's championship as well. It's a tough order, but the Redskins are tough and don't forget it."[96]

Despite the verbal sparring among the other coaches, the Oshkosh All-Stars were considered one of the favorites to win. Oshkosh competed well in the tournament but always found a way to come up short

FIG. 12. A native of the Caribbean, Bob Douglas owned, managed, and pro-moted the New York Renaissance team, one of the best professional teams from the 1920s to the 1940s. Courtesy of Bill Himmelman.

when it mattered most. Lon Darling, Oshkosh All-Stars coach, sounded optimistic on why this year's team might be the one to overcome past history. "We've been runner-up in two of the three tournaments, and it's about time we finished in that number one spot. Gene Englund will be a big help to us and our boys are keen to win. So will Eddie Riska, another new man, although we'll miss Bob Carpenter from last year's team, who is now an army lieutenant."[97]

Oshkosh jumped out to a quick start with an easy win in the first round versus Davenport, 44–29. The win set up a quarterfinal match-up with the New York Rens, who defeated Indianapolis, 55–37, as Sonny Boswell set a tournament record with thirty-two points for the Rens. The All-Stars-versus-Rens game was considered by many experts to be the game of the tournament; as Leo Fischer asserted, "That Oshkosh-Rens contest should be something to behold and may be the standout game of a tournament which has offered nothing but standout games."[98] The *Oshkosh Daily Northwestern* declared, "The Oshkosh-Rens battle tonight is one that is expected to turn out a large crowd of fans in Chicago as the teams long have been rivals."[99] This marked the seventh year that the two teams had faced each other with Oshkosh holding a 20-16 edge. The game was also a rematch of the 1939 finals, in which the Rens won the inaugural tournament. This marked the fifth time that the teams were facing each other this season. They had played a four-game barnstorming tour in Wisconsin in November prior to the start of the National Basketball League play.

This much-anticipated game turned into a hard-fought slugfest characterized by record-setting fouls by both clubs. Writing the following day Harry Wilson summed up the game, "Never has this author witnessed a more fiercely contested sport event than that ding-dong game that saw a plucky Oshkosh team beat down a determined bid by the Rens, to gain the semifinal round. . . . Fifty-two fouls, twenty-seven on the Rens and twenty-five for Oshkosh, set a new title tourney record. . . . Cashing in on 24 out of 29 attempts at the charity line, Oshkosh set another tourney record. . . . Blood, sweat and tears was in evidence at the conclusion of that epic game. . . . (Who said the pros didn't play for keeps)."[100]

Despite the fouls by both teams, Oshkosh jumped out to a strong start and held a 27–18 lead at halftime. Oshkosh held an eleven-point lead going into the final frame before a late spurt by the Rens closed the gap, but that surge could not get them over the hump. Oshkosh won 44–38. Oshkosh's defense on Sonny Boswell proved a key in the victory. After scoring thirty-two points in the previous game, he was held to fifteen points in defeat. Gene Englund led the All-Stars with thirteen points. Having escaped defeat, Oshkosh readied itself for a trip to the semifinals.

As the semifinals loomed, local interest soared to new levels. The previous night three thousand fans had been turned away from the Oshkosh-Rens game because the stadium had reached its capacity. Hoping to avoid a public relations nightmare, the organizers announced that "twenty-five hundred extra seats [would] be available for tonight's semifinals and tomorrow's finals in order to avoid having to turn away any fans."[101] The extra seats would be needed to see the marquee match-up featuring Oshkosh and the Harlem Globetrotters, winners of the 1940 tournament.

Oshkosh had won two early season games from the Harlem Globe-trotters and looked to continue its winning ways. The Globetrotters had the unfortunate distinction of losing tough games to the eventual champions in early rounds in 1939 (Renaissance) and 1941 (Detroit). Would this dubious distinction repeat itself in 1942? The game did not disappoint as "the Oshkosh team trailed the Harlem Globe Trotters by ten points late in the final half and then piled thrill upon thrill to pull out an amazing 48–41 victory that left the 8,200 crowd in a daze as the final gun went off."[102] Lon Darling's pre-tournament comment about newcomer Eddie Riska being a key player proved correct in the semifinal win. He turned in one of the most spectacular performances in the short history of the tournament. Leo Fischer reported, "Riska was superb last night as he rallied the Oshkosh team in the closing minutes and single handedly piled up point after point to snatch what looked like certain victory away from the brilliant Globe Trotters. Aside from his rival of tonight, it was the single greatest individual exhibition in the meet. When the box score was finally tallied up, it showed Riska with sixteen points for the final period—thirteen of them in about three minutes to pull Oshkosh far from behind into their championship game."[103] Eddie Riska's twenty points and Gene Englund's fourteen paced the All-Stars.

Waiting for Oshkosh in the finals were the Detroit Eagles. The Eagles, having squeaked out a 44–43 win over the Long Island Grumman Flyers in the semifinals, were back in the championship for the second year in a row and looked to become the first team to win two consecutive championships. The game was a repeat of Detroit's thrilling 38–37 win over Oshkosh last year, in which they held off a furious late rally by the All-Stars. Oshkosh was making its third trip to the finals and looking to avenge that defeat. This repeat championship game elicited the interest of the media; Jack Lieb of News of the Day, Emile Montemurro of Movietone News, and Floyd Traynham of Universal News Reel were all present to film and distribute the game. While Eddie Riska, a newcomer, was the star of the semifinal win, Oshkosh was led by old stalwart Cowboy Edwards in the finals. His tough play provided the emotional lift necessary for Oshkosh to finally claim the crown with a 43–41 win. Harry Wilson, writing the following day, described the all-out effort that Edwards provided for the team: "For the pluckiest player in the meet we give you Leroy 'Cowboy' Edwards, one of the two great centers on the new title-holding team. . . . Injured badly in the first play of the game last night, he came back in the second quarter, got hurt again, went limping out only to return in the fourth quarter taped up. He proceeded to dump in five consecutive points for his team then got hurt so badly he couldn't move. . . . But the big Kentuckian had a big grin when the final gun went off and thought the result justified his injuries."[104]

With Cowboy Edwards as its inspiration, Oshkosh fought its way to a tough victory. Oshkosh started well and built a 20–10 lead at halftime. But with the season on the line, the second half proved interesting. "In the last two quarters excitement reigned throughout as the Eagles soared to within two points at the third period, 31 to 29, and in the final session actually went out in front, dropped behind, tied the score with less than a minute remaining and then saw the Oshkosh team—an aggregation that wouldn't be denied—gain the precious two victory points on a pot shot by Gene Englund."[105] Englund's seventeen points led all scorers. For their efforts Gene Englund and Eddie Riska were named to the all-tournament first team. Each Oshkosh player received an Elgin gold watch for winning the tournament. Based in Elgin, Illinois, the Elgin National Watch Company had been an American tradition for seventy-seven years by the time of the tournament. Regarded as America's best-selling watch at that time, the Elgin watch was endorsed by former Michigan football great Tom Harmon. As the tournament program noted, the watch "is the official first prize award of the world championship basketball tournament. Every member of the winning team will receive the Elgin watch, supreme in time keeping as a worthy memento of being supreme in basketball."[106] The tournament itself had finally arrived as evidence by the fact that both baseball's Charles Comiskey and football's George Halas sat courtside to watch the game.

On the way to its first World Professional Basketball Tournament championship, Oshkosh beat the three previous winners in succession. The team earned the championship the hard way and proved to be the top professional basketball team in 1942. The city of Oshkosh was overjoyed by the victory; as one sportswriter described it, "A happy lot were the Oshkosh boys when upon arriving home in the town of a population of 40,000 souls, they were greeted at the station by 10,000 of the folk, who escorted them on fire engines to the center of town, where the Mayor lauded their energy and spirit."[107] Oshkosh would continue to compete annually in the World Professional Basketball Tournament for the first nine years (1939–47) and would be the only squad to play every year in the National Basketball League until the NBL merged with the Basketball Association of America (BAA) to form the National Basketball Association (NBA). Despite this consistency 1942 would be Oshkosh's best season. Although it won both the NBL and the World Professional Basketball Tournament, the team was still interested in continuing to compete and earn more hardware for its trophy case back home in Wisconsin. Shortly after winning in Chicago, the team headed out to compete in another tournament, this one located in Cleveland.

Among other tournaments the World Professional Basketball Tournament had the greatest reach in popularity and annually drew the strongest teams. In the early 1940s other cities hosted tournaments for professional teams, mainly as a way to include more eastern teams, which were snubbed by the World Professional Basketball Tournament. Sprinkled throughout the East, these tournaments drew fewer teams and attracted less national media exposure. Nonetheless, the purses were comparable, and top teams rarely declined an invitation to play.

One such tournament was one sponsored by Max Rosenblum in Cleveland, Ohio. Born in Austria-Hungary, Max had moved with his family as a young child to the United States and settled in Cleveland. After leaving school in the sixth grade to help support his family, he enrolled in Canton Business College to become a bookkeeper. Eventually, he found himself in the clothing and garment trade, where he worked as an errand boy for a clothier. He later rose to the ranks of manager for Enterprise Credit Clothing Company, and by 1910 he opened his own clothing store, where he sold clothes on credit.

Sports had always interested Rosenblum, and by the time he was thirty years old, he had started supporting baseball, football, soccer, and softball teams in Cleveland. Sports were a way to become more American and to give back to the community. Through the years Rosenblum was an active supporter of many local causes, including serving for fifteen years as the president of the Welfare Association for Jewish Children. In 1925–26 a new professional basketball league, the American Basketball League, was starting, and he jumped at the opportunity to sponsor a team. For six years the Cleveland Rosenblums were a mainstay for the league, and the team won the championship three times and reached the finals one other time. In December 1930, however, Rosenblum folded his team due to poor attendance and the

Depression. One of the ABL's founding members, Rosenblum preceded the league's disbanding by several months.

Without basketball Rosenblum continued to fund local sandlot and baseball teams, but the allure of basketball never left him. With the initial success of the World Professional Basketball Tournament, he became interested in creating a tournament in Cleveland to rival Chicago. In 1940 he began sponsoring the Max Rosenblum Tournament every March in Cleveland. For six years the tournament attracted top teams, including the SPHAS, who participated once in 1941. Always generous with his money and sponsorship, Rosenblum used the tournaments to assist local causes. In 1941 he donated $750.00 to the medical fund of the Municipal Basketball Association. In future years he underwrote the tournament to help benefit the Military Athletic Association as well as the Muny Basketball League in town. With his philanthropy and the recruiting of top teams, Rosenblum had created a highly successful counterpart to Chicago's March Madness.

The second tournament was held in 1942. The previous year, its first, the tournament had attracted four of the nation's top teams, three of which were generally regarded as the nation's best teams during the 1930s. The field included the Original Celtics, the New York Renaissance (Rens), the Philadelphia SPHAS, and the Detroit Eagles. In the finals the SPHAS halted the Celtics sixty-game winning streak, 43–38, as they claimed the prizes of $1,000 and a trophy. In the consolation game the Rens got by the Eagles, 49–45.

In the tournament's second year, eight teams competed, six of which—Chicago, New York, Detroit, Fort Wayne, Toledo, and Oshkosh—had recently finished playing in Chicago. Wilmington, which won the American Basketball League and did not enter the World Professional Basketball Tournament, made the short the trip from Delaware to Ohio. East Liverpool rounded out the eight-team field. Perhaps fatigued from winning the NBL and the World Tournament in succession, Oshkosh could not muster the effort and fell to newcomer East Liverpool, 47–39.

WORLDS PRO
BASKETBALL CHAMPIONSHIPS

WORCESTER
AUDITORIUM
MARCH
3 - 4 - 5
1943

ALL THE
WORLDS
BEST
BASKETBALL
STARS

FIG. 13. The Worcester Basketball Tournament was held in 1943 and 1944 in Worcester, Massachusetts, and featured the top professional and military teams. Courtesy of the author.

In the other games Chicago defeated Detroit, Wilmington beat Toledo, and the New York Renaissance (Rens) outlasted Fort Wayne. In the semifinals Chicago overcame Wilmington, while the Rens made quick work of East Liverpool. In the finals the Rens defeated a pesky Chicago team.

The Cleveland tournament lasted six years, from 1941 to 1946. The New York Renaissance was the tournament's top team, winning four times, including three consecutively from 1942 to 1944, and again in 1946. The Philadelphia SPHAS (1941) and the Detroit Mansfields (1945) were the other victors. The Rens were the only team to compete all six years.

Throughout the war additional second-tier tournaments popped up along the East Coast, including contests in Rochester, Buffalo, and Worcester. For several days in March, teams competed in tournaments in these cities, all the while spreading the game during the war. While these tournaments were popular locally, it was the World Professional Basketball Tournament held annually in Chicago that garnered the most attention and did the most to propel professional basketball onto the national stage. In the years to come, the World Professional Basketball Tournament would prove to be even more popular and important in supporting and advancing professional basketball during World War II.

2

THE COLOR LINE FALLS, 1942–1943

I went to the league and told them, "I don't know what you fellows are going to do, but if you want me to stay in I'm going to use blacks." Some of them didn't relish it, I suppose, because they thought it would bring problems. But I don't think any of them objected. —SID GOLDBERG, MANAGER OF THE TOLEDO JIM WHITE CHEVROLETS

There was only one game scheduled for the National Basketball League on Friday, December 11, 1942. It pitted the Chicago Studebakers, new to the league, against the Toledo Jim White Chevrolets, who were entering their second season of league play. For most followers of professional basketball, this game would take a back seat to the star-studded match-up featuring the two Wisconsin teams who were playing exhibition matches in Milwaukee. Normally, an exhibition match would not generate this much interest, especially against league play, but in this case the games did not disappoint. The double-header featured the Oshkosh All-Stars against the world famous Harlem Globetrotters, while the second tilt showcased the Sheboygan Red Skins paired against the New York Renaissance (Rens). The Globetrotters and the Rens were two of the best black basketball teams in the country, and their appearance always generated great interest and overflow crowds. One could be forgiven if all the basketball-watching focus was centered north in Milwaukee and not in Chicago.

It was an early-season game. Chicago stood at a surprising 2-2, while

Toledo had dropped its first two games to start the season 0-2. Cicero Stadium at Nineteenth and Laramie Avenue, not exactly Chicago Stadium, served as the host site. The tip-off was scheduled for 8:15 p.m., to be preceded by a preliminary game at 7:00 p.m., a game of local teams that might draw more interest than the main feature. Thanksgiving was a few weeks past, while Christmas still stood a few weeks away. College football was entering its bowl season, and the local newspapers had started the annual hype machine. Of the three main newspapers in town, the *Chicago Defender*, the *Chicago Herald American*, and the *Chicago Tribune*, only the *Tribune* sought fit to write a brief preview article. Notwithstanding the press's indifference to the contest in the days leading up to the game, the game was actually significant. Chicago and Toledo were both integrated, and the game pitted the first two integrated basketball teams to play against each other in a professional league in the twentieth century. It marked a significant milestone for the game of basketball, one that largely went unrecognized at the time and, to some degree, has still been underappreciated more than seven decades later.

Changes were afoot for the 1942–43 NBL campaign. Seven teams finished the 1941–42 NBL season, including the two-time defending league champions Oshkosh All-Stars; the Akron Goodyear Wingfoots, a charter member of the league since 1937–38; the Fort Wayne Zollner Pistons and the Toledo Jim White Chevrolets, both of which had just completed their first year in the league; the Indianapolis Kautskys, a charter member that sat out the previous season; the Sheboygan Red Skins; and the Chicago Bruins, who finished their third season in the league. With the war in full swing, the league was affected by players being drafted and teams being challenged by a shortage of available players.

Five teams were set to begin the new season, including Oshkosh, Sheboygan, and Fort Wayne. Long-standing member Akron withdrew, the last time the Goodyear company would field a professional basketball team. (Goodyear did, however, return to amateur ball.) Citing the effects of the war and the impact of the draft on its players, Indianapolis temporarily halted its league participation for three seasons and would not field a team again until the 1945–46 campaign, effectively missing three seasons during the height of World War II. At the end of the 1941–42 season, Indianapolis's owner, Frank Kautsky, addressed the local media and explained his decision to halt his team's operation for the duration of the war: "I felt as though I'd be doing something wrong."[1] Toledo returned for a second season. Meanwhile, the Chicago Bruins, George Halas and Bill Bidwell's team, withdrew, only to be reconfigured in a much different way. The biggest change for the upcoming NBL season was the inclusion of black players on two of the teams. The Chicago Studebakers and the Toledo Jim White Chevrolets would make history by becoming the first two integrated professional basketball teams to play against each other in a league game in the twentieth century.

Integration in basketball happened sooner and with less fanfare than it did in other sports. As Todd Gould has declared, "racial integration was born out of simple necessity."[2] This milestone came four years before Kenny Washington suited up for football's Los Angeles Rams, five years before Jackie Robinson broke the color barrier in baseball, and a full sixteen years before Willie O'Ree laced his skates for the Boston Bruins. Unlike those three sports, which integrated with a single player, professional basketball in 1942 integrated with ten players joining two teams. "Basketball was a great melting pot of all sports for all people," Bill Himmelman, basketball historian, noted. "Players are in shorts and shirt and bumping into one another. You do this a few times with people; you realize that there is no difference with people. Basketball was the great integrator of all sports. It did it easier and quicker than other sports."[3]

Bill Reynolds, writing in his book *Rise of A Dynasty: The '57 Celtics, The First Banner, and the Dawning of a New America*, reflects on the integration of the National Basketball Association (NBA) in 1950. Many of his comments are also applicable to integration in 1942. "It had been three years since Jackie Robinson had integrated baseball, but professional basketball's integration in 1950 took place almost quietly, with none of the demonstrable hate and public fervor that had accompanied Robinson's entrance into the Major Leagues. One theory was that basketball players had been to college and didn't seem to harbor the same vitriol against blacks as did many baseball players, most of whom had not gone to college. Many baseball players had also grown up in the South. Another theory was that college basketball had long been integrated in much of the country, so most players had played against blacks before."[4]

One of the game's least known stories concerns the inclusion of black players early in the game's history, particularly its formative years. The history that the Chicago and Toledo teams made in November and December 1942 at the outset of World War II in a Midwest-based professional league owed its beginnings forty years earlier to a young man from a small town in Massachusetts.

In 1902 the game that James Naismith had invented in the winter of 1891 was entering its second decade. Nascent professional leagues were forming all throughout the Northeast, and New England had a number of these ambitious leagues. In an otherwise unremarkable game in the winter of 1902, the New England Basketball League became the first professional basketball league to integrate. Harry "Bucky" Lew became the first African American to play in a professional basketball game when he played for Lowell's Pawtucketville Athletic Club against a team from Marlboro [now Marlborough], Massachusetts, on November 6, 1902. In 1958 Lew sat for an interview with sportswriter Gerry Finn of Springfield, Massachusetts, who chronicled Lew's place in basketball history. The story of Lew breaking the color barrier is best told by Lew himself.

I can almost see the faces of those Marlboro players when I got into that game. Our Lowell team had been getting players from New

York, New Jersey, Pennsylvania, and some of the local papers put the pressure on by demanding that they give this little Negro from around the corner a chance to play.

Well, at first the team just ignored the publicity. But a series of injuries forced the manager to take me on for the Marlboro game. I made the sixth player that night and he said all I had to do was sit on the bench for my five bucks pay. There was no such thing as fouling out in those days so he figured he'd be safe all around.

It just so happens that one of the Lowell players got himself injured and had to leave the game. At first this manager refused to put me in. He let them play us five on four but the fans got real mad and almost started a riot, screaming to let me play.

That did it. I went in there and you know . . . all those things you read about Jackie Robinson the abuse, the name-calling, extra effort to put him down . . . they're all true. I got the same treatment and even worse. Basketball was a rough game then. I took the bumps, the elbows in the gut, knees here and everything else that went with it. But I gave it right back. It was rough but worth it. Once they knew I could take it, I had it made. Some of those same old boys who gave the hardest licks turned out to be among my best friends in the years that followed.[5]

With his first game in the books, Lew finished the season with Lowell. A steady player, Lew stood five feet eight and was a strong defensive player for his era. His exploits did not go unnoticed as evidenced by a December 2, 1902, article in the *Lowell Courier-Citizen* that states, "His playing has been of the phenomenal kind, and his success in caging the elusive sphere has been remarkable." One month later Lew was again singled out for his exploits on the court, but this time for his defensive performance. Playing in Manchester, Massachusetts, Lew was guarding Harry Hough, an early pioneer of the game, and "he had the heralded champion player of the world on the weary list.

Three baskets were all that Hough succeeded in landing."[6] By the first week of January 1903, Lew was being recognized for his all-around efforts. Writing in the *Citizen* of Manchester, New Hampshire, the article noted, "Lew is now recognized as one of the very best floor workers in the business."[7]

Indeed, Lew was considered a very good player by his peers. Dan O'Connor, Lew's teammate in those years, recalled in an interview later in life, that "Bucky was considered the best dribbler in pro basketball, and it was almost impossible to take the ball away from him. He used two hands and kept spinning."[8] Players in those years were also tough; it was part of basketball's creed during those years. Lew was no exception. "Bucky Lew had a severe toothache, and we had to stop in Haverhill to see a dentist en route to the game," O'Connor recalled. "After having the tooth pulled, we continued to Gloucester, where Bucky played the entire game with a blob of gauze in his mouth."[9]

Those early professional basketball leagues were often regarded as the country's best with the top players testing their mettle against their fellow competitors. Lew recognized the fierceness of the competition but also how the game's early years and its roughness contributed to a much different game.

As Lew recalled in 1958,

> The finest players in the country were in that league just before it disbanded and I always wound up playing our opponent's best shooter. I like to throw from outside but wasn't much around the basket. Of course we had no backboards in those days and everything had to go in clean. Naturally, there was no rebounding and after a shot there was a brawl to get the ball. There were no out-of-bounds markers. We had a fence around the court with nets hanging from the ceilings. The ball was always in play and you were guarded from the moment you touched it. Hardly had time to breathe, let alone think about what you were going to do with the ball.[10]

It was on the defensive side of the ball, where players were guarded from the moment they touched the ball, that Lew not only made his mark but also distanced himself from his peers by his performance. As Himmelman notes, "He was probably one of the best defenders of his time on the planet."[11] "His real talent was as a defensive guard during a period when guards were responsible for guarding forwards, unlike today when forwards cover forwards and guards cover guards. He had a real talent for shutting down high-scoring forwards."[12]

In fact, his defense was so good that in some cases it was regarded as the reason, and not race, that some teams refused to play against Lew. In an early season game in November 1904, the sportswriter for the *Lowell Courier-Citizen* suggested, "Many are of the belief that the star basketball shooter of the Natick team had other reasons for not wanting to play Lew than the mere fact that he was colored. It has been noted in the past that [Harry] Hough has found that the goals from the floor do not come with the usual frequency when he is pitted against the Lowell boy."[13]

After one season with Lowell, Lew played the next few seasons with Haverhill, where he developed into a defensive player and set shooter. While playing for Haverhill, he scored 236 points in sixty-seven games during the 1903–4 season. The following year he returned to Haverhill and scored 102 points in forty-seven games. He played for Peabody in 1906. After the league disbanded in 1906, Lew organized his own team, the Lowell Five, and played for another twenty seasons up and down the East Coast. Lew's last game came in 1926 in St. Johnsbury, Vermont, at the age of forty-two. During his career he was regarded as an equal contemporary of Ed Wachter, Florenz "Flo" Harvey, Paddy Grand, George Renkert, Jim Crowley, and Francis "Flo" Haggerty, all early stars of the game in New England, particularly Wachter, who is a member of the Naismith Memorial Basketball Hall of Fame.

Lew was an anomaly, but his fine performance did not attract the attention of other teams wishing to integrate. It would be decades before another professional basketball team integrated. In many ways Lew was similar to Moses Fleetwood Walker, who integrated professional baseball with Toledo, Ohio, in 1884 but has largely been forgotten since Jackie Robinson integrated professional baseball in the twentieth century.

"The addition of both these players [Lew and Walker] to professional team rosters was singular, localized events. Neither started a movement in their time that allowed others of their race to gain playing spots," Bill Himmelman notes in a *Boston Globe* article in 1997. "Robinson was good, and owners realized there was money to be made by recruiting the best players, regardless of race, so we begin to see other blacks in professional baseball as part of a continuous trend."[14]

In 1997 Lew's daughter, Phyllis, reflected on her father's remarkable achievements and some of the adversity he faced. "My father talked often about playing basketball but I was too young to remember seeing him play. When people would talk about the discrimination that Jackie Robinson experienced in baseball, my father would chime in with his own experiences. When his team traveled to Fitchburg or Haverhill, he had to find different eating accommodations, for example."[15]

Despite his contributions, Lew has largely been forgotten by basketball historians for his singular role in breaking the color barrier. Martha Mayo, former director of the University of Massachusetts Lowell Center for Lowell History, spent many years researching and documenting the importance of Lew. In a 1997 interview she emphatically stated, "Lew deserves credit for not only being the first African-American professional player, but for his passion for the sport and his efforts to help it grow in New England."[16] Himmelman echoes these sentiments, stating, "There is a spot [in the Hall of Fame] for the breaking of the color line, and obviously Lew did it."[17] Himmelman, however, correctly points out that the game has changed considerably, and it is easy to overlook a player who scored few points and was a defensive specialist. "He averaged three to five points a game, which does not sound very good until you realize that back in the early days of basketball, teams won games with 19 or 20 points."[18]

While the story of Lew is remarkable in and of itself, his journey is best understood in the context of his family and their quest for freedom, equality, and the American dream. Theirs is an important and fascinating story.

Bucky Lew was born on January 4, 1884, to William and Isabell Lew. His family's lineage and their remarkable story began in the decades prior to the American Revolution. In the 1740s his great-great-great-grandfather and great-great-great-grandmother Primus and Margaret Lew were married. Both were former slaves in Groton, Massachusetts. Primus distinguished himself by fighting with the Americans in the French and Indian War.

During the American Revolution Lew's great-great grandfather Barzillia Lew fought in the Battle of Bunker Hill in 1775. Barzillia was a free man, and he later bought his wife, Dinah's, freedom for $400. Barzillia's remarkable life has been memorialized with an oil painting of him that hangs in the U.S. State Department Building in Washington DC. Duke Ellington also composed a song titled "Barzillia Lew." Barzillia's daughter, Lucy, and her husband, Thomas Dalton, were extremely active in an antislavery movement in Boston; Thomas served as president of an all-black antislavery society that predated the efforts of the noted white abolitionist William Lloyd Garrison.

In the 1840s Bucky Lew's grandfather and grandmother, Adrastus and Elizabeth Lew, purchased property near Riverside Street in Lowell. Over the ensuing two decades, this property became a well-known and documented stop on the Underground Railroad. The property was in a secluded forest area in Lowell, and the runaway slaves hid in the closet upstairs in the house. More than likely these runaway slaves were en route to Canada. Laura Ashe, a great-granddaughter of Adrastus and Elizabeth Lew, recalled decades later the remarkable role they played in this period of American history. "My [great] grandparents would put a pallet down there and the slave would sleep there during the day and come down to the kitchen at night."[19] After eating and telling stories, Ashe's great grandfather would gather the slaves and hide them in a horse-drawn carriage under piles of hay.

Ashe recalled, "They would take them to the Pelham, N.H. line. They were met by someone else to take them to Canada. If no one else was there to take them, then my [great-] grandfather or Elizabeth Lew would."[20] Nearing the end of her life, Elizabeth recalled her and her husband's participation in the Underground Railroad: "My husband and I helped many of the escaping slaves to get safely to Canada, giving them rest for the night, food and clothing and money to help them on their way. Those were terrible times."[21]

In the 1880s Bucky Lew's parents opened a dry-cleaning business in Lowell, and in 1891, the year basketball was invented, Lew's father, William, was a delegate representing Lowell at the 1891 Equal Rights Convention in Boston, Massachusetts.

Bucky's siblings were equally impressive in their achievements. His sister Theresa graduated as the salutatorian from Lowell High School and later earned a law degree from the Portis Law School in Boston. His brother Girard was a co-founder of the first African American museum, now known as the DuSable Museum. Among the artifacts in its collection is a powder horn used by Barzillia Lew in the American Revolution.

Lew's experience differed from that of most African Americans, who learned the game through the black YMCAs, club teams, and later a few of the African American–founded black leagues such as the six-member Interscholastic Athletic Association of Middle States (ISAA), which was created in 1906. It was two individuals, Edwin Henderson and Cumberland Posey, who proved to be most instrumental in introducing and organizing basketball in the black community.

Club teams formed immediately in the Northeast area and featured the best of black basketball. In 1906, the Smart Set Athletic Club of

Brooklyn was the first organized black basketball club. Two other teams quickly formed—St. Christophers and Marathone Athletic Club—which were part of the new league called Olympian Athletic Club, the first black club league outside of the YMCA circuit. Smart Set won the first championship in 1907–1908. During the next few years, several more clubs formed, and in 1909 a challenge match was formed between the ISAA and the Olympian Athletic Club. Smart Set won 27–11. The next year, Twelfth Street YMCA (ISAA) defeated the teams of the Olympic Athletic Club.

After 1910, a second wave of club teams was formed that included the Monticello-Dellaney Rifles, the Incorporators, and the Leondi Five, the first truly famous African-American basketball team. Based in Pittsburgh, Pennsylvania, the Monticello Rifles were led by Cumberland Posey, who later was known for his role in baseball's Negro Leagues. The Monticello Rifles enjoyed four successful seasons campaigning against eastern competition. In 1912, Cum Posey founded the Leondi Big Five that became the dominant team prior to World War I. Featuring an aggressive, fast-paced style; the team introduced a style of play later emulated by college and professional teams.[22]

Unlike baseball, basketball did not have "Negro Leagues" in which all-black teams competed. Out of necessity two all-black squads formed in the 1920s, the New York Renaissance and the Harlem Globetrotters. Founded in 1922 by Bob Douglas, a West Indian living in Harlem, the Rens, as they were known, played in the Harlem Renaissance Ballroom. Over their twenty-seven-year existence, the Rens won nearly three thousand games and were considered the best team in the country during the mid-1930s. Their Midwest counterpart was the Savoy Big Five, founded in 1927 in Chicago. Later purchased by Abe Saperstein, the team became known as the Harlem Globetrotters and traveled the country playing the best competition they could find. Both the Rens and the Globetrotters provided the only avenues for black basketball players to play professionally in the 1930s. During World War II this situation began to change more out of necessity than anything else. In 1942–43 the National Basketball League made history, forty years after Bucky Lew.

It was in November 1942, though, that the winds began to change. The league season began on Wednesday, November 25, as the Sheboygan Red Skins hosted the Chicago Studebakers. It marked the first time in three seasons that the Oshkosh All-Stars did not host the league opener. After finishing the previous season with a 10-14 mark good for fifth place out of seven teams, Sheboygan brought high hopes into their fifth league campaign. The team returned its lineup including Rube Lautenschlager, Kenny Buehler, Ed Dancker, Kenny Suesens, Bill McDonald, Moose Graf, Bill Schwartz, and Pete Lalich. The Red Skins tuned up for the game with easy victories over Camp Grant and the Harlem Globetrotters. The only thing missing was the arrival of the Chicago Studebakers, an unknown team that brought a lot of intrigue with them.

The Chicago Studebakers were born out of the failure of the Chicago Bruins. The Bruins, owned by footballers George Halas and Bill Bidwell, began play in 1939–40. In their three years in the league, the team took a step back each season as reflected in their win-loss records. Their first season, the team finished 14-14, a game behind both Oshkosh and Sheboygan for first place in the Western Division. The following season, 1940–41, the team finished with an 11-13 record, before dropping to 8-15, a sixth place finish in 1941–42. After a disastrous ending to their 1941–42 season, Halas wisely folded the franchise, making the smart move to focus on his Hall of Fame football career. In place of the Bruins rose the Studebakers, a compilation of white players from the Chicago area and former members of the Harlem Globetrotters. The United Automobile Workers Union local Studebaker was able to sponsor the team, which was important to league officials who wanted to keep a team in Chicago, the largest city in the Midwest and the largest city in the National Basketball League.

The remarkable story of the Chicago Studebakers was told by Michael Funke in an article titled "The Chicago Studebakers: How the UAW Helped Integrate Pro Basketball and Reunite Four Players Who Made History" published by the UAW. Here he describes how the team was comprised.

> Studebaker was where Mike Novak, a Bruins star, got a job in 1942, after his team discontinued play. And it was outside that plant where Roosie Hudson was standing one day in 1942 while another Globetrotter, Duke Cumberland, was inside applying for a job. Hudson was invited inside by a company official who recognized him from seeing him play with the Trotters at Studebaker's South Bend, Indiana plant. Urged to contact some other Trotters, Hudson called Bernie Price from an office phone. Price, in turn, contacted Sonny Boswell. In the meantime, Novak contacted Dick Evans and told him he could get a job at Studebaker and play ball, too. Hillery Brown, another Trotter, got wind of the plant and joined up. Tony Peyton was rooming with Duke Cumberland, and he was the last of the Trotters to join the team. Paul Sokody, who had played NBL ball with Sheboygan, and Johnny Orr, who'd played college ball, rounded out the team. Everyone, except the security guards Evans and Novak, was a UAW Local 998 member."[23]

Thus, Mike Novak, Paul Sokody, Dick Evans, Johnny Orr were the white players, while Roosie Hudson, Duke Cumberland, Bernie Price, Sonny Boswell, Tony Peyton, and Hillery Brown were the former Harlem Globetrotters.

As author David Neft and his colleagues note, "The Studebaker factory had been converted to war-industry production, so the workers there were exempt from the draft. When quite a few pro basketball players got jobs at the plant, the United Auto Workers union picked

FIG. 14. The Chicago Studebakers became one of two basketball teams to integrate in the 1942–43 National Basketball League season. Naismith Memorial Basketball Hall of Fame.

up the N.B.L. Chicago franchise and sponsored a team. Working in the plant were Mike Novak and Dick Evans of the Bruins, Paul Sokody of Sheboygan, and a host of Harlem Globetrotters led by stars Sonny Boswell, Duke Cumberland, and Bernie Price. Thus, the N.B.L. had its first racially integrated club, one that shaped up as among the strongest in the five-team field."[24] The players worked at the factory and also participated in basketball games on the weekend. Their commitment to the Studebaker factory was evident; as the 1943 World Professional Basketball Tournament program reminded fans, "This year the boys are all engaged in defense work for the Studebaker Corporation and have carried on through the basketball season without losing any time from work."[25]

The Chicago Studebakers drew interest in the press leading up to their first game against Sheboygan. In a preview article for the *Sheboygan Press*, the paper noted, "On the team, in addition to [Sonny] Boswell and [Bernie] Price, are Tony Peyton and Hillery Brown and 'Roosie' Hudson and Duke Cumberland all of the Harlem Globetrotters of last year and former great colored squads which were always formidable foes. These boys all know how to handle themselves on the court, can really shoot, and are expert ball-workers and passers. It is a snappy team that Chicago will put on the floor against the Redskins."[26] It was assumed that Chicago would play a fast-paced game with tenacious defense. Writing the day of the game, the *Sheboygan Press* stated, "All of these boys can shoot with the best of them, and when it comes to deft ball-handling and passing they don't come much better. It will be a classy team on the floor tonight."[27]

Despite the advance praise and top billing for the Studebakers, they were no match for the home team Red Skins. Playing in their newly built Municipal Auditorium and Armory, three thousand Sheboygan fans saw the home team defeat the Studebakers, 53–45. The Red Skins were led by Ed Dancker, who paced the team with sixteen points. His effort at disrupting Chicago's own tenacious defense led his team to victory. "Big Ed Dancker, a real scrapper, was better than ever and was forever in the Chicagoans' hair—literally as well as figuratively. He slapped out balls, zoomed into the air for rebounds and free balls, fought them off two at a time under the boards, and then found the energy to take high-scoring honors with seven field goals and a couple of free tosses for 16 points."[28] The game was close for the first period as Sheboygan enjoyed a slim 13–11 lead. In the second period Sheboygan increased its lead to 31–22. The third period was Chicago's undoing; it failed to score a field goal and managed only four free throws as Sheboygan built a comfortable 41–26 lead entering the final frame. Despite nineteen fourth-quarter points and a furious comeback, Chicago had dug itself too deep a hole to overcome against an experienced team.

Sonny Boswell and Roosie Hudson combined for twenty-seven points to lead the Studebakers.

With little time to mourn their opening loss, the Studebakers continued with their Wisconsin swing for a Saturday game against the defending league champion Oshkosh All-Stars. Arriving shortly before tip-off from Chicago in their game against the College All Stars, Oshkosh was in for a dogfight. A close game, featuring ten ties and fourteen lead changes, came down to the final minute as "that old bugaboo" Leroy "Cowboy" Edwards scored "three points on a free throw and field goal . . . to turn what appeared to be a 40–38 defeat at the hands of the Chicago Studebakers to a 41–40 victory for Oshkosh."[29] Roosie Hudson led the way for Chicago with twelve points.

The Studebakers faced challenges wherever they played, and the city of Oshkosh proved to be one of the cities where the team encountered some difficulty. As Bernie Price remembered, "They didn't like us up there, though I imagine it was because we were black; but it could have been because they were crazy about the team they had up there. And they had a good team. The fans used to shoot staples and everything at us."[30] They also knew that some of the calls might not go their way. As Tony Peyton explained, "We knew we weren't going to get the calls from the refs with a mixed team."[31]

With two losses in its first two games, Chicago had one more road game before it headed to Chicago for its home opener and rematch against Oshkosh. Next up for Chicago was the Fort Wayne Zollner Pistons. Fort Wayne acquitted itself quite well in its inaugural campaign the previous year by losing the championship series in three games to Oshkosh. Seeking to improve, Carl Bennett addressed the team's weakness: size. "They have what may be classed now as a veteran squad, with two of the three newcomers experienced in the pro sport and furnishing much size that was needed last season. They are Jerry Bush and John Pelkington, veterans of several years' experience. The other newcomer is Gus Doerner, the Evansville College southpaw who set a new state college scoring mark last season."[32] Pelkington had played his college ball at Manhattan College, while Bush played at a New York college, St. John's. All three were expected to contribute to Fort Wayne.

The city of Fort Wayne was concerned about the effects that the war might have on the team and the ability of the fans to support them. Writing on December 1, 1942, the night of the team's home opener, the *Fort Wayne News-Sentinel* raised these questions, "How the gas rationing and defense work at nights will affect attendance at the pro games this year remains a mystery. Advance interest has been high and there has been a good sale of season tickets. The fans took the Pistons to their hearts last year and the strengthened squad of this season gives the city good representation in the pro sport. It remains to be seen, however, how well the fans can get to the games and how well the Pistons can do in the league to make them want to get there."[33]

Despite this initial concern over rationing, the focus was clearly on the upcoming season and the home opener against Chicago. An interesting item in the article on the night of the game stated, "The Studebakers sent word late Monday that they planned to start an all-Negro lineup here, this one having clicked in a 41–40 loss to the vaunted Oshkosh cagers at the Wisconsin city Saturday night as the loop campaign got under way."[34] Certainly the notion of starting an all-black lineup was novel in 1942, but curiously this was not mentioned in the write up of the Oshkosh game in the *Oshkosh Daily Northwestern*. In fact, it was not mentioned in any other article that covered the Studebakers all season. Starting an all-black lineup in 1942 did not carry the same weight or meaning as Texas Western University fielding an all-black starting five in 1966 versus the Adolph Rupp–coached University of Kentucky in the NCAA championship game. Nor did it measure up to Red Auerbach employing an all-black starting lineup for the Boston Celtics in the early 1960s.

Regardless of the lineup, the Studebakers were clearly ready to avenge two early season losses as strong defense and timely offense led them to a 54–47 win, their first of the season. Ben Tenny, the beat writer for the Zollner Pistons for the *Fort Wayne News-Sentinel*, wrote that Chicago was "possessed of plenty height, speed galore, experience and all-around scoring ability" in defeating Fort Wayne. Tenny noted that the Studebakers played as a unit and complemented each other well, particularly "when [Sonny] Boswell cooled off in the last half, there were plenty other former Rens and Globe Trotters to take up the sniping work and the white players of the squad, furnishing much of the size and rebound work, teamed remarkably well with their colored mates in a basketball experiment that seem[ed] sure to succeed."[35] Fort Wayne's other newspaper, the *Journal Gazette*, wrote in their game story, "The little, speedy colored boys on the Chicago club seemed to be in great shape, and their tireless play and accurate shooting were the big factors in the Pistons' downfall, although the entire Chicago club looked good."[36] Clearly the notion of an integrated team intrigued both Fort Wayne papers and many other observers, who realized that this was a basketball experiment, but one that could be successful.

In the decades following Chicago's experiment, a rumor emerged that the team was affected by racial strife and dissension. However, the players to a man disputed that notion, although their memories of those days may have faded over time. Nevertheless, Dick Evans recalled, "We were proud to be together. We admired each other." Tony Peyton concurred, noting, "We were proud of what we did. Just playing our home games in Cicero [a Chicago suburb] was groundbreaking, man, because black people weren't even allowed to walk there back then."[37]

The team got along, and the notion of playing blacks and whites together did not present a problem for the players. According to Roosie Hudson, "It did not matter if there were three black players and two whites in the game, or three whites and two blacks, we played as a team. There was no difference."[38] The coach Johnny Jordan disputed any claim of racial problems, noting, "There was no strife at all and the blacks were treated well by players and fans because, you know, people knew the Globetrotters as great ballplayers. They were well received." Bernie Price agreed with this assessment, declaring, "We played all year together and didn't have any problems. The only time we had a break-up was for the World Tournament at the end of the year. I think it was a matter of egos. I don't believe it was racial."[39]

As with most teams, problems arise from players taking too many shots, not passing enough, or missing defensive assignments. It's about the basketball and not about the composition of the team. The Studebakers were no different. Roosie Hudson believed that the problem was between Mike Novak and Sonny Boswell. "It had nothing to do with race. It was just about Sonny (Boswell) taking too many shots and not giving up the ball. That's all that was."[40] As it went, Boswell shot too much, and Novak believed that Boswell should pass the ball more often. Sonny was a good scorer who in twenty-two games that season tallied 229 points. His average of 10.4 points per game was good for third in the league.

Although problems arose on the court, there seemed to be little dissension at the workplace in the plant. As Michael Funke recounted about one incident, "Peyton recalls one incident in the plant when he got into a fight with a white worker who challenged his right to use a restroom. Peyton starting chasing the guy through the plant. Novak, on guard duty, took up the chase, caught the man, and hauled him to a supervisor's office. It was Peyton's word against the white worker. But other workers, white and black, agreed with Peyton's version of what happened and the white worker was fired."[41]

After their first league win against Fort Wayne, the team headed home for a match-up against Oshkosh. Seeking to avenge its close loss the previous week, Chicago came out strong in front of its home crowd at Cicero Stadium as the team built a 12–7 lead after the first period. Behind the scoring of Bernie Price, the Studebakers built a 27–12 lead at halftime. The team went on to a 46–35 victory behind Price's fourteen points. With its first home victory under its belt, Chicago looked ahead to its next match-up against Toledo, the only team it had yet to face in the league.

The other team that made history that season was the Toledo Jim White Chevrolets. The season marked Toledo's second as a member of the National Basketball League. As Sid Goldberg, the team's manager, recounted, "They were after me. They wanted Toledo and they needed teams. I paid $350 for a franchise. They also insisted on a $1500 deposit in case of forfeits, which I couldn't raise, but I got the backing of Jim White Chevrolet. Jim White also bought us uniforms and gave us two station wagons to use."[42] In its inaugural season the team finished with a 3-21 record and in last place among seven teams. It was a terrible season marked by poor play, bad coaching, and first-year jitters playing in the NBL against top-flight competition.

The Toledo experiment in integration and playing in the NBL in 1942–43 was not nearly as successful as its counterpart Chicago. The team played only four league games, all of which were on the road against Oshkosh, Sheboygan, Fort Wayne, and Chicago. All were losses. After finishing with a 0-4 record, the team decided to disband days before Christmas 1942. As opposed to Chicago, Toledo did not start off with league play immediately. In fact, the team did not play its first game until well into the first week of December. While other league teams had played a few games, Toledo had yet to play. This might have contributed to some of the team's problems.

Toledo's first league game was scheduled for December 8 at Fort Wayne. However, a blackout caused the teams to reschedule the following evening. The *Fort Wayne News-Sentinel* reported,

Toledo willingly agreed to the postponement to help out officials here. Because the time of the blackout remained a surprise, Zollner officials were fearful that it might come at some time in the game when it would be tough on either or both quintets, as well as the fans. It is rather difficult to black out North Gym and continue play.

In addition, many of the persons involved in staging pro games here are in Civilian Defense work of some sort and wanted to be on the job tonight. In addition, many persons who hold season tickets or already had purchased ducats for the game tonight were in the same fix and it was deemed only fair to enable them to fulfill their duties this evening and still get to use their tickets Wednesday evening, the move being the most advisable of several possible ones suggested.[43]

Rescheduled for the following evening, the Zollner Pistons pounded Toledo for a 70–51 victory. The postponement of the game one day greatly impacted Toledo as its star player, Chuck Chuckovits, and Johnny Townsend were unable to play due to other coaching and officiating responsibilities. Instead, the team was paced by Bob Gerber, who tallied twenty-two points. However, his effort was not nearly enough as balanced scoring from the Zollner Pistons led them to an easy victory.

The Toledo squad was led by Chuck Chuckovits, a former standout at the University of Toledo and a popular player in the Midwest. Chuckovits was an instant sensation due to a breakout performance in his first year in professional basketball the previous season. "His debut in the pro circuit last season was marked by the record breaking feat of scoring 406 points in 22 games."[44] The team was built around players who had good college careers in the Midwest, many of whom had played at the University of Toledo and for the Detroit Auto Club, a semiprofessional team. The latest sensation from the University of Toledo was Bob Gerber, who "was even more outstanding in college than Chuckovitz" and "smashed Chuckovits' [sic] record while at Toledo University last year."[45] He tallied 1,319 points for Toledo. Gerber was a sensational player, and his senior year at Toledo made him this year's Chuckovits. "So well-known was his scoring ability that he was named the No. 1 man on the College All Star squad this fall and played with the collegians in the Chicago Stadium when they defeated the Oshkosh All Stars, 61–55."[46]

Other players included Al Price, the brother of Bernie Price, who was playing for the Chicago Studebakers. An interesting side note is that both Price brothers had a role in integrating the NBL in this season. Other black players on the Toledo team included Casey Jones and Shannie Barnett. As the *Oshkosh Daily Northwestern* reported,

> Also with Toledo will be John Townsend, University of Michigan All-American, who is considered one of the best passers in the league. Toledo will be strong inasmuch as several of the players were together last year on the Toledo university team and should develop a smooth-working quintet. Some of them played at Toledo a year or two ago so all have worked under the same system of coaching. They include Marshall Carlson, who was named to the College All Star team a year ago; Pat Hintz, captain of the 1940 Toledo five; Bill Jones, a Negro who was with Toledo university last season and was named all-state guard among players of all Ohio universities and colleges, including Ohio State.[47]

A Toledo native, Bill Jones grew up playing basketball in the city. He first entered the University of Toledo in 1932. Since it was during the Depression, Bill earned money for tuition by working the night shift at the Fort Meigs Hotel. His long day began with classes in the morning, basketball practice in the afternoon, then his shift at the hotel. After basketball practice he would walk home and take a short nap before heading out to his night job. He performed this routine each and every day. Jones played one semester his sophomore season in 1933–34 and led the team in scoring, but the economic hardships of the day forced him to quit school in 1934. For the next two years, he worked to support his family and eventually re-enrolled for the second semester of the 1935–36 season. The team was now coached by Harold Anderson, who later became a Naismith Memorial Basketball Hall of Fame coach. Jones played the next two seasons, 1936–37 and 1937–38, and led his team with local star Chuck Chuckovits. The 1936–37 team finished with an 18-14 record. Because Jones had already earned three varsity letters and the university policy only allowed three letters, he was unable to play in the 1938–39 season, in which the team traveled to Madison Square Garden in New York.

After he graduated, Jones continued to look for opportunities to play basketball. He joined a series of professional and semiprofessional teams in the Toledo area. He played for the Brown Bombers and Joe's Toledoans, which later became the Ciralsky Packers. These African American teams traveled the region playing other black teams. Jones integrated the Toledo Jim White Chevrolets in 1941, but the team did not play in the 1940–41 National Basketball League. However, the team did compete in the 1941 World Professional Basketball Tournament. Toledo fielded an integrated club and won two games against the Sheboygan Red Skins and the Chicago Bruins before losing to the Oshkosh All-Stars in the semifinals. Jones tallied three points in those three games. Toledo finished in fourth place after losing to the New York Renaissance in the consolation game, a contest in which Jones scored two points. Jones continued playing professionally before joining Toledo in the NBL for 1942–43. Years after helping integrate the NBL, Jones spoke positively about his experience that year, "There was never any bench jockeying like in baseball. We never had problems on our own team. Players on the court for and against were fine."[48]

The game between Toledo and Chicago, the first basketball game between two integrated teams in a professional league in the twentieth century, barely registered on the sporting landscape. The Toledo newspaper made no mention of the game. The Sheboygan, Fort Wayne, and Oshkosh papers just mention a final score, Chicago 42, Toledo 30. Among the Chicago papers the *Herald American* listed the game in its sports schedule listing but did not follow up with a score. The *Daily Tribune* provided a two-paragraph story recounting the game and high scorers. The only Chicago paper to devote any coverage of note was the *Defender*, the much-heralded black press in that city. The *Chicago*

Defender's story was five paragraphs, noting among other things that the "game was late in starting—two hours to be exact—because of the lateness of the train bearing the Toledo squad."[49] The article went on to recount that the Studebakers jumped out to a 5–3 lead after a sluggish first period by both squads. The scoring picked up considerably in the second quarter as Chicago held a 20–16 lead at halftime. Paced by Bernie Price, who tallied ten points on four field goals and two free throws, Chicago won 42–30. An interesting aside is that no box score exists for this landmark game in any of the newspapers.

Two noteworthy developments resulted from this game. The first was that the *Chicago Defender* covered the game and would continue to follow the team on a weekly basis throughout the season. As Murry Nelson notes in his history of the National Basketball League, the *Defender*'s coverage of the Studebakers marked "the first time the NBL had been covered in the top African American newspaper in the country."[50] The second was the growing popularity of the team. "In order to accommodate their many friends and followers, the Studebakers [would] play the remainder of their home schedule at the Sixteenth and Michigan avenue armory instead of the Cicero stadium out on West Fifty-second street."[51]

While the Chicago Studebakers were playing well in the early part of the season, compiling a 3-2 record, the Toledo Jim White Chevrolets were headed in the opposite direction and fast. After losing to Chicago, Toledo prepared for its trip to Wisconsin to face both Oshkosh and Sheboygan. This weekend trip to Wisconsin would ultimately prove the final straw for the team. Despite not playing with Gerber, who earlier that morning was inducted into the U.S. Army and assigned to Camp Perry, and Chuckovits, who was coaching a high school team, Toledo kept the score close, only to fall in the final period, 46–41. Trailing 36–32 heading into the final period, Oshkosh staged a late rally, outscoring Toledo 12–5 in the final frame. The All-Stars were paced by Gene Englund, whose inside baskets and foul shots proved the key in the win.

As it turned out, the game was the least of Toledo's challenges. As an integrated team traveling on the road in the Midwest in the 1940s, the team faced its share of hardship and racial discrimination. Years later manager Sid Goldberg recounted the incident of one terrible night in Oshkosh:

> I never thought I'd encounter the problems I did there. I went into a hotel to register the team, and they said, "We don't accept blacks." So I had no place for them to sleep. The blacks couldn't even go to a hamburger place. I had to go in and get the hamburgers. The blacks had to sleep in the car. It was cold, and I remember taking the uniforms out and putting them in the car to use for blankets. I had a room, but I felt guilty so I went out and slept in the car with them. We were there for a two-game series, and the second night I finally found a place in Oshkosh. This guy had one room, and the blacks and I slept there.[52]

The following night the team traveled to Sheboygan to finish its two-game Wisconsin swing. Mustering the same fight as they had the night before, Toledo again held a second half lead before losing, 38–31. Leading 16–13 at the half, Toledo stumbled to start the second half as Sheboygan's Kenny Buehler scored six straight points to give the Red Skins a 19–16 lead, one they would not relinquish the rest of the way. For the second straight night, Toledo played without its best player, Chuck Chuckovits. In its preview article about the Toledo-Sheboygan game, the *Sheboygan Press* disappointedly noted,

> Toledo will bring a galaxy of stars here for the 3 o'clock Sunday afternoon game. Bad news for Redskins fans, however, comes by special delivery; the air mail letter from Manager Sid Goldberg to the effect that the great Chuck Chuckovits may not be here. "Chuck's high school plays Friday night. I want him to come over to Oshkosh and Sheboygan Saturday and Sunday, but I don't know if he will.

He made more money last year than anyone in basketball, but he's intent on making good as a coach, and while he wants me to keep his name on the list, he doesn't want to play in the first few games."[53]

In fact, Chuckovits never did play professional basketball again. Instead, he became a well-regarded basketball referee.

Even though the team lost another tough game, it did not encounter any of the off-court problems of the previous night. As Sid Goldberg recounted,

> So now we go to Sheboygan for a game. A great guy, Carl Roth, ran the team there—a wonderful fellow. I called Carl and said, "I don't want what happened in Oshkosh to happen again." A minor league first baseman named Joe Hauser owned a hotel on the waterfront, and Carl called him. He told me, "Joe says you can stay in the hotel." I said, "Should I bring them in the back door?" and Joe said, "You can bring them in the front door and they stay right here." So that helped the situation. The crowds were good and the players cooperated. I can't recall any of the black players coming to me and saying they heard the remarks that Jackie Robinson got later as the first black major leaguer. They were accepted because they were good ballplayers.[54]

Asked if the black players on the team blamed him for the incident in Oshkosh, Goldberg replied, "No, they didn't blame me, because hell, I slept right with them. How could I feel right? I was no martyr, but I just didn't feel right. Hell, they couldn't even go to the hamburger place, not even through the back door. I couldn't understand it. It was not Lon Darling. He tried. I've got to hand it to him. And the crowds were good. We didn't get any guff."[55] Many years later Goldberg did not think much about his role in integrating the sport. "I was just trying to fill out a team and save my deposit."[56]

On December 23, 1942, after only four games in the league, the *Toledo*

Blade ran a three-paragraph article announcing that the team was disbanding. The article noted that "Toledo had been granted a 'bye' for the remainder of the season. Toledo withdrew, the announcement said, because of loss of personnel to military service and transportation difficulties. The action, however, [would] not affect the standings since the Ohio pros played only four games and lost once to each of the league's other clubs—Chicago, Sheboygan and Oshkosh, Wis., and Fort Wayne, Ind."[57] The *Sheboygan Press* wrote, "Toledo withdrew because of loss of personnel to military service and transportation difficulties according to the announcement. When the team played here it was without the services of several stars, Bob Gerber being inducted after the first game (he scored 22 points in that game), Jewell [*sic*] Young having an appendectomy, and Chuck Chuckovits having a coaching position to fill."[58]

Toledo's withdrawal left the league with four teams to finish the season. With only four games played, all of them on the road, Toledo had little to show for its effort to integrate professional basketball. Unlike its counterpart Chicago, Toledo's integrated team was not a big news story either in its hometown, Toledo, or in the visiting cities. The *Fort Wayne News-Sentinel* was the only newspaper to mention that Toledo was fielding an integrated squad. In its game article on December 10, 1942, when Fort Wayne defeated Toledo, it noted, "The Pistons were unable to shake off the mixed Toledo five (it had half white and half colored players this year like the Chicago Studebakers)."[59] Sheboygan, Oshkosh, and Chicago did not mention this fact. Even the *Toledo Blade* gave scant coverage to its own team. Game articles, box scores, or just plain scores were never mentioned. The biggest article devoted to the team occurred when it was withdrawing from the league. Several factors may have contributed to this. Toledo was a much smaller city than Chicago, and the Toledo team was largely composed of former University of Toledo players, some of whom had integrated the college team. Also, the Harlem Globetrotters were well known throughout the

Midwest, and the players were a known commodity. That certainly helped the Studebakers as they traveled the Midwest. Finally, Toledo did not have a black newspaper like the *Chicago Defender*, which covered the Studebakers for that season. All in all, Toledo's role would go down as a mere footnote in basketball's integration. As Bill Jones lamented in 2001, "Very little recognition has been given to the National Basketball League. People have not properly recognized it today. The league was ahead of its time in the integration and utilization of black basketball players."[60]

With Toledo out of the league, the remaining four teams set their sights on a league championship. The general consensus among the remaining four teams and their followers was that "each of the four teams remaining [was] believed capable of defeating each of the others so that the winner of the crown [would] probably lose a number of games before emerging as champions."[61] The surprise of the first few weeks was the Chicago Studebakers, and the eyes of the basketball world would continue to follow them to see if they could continue their strong play. One positive sign of both the strong early season play and the historic nature of the team was the fact that the *Chicago Defender,* the black press in town, started to cover them for the rest of the season. Each week the *Defender* filed a story about the team and did so through the end of the National Basketball League postseason. Late in December Chicago played a home-and-home series against Sheboygan. In the first game, on December 20 in Chicago, the Studebakers pulled out a two-point win to pull into a tie for first place in the league. That would be the high-water mark for Chicago the rest of the season. In a rematch on Christmas Day in Sheboygan, the Red Skins won 55–46, dropping Chicago out of a tie for first place. Inconsistency plagued Chicago for the remainder of the season as the team finished in last place with an 8-15 mark.

The rest of the regular season saw the Fort Wayne Zollner Pistons, in only their second year, cruise to a 17-6 record for a first-place finish.

The two Wisconsin teams hovered around .500 all season, with the Red Skins finishing with a 12-11 record, while Oshkosh finished with a 11-12 record for third place. It was the worst regular season finish for the All-Stars since they joined the NBL in 1937–38. But with four teams in the league, all made the league postseason. The opening round saw Sheboygan outlast Oshkosh, while Fort Wayne handled Chicago, thus setting up a championship series between Fort Wayne and Sheboygan.

The series figured to be evenly matched even if Fort Wayne held the edge in the regular season. For the first time in a while, Sheboygan had a healthy roster, and that gave the team confidence heading into the series with Fort Wayne. The center position was considered a draw with Blackie Towery and John Pelkington of Fort Wayne facing off against Eddie Dancker and George Jablonsky for the Red Skins. Sheboygan felt that it had two advantages going into this series. The first was at the forward position in which Buddy Jeannette, Rube Lautenschlager, Eddie Sadowski, and Dick Schulz were all finally healthy and could match up against any forwards that Fort Wayne would throw at them. Second, Sheboygan was confident that its guards, Kenny Suesens and Bill McDonald, defensively could contain the offensive-minded back court of Fort Wayne. Suesens and McDonald were iron men all year, missing a total of three minutes between the two of them. The first game, held in Fort Wayne, proved that Sheboygan was correct about its four forwards. Fort Wayne started off strong, building a 27–21 lead at the half. The tide turned in the third period as "the Redskins bounded back with a will that simply couldn't be beat and they turned the trick. In a torrid third quarter the Skins poured in nineteen points and allowed the Pistons just seven, and thereby hangs the tale. Going into that frame the Skins were trailing by six points but after ten minutes of play they had changed things decidedly, giving them a 40–34 third quarter margin."[62] Dancker (sixteen points), Lautenschlager (fifteen points), Jeannette (thirteen points), and Sadowski (three points) proved the difference as the four forwards scored forty-six of the team's fifty-five points. The big addition for Sheboygan during the season was Buddy Jeannette. A graduate of Washington & Jefferson College, Jeannette was considered a clutch player. In 1941 he helped lead the Detroit Eagles to the World Professional Basketball Tournament championship.

The series shifted back to Sheboygan for the second game with the Red Skins hoping to close out the series. In a thrilling game that went into overtime, Fort Wayne outlasted Sheboygan, 55–50. This set up a winner-take-all-game back in Fort Wayne. Based on the previous game, the final contest did not disappoint. A defensive struggle all game, the contest was low scoring, and each basket came at a premium. The score was knotted at 28-all with six minutes left in the game. The two teams would not score again until there was a minute and a half left, when Fort Wayne's Curly Armstrong hit one foul shot to give the Pistons a 29–28 lead. A foul by Sheboygan gave the Pistons the ball again, but sloppy play turned possession right back to Sheboygan. And then the game came down to the final play. "With the seconds flying by the boys were all on edge as Eddie Dancker took the ball way over in the corner and suddenly looped in a long one-handed hook shot at the basket and IT WAS GOOD and the Redskins were crowned National champions as the horn sounded a few seconds late. The final score 30 to 29, a slim one-point margin but the Redskins were CHAMPIONS."[63]

The win was a significant milestone for the city of Sheboygan. For Fort Wayne it was a bitter defeat; as Carl Bennett, the Pistons' manager recalled decades later, "It was the most heartbreaking moment in my career with the Pistons."[64] A few days later a banquet was scheduled to recognize and celebrate the fine achievements of the Red Skins. Sheboygan's mayor, Charles H. Bau, spoke for the entire city when he declared, "It isn't often that a city the size of Sheboygan can win a national championship in any type of sport, and citizens of Sheboygan will want to fill the dining room of the Hotel Foeste to show their appreciation of this team which has brought the championship to our city. They played great basketball all season and worked their way up to

FIG. 15. The Sheboygan Red Skins won their only National Basketball League championship, in 1942–43, by defeating the Fort Wayne Zollners Pistons in three games. Courtesy of Bill Himmelman.

the top of the list by their fine team play."[65] This achievement marked the only league championship that Sheboygan ever won.

With their Midwest counterpart finding ways to be successful despite the restrictions of war, the American Basketball League did its best to stay creative in fielding a competitive season. The league faced challenges of player shortages, teams ceasing operations until the war ended, and a reduced schedule. While the NBL sought to address player shortages by signing black players, its eastern counterpart, the ABL, did not follow the same path during the war years. Only after the end of the war, in 1947–48, did the American Basketball League field an integrated team. Nevertheless, the war greatly impacted the operation of the ABL for the 1942–43 season, much as it did for the NBL.

In 1941–42 the ABL played a two-half schedule. The first-half winner would face the second-half winner in the championship round. For the only time during the history of the American Basketball League, no championship series was contested as the Wilmington Blue Bombers won both halves and were declared league champions. As a new season prepared to get started, the assumption among league officials and its followers was that Wilmington was the team to beat. Prior to the start of the season, Wilmington's owner, Robert Carpenter, informed John J. O'Brien, the league commissioner, that his team would not play in the upcoming season because "the Armory in Wilmington had been commandeered by the Army for the housing of approximately 195 soldiers, and that, therefore, this building would not be available for other than military activities for the duration. He also expressed his willingness to become associated with the League at such times as conditions are altered."[66] With Wilmington sitting out for a year, the landscape reshuffled as other teams now believed that this might be their year.

Wilmington was not the only team forced to withdraw for the upcoming season. The Washington Heurich Brewers, who finished the previous season with a 10-13 record, informed Commissioner O'Brien "that it had not been possible to obtain an auditorium in Washington for the season 1942–1943, and that Mr. Heurich would like to withdraw his membership for the duration and to have it made available when conditions are altered."[67] Thus Washington and Wilmington were two notable teams that withdrew due to the effects of the war on their cities. The Trenton Tigers, the Philadelphia SPHAS, and the New York Jewels were the three teams that committed to another campaign. Both Trenton and Philadelphia were stable franchises that were believed capable of completing the season in good standing. The New York Jewels, however, presented another challenge: the Jewels played in Brooklyn, New York, a great driving distance from the other teams. Due to gas rationing and other war restrictions, the other franchises decided at the December 4, 1942 board meeting to "assist in the financing of the New York Jewels at Brooklyn to the extent of $15 each per home game played by the New York Jewels." The board further stated,

"If this contribution is not necessary it will not be paid and if any contributions are paid and the New York Jewels enjoy a profitable year it is the understanding that reimbursements are to be made by the Manager of the New York Jewels for each advance previously made to him. It is also understood that these advances of the various clubs will be taken out of the $55 per home game assessment treated above, and no club will be liable for any greater proportion of the New York Jewels expense."[68] The success of the league was predicated on all the teams working together and sharing in the sacrifice.

With Trenton, Philadelphia, and New York all in the fold, the league sought to add more franchises. While the league confronted the withdrawal of teams, it also faced the issue of new franchise applications. Interestingly, the league offices received applications for seven new franchises as evidenced by the minutes of the league meeting.

The President reported that he had discussed with Mr. L. A. R. Pieri of Providence, R.I., Mr. F Dubinsky and Mr. J. Lawrence of Hartford, Conn., and Mr. A.W. Broden of Springfield, Mass., the possibility of having these cities represented in the American Basketball League. However, in view of the inability of these cities to play other than mid-week games, the applications were dropped for the duration because of travel restrictions.

The President also announced that he had received an application from Mr. A. Ehlers of Baltimore MD, but that no auditorium could be made available for the present time.

Another application had been received from Mr. J. Russell representing Paterson, but it was ascertained on Monday, November 30th, that the high school gymnasium in that city could not be heated after 3:00 P.M. on any weekday because of fuel restrictions.

After discussion, it was the sense of the meeting that all these applications be filed with the Secretary and considered at a later and more propitious opportunity.[69]

Although the league and team representatives denied five applications, there were two that were received positively. The first was from Harrisburg, Pennsylvania. Mr. Carl B. Shelley of Harrisburg applied to operate a franchise, and after consideration, it was "RESOLVED that a franchise be awarded to Carl B. Shelley and Associates for use in the city of Harrisburg, Pa., during the season of 1942–1943, carrying with it all right, title, and interest to the territory adjacent to Harrisburg, Pa."[70] The Senators played that season and finished with a 4-8 record. It would be the only season for the Senators in the ABL.

The other city to make a positive impression on the league was Camden, New Jersey. Barney Sedran, a great player from New York in the second decade of the twentieth century who had a successful coaching career in the ABL, most recently the previous year with the league champion Wilmington Blue Bombers, presented on behalf of the Camden syndicate. His good name and history with the league might have been beneficial in securing a franchise for Camden. In his presentation to league officials, he noted that "arrangements had been effected to use the auditorium in that city for the playing of American Basketball League games."[71] The league owners approved the new franchise with the caveat that Camden would not "in any way [affect] the rights of the Philadelphia SPHAS."[72] With that the league cobbled together five teams to start the 1942–43 campaign. It would be a different season for all involved as play did not start until right before Christmas, a month later than normal. There would not be two halves; instead the top two finishers in the regular season would meet for the championship. Each team would play fewer games—Philadelphia SPHAS (fifteen), Trenton Tigers (thirteen), Harrisburg Senators (twelve), New York Jewels (eleven), and Camden/Brooklyn Indians (eight)—in an unbalanced schedule. All in all, the league was cautiously optimistic that a successful campaign could be waged with fewer teams and a limited schedule.

In a shortened season greatly impacted by the toll the war was having on the nation, the league came down to a two-team race between the Trenton Tigers and the Philadelphia SPHAS. The Tigers led the league from start to finish, compiling an 11-2 record with only one loss at home. Sitting in second place was the SPHAS, whose season was lackluster from the opening game. The team finished with a 9-6 record, but it was a struggle. Inconsistency plagued the team, and aside from two three-game winning streaks, it rarely found the spark it needed. It also did not help that manager-coach Eddie Gottlieb missed two games while spending time in Warm Springs, Georgia, the same site made famous by the death of President Franklin D. Roosevelt in April 1945. For those two missed games, his players—first Shikey Gotthoffer and then Red Wolfe—took turns coaching the team. Needless to say, this experiment did not work, and Gottlieb could not wait to return and restore order to his team.

The championship series came down to Trenton and Philadelphia, and most followers of this Delaware River rivalry predicted a highly competitive match-up. During the regular season, the teams faced each other four times, each winning once at home and once on the road. Each won a close game and a blowout. The championship figured to be a repeat of the regular season. Indeed, that was the case from the opening tip-off. It is often said that a series does not actually become a series until the home team loses a game on its home court. Well, this series became one after the first game. The series opened at the Broadwood Hotel, and the SPHAS, as was their custom, jumped out to an early advantage, playing a confident brand of ball as they compiled a 15–9 lead after the first frame. As the second period began, the tenor of the game change as Matt Goukas entered for Trenton. As recounted the following day in the *Philadelphia Inquirer*, "The entry into the game of Matt Goukas for Trenton in the second period changed the entire complexion of the play. Around Matt the Trenton plays were built.

He worked the pivot to perfection, his handling of the fast whirling sphere on par of the one-time great Dutch Dehnert who was famed for his pivot playing and he caged three goals, one coming one minute after his entry into the fray to start the Jerseymen on their victorious way."[73] Behind Goukas and his six points, Trenton outscored Philadelphia 27–12 over the final two periods for a 36–27 win and 1–0 lead in the series.

The series resumed across the river in Trenton, and the game started much like it had the previous night. The SPHAS led 13–6 after the first frame. Unlike the first game, the Tigers could not jumpstart their offense with Goukas coming off the bench, and the SPHAS cruised to a 42–35 win behind thirteen points from Inky Lautman. The visiting team had won the first two games, and it would be a trend that would continue. Trenton won Game Three on the road, and the SPHAS countered with another victory in Trenton in Game Four. In Games Five and Six, the theme repeated itself, which set up a decisive Game Seven. The road team had won all six games. Would the trend continue for the decisive seventh game? Could Philadelphia finally win at home, or would Trenton win all four games on the road to claim the series?

The game had all the makings of a classic decisive seventh game. From the start it was a hard-fought contest; "the play was desperate, fast and bitterly fought and the teams were never matched better."[74] The SPHAS had only six players as Irv Davis had been inducted into the army the previous day. Trenton got off to a quick 6–0 lead before Philadelphia scored its first basket. Despite playing short-handed, the SPHAS slowly climbed back and soon had opened a 14–6 lead before Trenton narrowed the deficit to 14–10 after the first period. The second period was equally hard fought with the score tied at 20 and 21. Trenton held a slim 24–23 margin as the final seconds of the second period dwindled. It was at that moment that the game and the series changed on one basket; "a sensational 70-foot throw, with only a second to finish the second period, by Irv Torgoff, proved the turning point and eventually won the game."[75] Capturing the excitement of the play, William Scheffer of the *Philadelphia Inquirer* wrote the following day, "The timers were yelling 'just one second to go,' when Irv Torgoff secured possession of the ball near the end of the second period. He took a desperate chance. Instead of making a two-hand push shot, he made a remarkable one-hand throw, as in making a long throw in baseball. The ball was in the air, mid-way down the court, when the gun sounded and the crowd sat breathless as it sailed through the net. The floor is 80 feet long and Torgoff was just about 10 feet from the end line."[76]

The miracle shot by Torgoff gave the SPHAS a 25–24 lead entering the final period. With momentum on their side and a boisterous crowd supporting them, the SPHAS continued to play aggressively, building a 38–31 advantage midway through the final frame. As in previous games Trenton was feisty and clawed back. With less than a minute to play, Philadelphia held a slim 43–42 lead. Seven seconds remained as Trenton grabbed the ball. Looking to set up the final play to win the championship, Trenton called a time-out to map out its strategy. The only problem was that Trenton did not have any more time-outs left. A technical foul was assessed, and Philadelphia's Sol Schwartz calmly stepped to the foul line and made the shot for a 44–42 win. The SPHAS celebrated a championship, one in which Trenton outplayed them for long stretches in the series. For Trenton it was one that got away, while Philadelphia celebrated its sixth American Basketball League championship and third in four years. For the league the season was also a success as the ABL completed another season despite only five teams, a reduced schedule, and significant player shortages experienced by all teams.

The story of the 1942–43 basketball season was the game's integration, and that signature event carried over to the fifth annual World Professional Basketball Tournament. By now supporters of this professional single-elimination tournament believed it to be the best in the nation. Noted Chicago sports columnist Jimmy Corcoran enthusiastically declared, "Every year there comes the basketball treat of the season. . . . Ned Irish and his Madison Square Garden staff may think they have it when the top-notchers of the college parade get together . . . or the folks out in Kansas City may think they have a great show coming up when some of the lesser college teams get together. . . . I prefer to think that The Herald-American's world championship basketball tourney, which starts next Sunday at the Michigan av. Armory, 16th and Michigan, will have it on 'em all."[77]

The biggest change for the tournament organizers was the location of the games. The games were moved to the Michigan Avenue Armory at Sixteenth and Michigan Avenue because the amphitheater, the site the previous four years, had been requisitioned by the army. Thus all games, except the championship, were played at the armory. The finals were played at Chicago Stadium, thus ensuring a larger venue for the finale. The only drawback was that the armory seated five thousand spectators, which only increased demand for tickets, which the *Chicago Herald American* took to promoting at every chance in the weeks leading up to the tournament. Despite the change in venue, the organizers of the tournament were extremely enthusiastic in previewing the field and building the necessary hype. Writing his Sidelines column in the *Chicago Herald American*, Leo Fischer patriotically declared, "War has taken a heavy toll of players on professional cage teams, but like baseball and football, there are enough remaining to make this coming championship meet a fitting successor to the four which have preceded it."[78]

By March 1943 the war was in full swing, and naturally it impacted the tournament much as it did the National Basketball League and the American Basketball League. The war, the sacrifices needed to be made by everyone, and the connection between sports and war were emphasized in a column by Leo Fischer. Writing a piece about democracy and sports for the tournament program, Fischer evoked the spirit of determination, sacrifice, and courage.

"Sports—an all-American democracy that recognizes neither color, race nor creed!

Out here on the basketball floor you'll find a vivid demonstration of the principles for which our boys are fighting in every corner of the globe. We don't stop to ask whether a man is white, black or yellow, whether he worships at this church or that, whether his purse is overflowing or empty. It's what he does and how he does it that counts.

The Herald-American is proud to present for the fifth consecutive year this climax of the basketball season—the world's championship tournament. The twelve great teams engaged in the struggle for top laurels in the sport represent the best in skill and fight. They are giving everything they have in pursuit of victory—just as many of them will do on the battlefields of the world before victorious peace dawns once more on this embattled globe.

This tournament is symbolic in a small way of America's drive to victory. No nation can be successful in war if its people are not physically fit. Organized physical activity, such as basketball and this world's championship tournament, have prepared the way for America's amazing production miracle and the heroic might of our armed forces.

That underlying spark of courage which stands off impossible odds in battle is only the extension of the last-minute rally which ends with a winning basket. The team-work which carries a giant bomber through to successful culmination of its mission is the outgrowth of the teamwork which moves the ball into position for the scoring shot.

War and sports are so closely associated that one can scarcely draw the line—except that in one the effort is for the team, in the other for the nation.

We feel that these tournaments and every other phase of competitive sport is well worth while. With this in mind, we dedicate the

Fifth Annual World's Championship tournament to the American spirit—

VICTORY!"[79]

In 1942 sixteen teams competed in the tournament, including teams from New York and Maryland. The 1943 World Professional Basketball Tournament featured twelve teams, and all were based in the Midwest except one. The four teams that completed the National Basketball League season—the Oshkosh All-Stars, the Fort Wayne Zollner Pistons, the Sheboygan Red Skins, and the Chicago Studebakers—all accepted invitations to play in the tournament. The tournament also featured the previous four tournament champions including the Oshkosh All-Stars (1942), the Detroit Eagles (1941), the Harlem Globetrotters (1940), and the Washington Bears, a team that was in fact the New York Renaissance, which won the inaugural title in 1939. Due to the war the Rens reconstituted as the Washington Bears and were sponsored by A. E. Lichtman, a theater-chain owner in Washington DC. Pop Gates, who played for the Rens and the Bears, remembered being a Bear:

> The Washington Bears was practically the same team as the Renaissance with just a different uniform. The Bears were owned by a white fellow in Washington. They started the Washington Bears around Tarzan Cooper, who had also left the Renaissance when I went to Grumman. I went to the Washington Bears later. We just played local teams around Washington. When I was there every Sunday we played two games in the Turner's Arena. Every once in a while they would get an offer to play somewhere else, but mostly it was in the Washington area. The Bears paid by the game. I was getting $40 per game and all expenses, except my transportation down there.[80]

The Washington Bears were coached by Tarzan Cooper, a great player in his own right, but this marked the first time in the history of the tournament that a team was player-coached by an African American player. Previewing the Bears in the days leading up to the start of the tournament, James Enright, a writer for the *Chicago Herald American* and a referee, wrote, "The Bears won't lack for canny leadership as they attempt to turn the Michigan av., Armory and Stadium tourney sites into shooting galleries. Boss Bear is 'Tarzan' Cooper, and if there's a smarter head in basketball anywhere it is still to be discovered. He's been through the mill for the past 14 years and has played in about every major and bush league joint in the nation."[81] The other two black teams, the Harlem Globetrotters and the New York Renaissance, were coached by Abe Saperstein and Bob Douglas, respectively, both of whom were nonplaying coaches. In 1945 the Long Island Grumman Hellcats, an integrated team, were coached by Dolly King, another great player for the New York Renaissance (Rens). King's coaching marked the first time in the history of the tournament that an integrated team was coached by a black player. In subsequent decades this concept would gain a little more currency when Bill Russell became the player-coach for the Boston Celtics in 1967, thus becoming the first African American head coach in the National Basketball Association. In this tournament Cooper proved to be a more effective coach than player: he scored a total of two points in three games.

The other teams included the Akron Collegians, the Indianapolis Pure Oils, the Dayton Dive Bombers, the Chicago Ramblers, and the Minneapolis Rock Spring Sparklers. Minneapolis was comprised largely of players from the University of Minnesota, including a young John Kundla, who led the University of Minnesota in scoring for three years. In the years to follow, Kundla would coach the first great dynasty in the Minneapolis Lakers, which starred George Mikan, Vern Mikkelsen, and Jim Pollard, all of whom would one day join Kundla as members of the Naismith Memorial Basketball Hall of Fame. Those three made up the game's best front line in the early 1950s. The Chicago Ramblers were composed mostly of players from Loyola University, while the Akron Collegians were players from the Akron, Ohio, area. The Ramblers plus

FIG. 16. In 1945 Dolly King became the first black coach of an integrated team in the World Professional Basketball Tournament when he coached the Long Island Grumman Hellcats. Courtesy of Bill Himmelman.

the Globetrotters and the Studebakers gave the host city of Chicago three teams. The Dayton Dive Bombers were the only military team in the field. The Pure Oils roster was peppered with players who were once members of the Indianapolis Kautskys. Byes were granted to Sheboygan, the Washington Bears, and the Harlem Globetrotters.

Another team earning a first round bye was the defending champions, the Oshkosh All-Stars. Although they lost in the NBL playoffs, the All-Stars had been one of the most consistent teams in the World Professional Basketball Tournament, winning the previous year, and advancing to the finals in 1939 and 1941. Despite a less-than-stellar league campaign, finishing the regular season at 11-12, the All-Stars had their sights set on defending their title. Upon accepting the invitation to play in the tournament, Lon Darling, Oshkosh's coach, declared, "Don't worry about us. We've lost a lot of men to Uncle Sam, but we're going to go into the world's championship tournament with one of the strongest teams you've ever seen. I'm just waiting for the college season to end, that's all."[82] Among the Oshkosh players who were called for military duty during the course of the season were Eddie Riska, Herm Witasek, Lou Barle, Warner Engdahl, and George Nelmark. Former University of Detroit star Bob Calihan was the most prominent of all professional players in the service at that time because he was working on submarines in New London, Connecticut.

Due to the effects of war, the tournament organizers made a decision to allow teams to sign college players to participate in the tournament, but only after the player's college season had ended. The Sheboygan Red Skins looked to shore up their scoring punch by signing University of Wisconsin star Johnny Kotz, who held the scoring record in the Big Ten Conference before Illinois's Andy Phillip, part of the Whiz Kids, broke the mark. Kotz played three years for the Badgers under head coach and future Naismith Memorial Basketball Hall of Famer Bud Foster and set a record with 242 points. Lon Darling signed Fred Rehm, who played his college ball at the University of Wisconsin, and Bill Crossett from Lawrence College a few days before the start of the tournament. Other teams quickly scoured the sports pages to secure the talents of players who had recently finished their college careers. This move would give an added spark and jolt of publicity to the tournament.

Capitalizing on the success of last year's star-studded performers before and at halftime of the games, the tournament organizers sought to provide even better entertainment that would also be reflective of the ongoing war. For this tournament they hired an all-black drill team. The *Chicago Herald American* described the team in glowing terms: hailing from Wyoming, "the outfit consists of nine jive-minded Negro soldiers from the Quartermaster Replacement Training Center in Wyoming, who have been creating a terrific sensation wherever they've appeared. With uncanny precision and faultless performance they present the regular manual of arms and marching steps and then go into what western newspapermen have labeled the 'rhythm jive' drill. The team goes through a razzle-dazzle repertoire of tricky side steps, reverse marches, rifle gyrations and boogie-woogie cadence that holds the audience spellbound. All the maneuvers are done with regulation 30-caliber army rifles which the boys handle with the ease of a drum major twirls."[83] So popular was this drill unit in the West that one western writer declared, "Suggest you put the Camp Warren 'jive squad' on last—at the very end of your program. They are so sensational your fans will never permit them to leave the floor. It is without question the greatest service show of any produced in World War No. 2. Plan on extra time for 'em or your schedule will be ruined."[84]

With the field and entertainment set, play began on the afternoon of March 14 with two first-round games. In the first contest the Detroit Eagles, led by Charlie Butler's ten points, narrowly defeated the Akron Collegians. Akron held the lead throughout, but Detroit slowly chipped away as "the Eagles kept pounding along and near the windup finally emerged with enough points to finish with a 33–31 victory."[85] Chuck Chuckovits, formerly of the Toledo squad that folded in December, signed on to play with Detroit and scored six points. It was the second afternoon game, however, that led to the tournament's first big upset. The hometown Studebakers, making their tournament debut and hoping to ride the momentum of a solid season, faced the Minneapolis Sparklers. The game was back and forth throughout, and it came down to the final play. As recounted the following day in the *Chicago Herald American*, "Probably the most spectacular game of the day was the Minneapolis victory on a shot from mid-floor by Willie Warhol with 10 seconds remaining. Less than 10 seconds previous, 'Duke' Cumberland had put Chicago in front by a point with a similar hair raiser, but even before the noise died down, Warhol let fly—and there was a game in the bag."[86] The *Chicago Defender*, meanwhile, laid blame for Chicago's loss squarely at the feet of Ted Strong: "Strong was goat, among other things. He failed to take a shot at the basket with less than three minutes to play. He might have been rushed. We will let it go at that but when [Tony] Jaros [*sic*], a Minneapolis player, stole the ball right out of his hands under the Minneapolis basket and made a field goal which tied the score 42 all, things didn't look so hot for a team that had any idea of winning the championship."[87] Minneapolis won 45–44, and Chicago's historic season came to an end. The Studebakers would no longer play professional basketball.

The evening session included three games, the first of which was the lone quarterfinal match-up on the first day. It featured Oshkosh facing Detroit, which had won earlier in the afternoon. Daunted by the prospects of playing their second game of the day, the Eagles were no match for a well-rested Oshkosh squad that easily won 65–36. In the second game the Dayton Bombers slipped past the Chicago Ramblers. The day's fifth and final game saw the Fort Wayne Zollner Pistons win a hard-fought contest against the Indianapolis Pure Oils. The Indianapolis squad featured players from Indiana, Purdue, and Butler Universities as well as smaller colleges in Indiana. "Trailing 17–6 at one time in the first quarter, the Pure Oils started to fight and not only knotted the count, but actually went ahead. From then on it was a ding-dong affair right to the windup, when Fort Wayne's reserve strength began to tell. Even then, Indianapolis wound up with a flurry of shots that would have caused plenty of worry had the gun not ended the battle."[88] Fort Wayne won 46–41, but the interesting side note that was lost in the game stories was that Indianapolis had integrated with George Crowe, who scored eight points.

The following evening saw three quarterfinal contests. In an NBL match-up Fort Wayne defeated Sheboygan, 48–40. In the second game on the card, Dayton continued its surprising run by defeating the Harlem Globetrotters to earn a spot in the semifinals. The evening's final game featured the Washington Bears, who were one of the tournament's preseason favorites, against the Minneapolis Sparklers, surprising winners the day before. After a slow start Washington poured it on to win in convincing fashion, 40–21. The Bears' defense was so strong that they limited Minneapolis to only six field goals for the game.

Washington's convincing win made it the odds-on favorite to win the tournament. In the semifinals the Bears handled the surprising Dayton squad, while Oshkosh eased by Fort Wayne by a single point. This set up a highly anticipated final between Washington and Oshkosh. It was the second time that two former champions, Washington (1939 Rens) and Oshkosh (1942), had met in the finals. The other was in 1942, when Oshkosh and Detroit reprised their 1941 championship game. The Washington-Oshkosh game was also a rematch of the 1939 finals, in which the Rens won, 34–25. The game marked the fourth time in five years that Oshkosh was playing for the championship. High expectations preceded the contest, but despite the advance billing, the game itself was one-sided. Playing the final before twelve thousand screaming fans at Chicago Stadium on St. Patrick's Day, the Bears jumped out to a sixteen-point margin and never looked back. Led by Johnny Isaac's ten points, the Bears put on a show of brilliant ball-handling that left the All-Stars gasping for air, as they won, 43–31. As one writer reported the next day, "A squadron of bronze speed merchants, darting like new Thunderbolt pursuit planes in and around slow air freighters, completely outclassed the defending champions of Oshkosh and the National league."[89]

Washington's dominating performance was covered by the black press, including the *Call* from Kansas City. So impressed was the paper with the team's performance that it sought to compare it to the 1939 Rens team: "The Bears looked even greater than the '39 Rens. Their teamwork was well nigh perfect and their speed so blinding that the other 11 entries resembled novices. That starting team of Sonny Wood, Pop Gates, Dolly King, Johnny Isaacs, and Zack Clayton is the smoothest combination the tournament has ever seen. It's greater than any '39 Ren five of Cooper, Smith, Gates, Fats Jenkins, Isaacs, Puggy Bell and Eyre Saitch."[90] The Bears had now gone undefeated in forty games over a two-year period. The Bears also became the third black team to win the tournament in five years, and helped make "Washington first in basketball as it [was] first in war and first in peace."[91]

3

WARTIME BASKETBALL, 1943–1944

Besides its use as a general body conditioner and a builder of physical stamina, basketball also develops precise optical, muscular, and mental coordination, body balance, deft touch and quick perception—factors which are benefit of to pilots. It improves the cadets' alertness and aids them in making instantaneous judgments and decisions. —LIEUTENANT COMMANDER FRANK H. WICK- HORST, HEAD OF PRE-FLIGHT AND PHYSICAL TRAINING, BUREAU OF AERONAUTICS

By the time November 1943 arrived on the calendar and sports con- sciousness shifted toward the upcoming basketball season, World War II was in the midst of its darkest days. The tide, though, was slowly turning. In February 1943 the Germans were defeated at Stalingrad, a decisive victory for the Soviet Union. Eventually, that battle would be a turning point, and what would become the beginning of the end for the Germans. Several months later the Allies conducted massive air raids on Berlin. In late November Winston Churchill, Franklin Roosevelt, and Chinese leaders met in Cairo to discuss aid to China and to reassure the Chinese that any territory taken from the Japanese would be returned after the war. Shortly thereafter Churchill and Roosevelt conferred with Josef Stalin in Tehran to confirm an invasion of Western Europe by the Allies. General Dwight D. Eisenhower was also confirmed to command the invasion of Normandy. While war raged, its effects could be felt on the home front as gas and food rationing impacted how Americans lived their lives. Factories were operating around the clock to produce the necessary munitions to assist with the war effort. Every facet of American life was affected, including sports.

While all sports adjusted to the new rhythms and realities of a country at war, baseball, the nation's pastime, received its biggest boost from America's first fan, President Franklin D. Roosevelt. On January 15, 1942, a little more than a month after Pearl Harbor, Roosevelt wrote baseball commissioner Judge Kenesaw Mountain Landis a letter, later to be known as the "green light" letter. The letter stated:

My dear Judge:

Thank you for yours of January fourteenth. As you will, of course, realize the final decision about the baseball season must rest with you and the Baseball club owners—so what I am going to say is solely a personal and not an official point of view.

I honestly feel that it would be best for the country to keep baseball going. There will be fewer people unemployed and everybody will work longer hours and harder than ever before.

And that means that they ought to have a chance for recreation and for taking their minds off their work even more than before.

Baseball provides a recreation which does not last over two hours or two hours and a half and which can be got for very little cost. I hope that night games can be extended because it gives an opportunity to the day shift to see a game occasionally.

As to the players themselves, I know you agree with me that the individual players who are active military or naval age should go, without question, into the services. Even if the actual quality to the teams is lowered by the greater use of older players, this will not dampen the popularity of the sport. Of course, if an individual has some particular aptitude in a trade or profession, he ought to serve the Government. That, however, is a matter which I know you can handle with complete justice.

Here is another way of looking at it—if 300 teams use 5,000 or 6,000 players, these players are a definite recreational asset to at least 20,000,000 of the fellow citizens—and that in my judgment is thoroughly worthwhile.

With every best wish,

Very sincerely yours,

Franklin D. Roosevelt

With that, baseball continued. While Roosevelt's letter was largely focused on baseball, basketball and other sports interpreted it liberally to include their own sports as well. Soon other sports executives were making plans and contingencies for their own leagues and teams. Issues such as reduced travel, players being drafted, league contraction, fuel restrictions, and participating in charity games all earned the attention of league officials and commissioners and forced them to conform to the new realities. Much like the other sports, basketball became an integral part of sports being played on military bases around the country. Armed service basketball factored heavily into the transformation and growth of the game during the war years. The advent of college basketball doubleheaders allowed players and teams from different parts of the country to play *against* one another. This offered players an opportunity to see new teams and different styles of play, some of which were characteristic of certain regions of the country. The big change, however, occurred on military bases, where the teams were composed of players from all around the country. What happened next was that players from different parts of the country, bringing their own styles of play, soon were on the same team playing *with* one another. As this happened, regional differences in styles of play soon evaporated and a more homogenous style of play emerged. Slowly, the game became more national, and in the process, it became more recognizable to

Americans across the country. "Service basketball loosened the game up. In the beginning of WWII to the end of WWII, scoring picked up. The game became more modern," Bill Himmelman, basketball historian, has noted. "Service basketball promoted the integration of the sport. When they came out of WWII, they did not give as much thought to integration as football and baseball did. Basketball players did not give it a thought. It was considered natural."[1]

The Special Services division of the Joint Army and Navy Committee on Welfare and Recreation had an immediate role in creating and administering service basketball. As it stated in its publications and marketing material, "Every red-blooded American youth, in and out of uniform, is a lover of sports. The Army has found it desirable to maintain and foster this competitive ideal. Mass participation in sports and games of every description is the Army goal."[2] Shortly thereafter a comprehensive plan was created on bases around the country to administer basketball and its incorporation into military life.

One of the great teams in all service basketball was the Great Lakes Naval Training Station in Illinois. Located in North Chicago, Great Lakes became a powerhouse for baseball, football, and basketball. The tradition of Great Lakes athletics began during World War I, when Captain W. A. Moffett, commandant of the Great Lakes Naval Training Station, and Commander John B. Kaufman, athletic director, developed an athletic program "at the station during the war years [composed of] some of the greatest athletes in the annals of sport and won for Great Lakes the acclaim of the entire world."[3] They believed something was missing in the training at Great Lakes, "something that would transform them into fighters that would have no equal. That finishing process, [they] believed, was athletics. This athletic program would extend to all sailors as a 'sports-for-all' program was set up, under which every man in the station took part in some sport, making themselves clean of mind and body for the day when they would go to sea."[4] Top-notch teams were developed beginning in 1917. The baseball club was led by Felix (Phil) Chuinard, who had played for the Chicago White Sox. The football squad included Pat Smith of the University of Michigan and Jimmy Conzelman, who during the 1940s was coach of the Chicago Cardinals football team. A basketball team was also developed and led by George Halas, who later gained fame as coach of football's Chicago Bears. World War II again conjured up memories of the great athletic teams of World War I. As the *Chicago Stadium Review* noted, "Now, as in the past war, men from all walks of life are enlisting in the United States Navy and the athletic program has again been extended to permit competition with the finest college teams in the middlewest and once again the Great Lakes team is gaining national acclaim by its victories."[5]

From the outset of World War II, developing a top-notch program was a priority for the training station. As Lieutenant Commander J. Russell Cook, the athletic officer at Great Lakes, noted, "From the moment our plans to form a basketball team first were announced last fall, the response was tremendous. A squad of 72 men reported for the first practice. In no time a tentative schedule of 26 games was arranged through the cooperation of collegiate athletic directors who made room on schedules already crowded. Other games were added as the demand for more Navy appearances increased."[6] Commander Cook was a native of Indiana and had competed in pole vaulting while in high school, winning the national high school championship. As a college student at DePauw University, he was a member of the football and basketball teams in addition to continuing with pole vaulting. He entered the navy in 1917 and completed aviation school at Great Lakes. He did not see any action during the war but instead was engaged "teaching motor theory and assisting in training the great football, basketball, and track teams produced at Great Lakes."[7] He later became a college head coach, worked with the American Legion, and was employed in the Office of Education in Washington DC. When war was declared, Cook was called back; "as Athletic Officer at the U.S. Naval Training Station, [he was] back at Great Lakes again, with the record of the 1917–1918 teams and his own Indiana teams setting the pace for the future."[8]

Indeed, under Commander Cook's leadership, Great Lakes quickly assembled a highly competitive team. There were three purposes in fielding such a team: it was "a morale builder for the thousands of recruits in training at the Station; a means of recruiting of bringing the Navy before the eyes of natives of the 13 inland states comprising the Ninth Naval District; and a means of adding receipts to the Navy Relief Fund."[9] It was noted that recruiting benefited as "a survey indicated that enlistments jumped from 20 to 40 percent in areas visited by the Navy team."[10] So important was the role of basketball on base for Great Lakes that for the 1942–43 season, "a survey . . . revealed that approximately 1,000 teams [would] compete in the sport during the season. More than 900 quintets [would] be formed among companies in recruit training. Thirty-eight squads ha[d] been organized in the Service Schools, and an additional 38 teams [would] be playing in two Ship's Company Leagues."[11] It was believed that "competition in basketball [would] aid tremendously in the physical development of Great Lakes sailors."[12] The Great Lakes' basketball team directly aided and benefited the navy as a whole.

Another theme that emerged in the growth of service basketball was the correlation between sports fitness and readiness on the battlefield. As Commander Cook explained, "Basketball at Great Lakes brought out something additional—means of achieving physical fitness—and as the season drew on athletics became recognized as an important factor in the Navy's vast physical hardening program to condition its men for wartime duty."[13] This theme was echoed throughout the war, in speeches, articles, tournament programs, and recruiting visits. Lieutenant Joseph G. Daher continued along this thinking when he stated,

The inclusion of athletics in the physical training program is strongly advocated. Regular sports and games which the boys enjoy possess great value from a conditioning standpoint in addition to their other merits. The boys will gladly engage in calisthenics, guerilla exercises, or grass drills if they know they will be able to play the various sports afterwards. Team-work, a highly emphasized objective to be acquired through participation in basketball, develops the principals of coordination that are invaluable on the battlefield. Basketball will develop aggressiveness, a fighting spirit, confidence, the will to win, and the ability to think and act decisively under fire.[14]

During the war years the Great Lakes Bluejackets were led by Tony Hinkle. A basketball lifer, Hinkle spent nearly his entire life involved with the game of basketball as a player, coach, or administrator. Born in Logansport, Indiana, Hinkle began playing the game at an early age. After a successful high school career, he enrolled at the University of Chicago, where he excelled as a player. During his college career he lettered three times, was twice named All-Big Ten, was twice team captain, and was named to the Helms All-America team in 1920 while leading the University of Chicago to the Big Ten Conference championship in 1919–20.

After graduating Hinkle took a job at Butler University in Indianapolis, Indiana, where he remained for the rest of his life. He coached the football and baseball teams but made his mark as a basketball coach, leading the Bulldogs to the 1929 national championship. He won 560 games and held top positions with the National Association of Basketball Coaches (NABC). He was inducted into the Naismith Memorial Basketball Hall of Fame in 1965. The Butler Fieldhouse was later renamed the Tony Hinkle Memorial Fieldhouse in 1966. The fieldhouse served for many decades as the site of the Indiana state high school championship. The site has become better known because the final scene in the movie *Hoosiers*, when Hickory High School wins the state championship, was filmed there.

Under Hinkle's direction and guidance, the Great Lakes Naval

Training Station became the top service team during the war years. In 1941–42 Great Lakes was the class of service basketball as they compiled a 31-5 record while being led by Bob Calihan, Frank Baumholtz, and Forrest "Forddy" Anderson. That team featured seven former college All-Americans, and two players, Frank Baumholtz and Ernie Andres, were two-sports professional athletes. Playing top college squads Great Lakes dominated the opposition. The *Great Lakes Bulletin,* a weekly publication on base, devoted one page to covering the sports exploits of Great Lakes. On January 17, 1942, the *Great Lakes Bulletin* summed up the previous week's basketball games, writing, "Sparked by the sensational left-handed hook shooting of Big Bob Calihan in the second half, the Great Lakes basketball team put on a closing minutes rally Wednesday night that let them win going away from Northwestern University, 47–38, and chalked up their fourteenth victory in 16 starts."[15] While Calihan led the team with eight points, it was George Rung's defense on Northwestern's Otto Graham, later a professional football star with the Cleveland Browns, that turned the game in the Bluejackets favor. "Rung stuck to Graham with leechlike tenacity, and until fouling out with but five minutes remaining, he held the Wildcat sophomore to a short seven points—quite a comedown from his usual 18 or twenty."[16] In late January the team won three games in five days all on the road, defeating in succession, the University of Chicago, the University of Nebraska, and St. Joseph's. The first week of February saw another tough schedule with four games in five nights against Iowa State University, Creighton University, the University of Kansas, and the University of Wisconsin. The Bluejackets faced all comers and by season's end, "now with 36 games under their belt and season end still a matter of conjecture, the boys in Blue and Gold ha[d] suffered but five losses in their entire season."[17]

The team was well balanced and included "Bob Calihan, former Detroit University star, [who] led the 1941–1942 team in scoring with 308 points. Frank Baumholtz, Ohio University, was second with 297. Others

FIG. 17. The Great Lakes Naval Training Station team compiled a 31-5 mark in 1941–42 and dominated service basketball. Naismith Memorial Basketball Hall of Fame.

included Ernie Andres, Indiana; Jim Currie, Northwestern; George Rung and Jim Van Orsdel, Miami University of Ohio.; John Lobsiger, Missouri; John Adams, Arkansas; Les Bruckner, Michigan State; Bob White, Dartmouth, and Lee Huber, Kentucky. All now [were] ensigns. Bill Menke of Indiana [was] training to be a Navy flier."[18] So impressive was the team's play and overall dominance, it evoked a passionate and emotional letter written by Captain T. DeWitt Carr, U.S. Navy Executive Officer, to Robert Calihan, EM2c of the U.S. Naval Training Station, at Great Lakes in March 1942.

> Never for one moment have you and the rest of the boys on the team been anything but the finest examples of Navy manhood. On trains, in hotel lobbies, at luncheons and on the basketball court your

conduct has been so splendid that the entire Navy recognized you and your team as the best recruiting "poster" in the Ninth Naval District. You carried the Navy story to colleges and towns and you did it in the Navy way. You ignored inconveniences, you fought harder when you were tired, and you asked for no special privileges during all the time you were doing a double job for your Navy.

In traveling the road, your basketball activity was comparable to a fleet arrangement of the United States Navy. Like our own fleet, the further you got from the home base of supplies the more difficult was the attainment of victory. Yet, in foreign "waters" you met the enemy and scored victory. True, five games were lost, but only five out of 36. In Navy terms, losing five while sinking 31 of the enemy ships means complete victory.[19]

With a year under its belt, Great Lakes professed high aspirations for the 1942–43 season. In previewing the season the *Great Lakes Bulletin* noted, "Twelve of the 14 boys who rang up that imposing record have been transferred from Great Lakes—and most are now engaged in combat duty on the high seas."[20] A great challenge awaited Coach Hinkle, the article continued. "For his new squad Lt. Paul D. (Tony) Hinkle is combing the thousands of boys in training here. From them he must choose a group to equal the strength of the best the Midwest can offer—a team which will approach or exceed last season's great record not only in wins, but in entertaining the recruits at Great Lakes, in aiding recruiting throughout the Ninth Naval District and in raising money for the Great Lakes Welfare Fund."[21]

Excitement was building as the season was close to starting, and it was hoped that all the sailors on base would continue to support the club as they had the previous season. "The Great Lakes home games [would] be played in one of the giant drill halls on the Station, as was the case last year, when a crowd of 5,000 recruits witnessed each of the nine games at Great Lakes. This season, again 5,000 boys [would]

FIG. 18. Tony Hinkle coached the 1942–43 Great Lakes Bluejackets to a 34-3 record. Photographer unknown. Naismith Memorial Basketball Hall of Fame.

watch the 1942 Sailor squad in action at each game. The general public [would] not be permitted to attend."[22] If it was possible, the Bluejackets bettered their mark from the previous season by compiling a 34-3 record, highlighted by wins over Ohio State, Butler University, Stanford University, Michigan State, Marquette, Notre Dame, and Kentucky. The win over Notre Dame, 60–56, came in overtime at Chicago Stadium before fifteen thousand fans.

The following season, 1943–44, they compiled a 32-4 record, again marked by big wins over top college teams. The Great Lakes team was led by Forrest Anderson and Dick Klein. Anderson, a native of Gary, Indiana, had starred at Stanford University, where he "won an all-Pacific conference berth and was fourth in scoring."[23] In his first year at Great Lakes, he averaged 5.4 points per game in thirty-three

FIG. 19. On February 20, 1943, the Great Lakes Naval Station played the University of Notre Dame in a game benefiting the Navy Relief Fund at Chicago Stadium in Chicago, Illinois. Author's collection.

games. In terms of his military career, Anderson was a "boatswain's mate, second class, [who] so impressed training station officers with his work as a company leader that he was made a regimental adjutant."[24] One of Anderson's teammates was center Dick Klein, who in only one season at Northwestern University was named to the All-Big Ten team and was an All-America. In his first season with Great Lakes, he averaged 6.7 points per game and scored 17 points in three consecutive games midseason. Klein eventually was an executive with the National Basketball Association's Chicago Zephyrs. In summing up the season, Coach Hinkle stated,

> We have no apologies to offer for our showing this year. The three teams that caught us were keyed to peak performance on those nights. This year's Great Lakes team is one of the greatest teams the country has seen. When the going got tough, they came through with points the hard way. Every game was a tough one, because there wasn't a team on our schedule that wasn't keyed to a feverish pitch to beat us. When you face a schedule like Great Lakes had, and come out with a victory over every team you play, that's some grind, and no other team in the nation can match that performance.[25]

For their effort, Great Lakes earned the distinction of being ranked the top team by Dick Dunkel and his rating system.

An interesting aside to the 1943–44 season was that Great Lakes fielded an all-black basketball team, which received some attention weekly in the *Great Lakes Bulletin.* Coached by Chief Specialist Forrest Anderson, the Great Lakes Negro varsity team, as it was called, played a number of company-based or independent teams, including Halliecrafter Company, Wehr Steel Company, Kadin Jewelry, and the Falk Corporation team among others. The team was led by Charley Harmon, a former University of Toledo player, and Jimmy Brown, a player at Southern University. One of the other players on the team was Larry Doby, who in 1947 integrated the American League with the Cleveland Indians shortly after Jackie Robinson broke baseball's color barrier. Other players on the roster included Sam Williams, Carl Brown, Grant Gray, Edward James, Jerry Cooper, Arthur Grant, and Leo Brinkley. As might be expected, the Great Lakes Negro team dominated its opponents as evidenced by the following wins; 53–30 over Halliecrafter Company, 67–41 over Wehr Steel Company, 78–26 over Wright Corporation in Cincinnati, and a 58–36 win versus Fort Sheridan. Throughout the season Harmon and Brown waged a personal battle for team scoring honors.

One of the players on Great Lakes during the war years was Pete Newell. Newell would eventually become a highly regarded college coach, earning a place in the Naismith Memorial Basketball Hall of Fame. But for now he was just an enlisted man in the navy. With the help of Sam Barry, his college coach at the University of Southern California and eventually a member of the Naismith Memorial Basketball Hall of Fame, Newell was assigned to the Great Lakes Naval Training Station. "I met people like Johnny Mize, Bob Feller, Joe Kuharich and Red Auerbach on the base," he recalled. "I played on the basketball team under Tony Hinkle, who became a great coach at Butler. It was the biggest Naval base in the country, and there were college stars all over the place. One time the boxing coach asked me to find some burly-looking guys for the program. This one guy looked like a prospect, so I asked him if he had any experience. 'Yeah, a little,' he tells me. Turned out to be Tony Zale, the middleweight champion of the world. I thought he looked a little familiar."[26] After his time at Great Lakes, Newell had an opportunity to enter the armed guard but passed on this chance and instead headed back home to California and joined up with an amphibious group out of Coronado. He later described his wartime experience:

I was on a ship for about a year and half. It seemed like ten. We went straight to the Philippines, got involved in the second Manila operation and the landing at Okinawa when the battle was still going on. We were in the harbor every night, and this was some of the damndest fighting you ever saw. Incredible shows in the air. Our picket boats with their lights would attract the kamikazes away from the fleet, and we used to marvel at those guys. To me, that was the toughest duty in the Navy. Every night they'd get smashed, guys just dying out there, routinely. And it was a big fleet. In the daytime, it was just ships as far as you could see.[27]

Later in 1944 Newell was in Samar, an island in the Philippines, and then went to Guadalcanal and Iwo Jima and experienced heavy fighting.

"I was a different man when I got back to the Bay Area," Newell recalled. "I swear that experience aged me at least ten years. I was so lucky to have a wonderful woman like Florence and a nice place to raise our family."[28] Newell now began his long-awaited coaching career.

Great Lakes was just one of many service teams who excelled during the 1943–44 season. Ned Irish, recapping the basketball season, wrote, "Service basketball, with its many star players from college ranks, was given considerable impetus last winter. The 48-hour restriction on travel kept many of the more powerful naval and maritime trainee teams from showing in New York, Philadelphia, Chicago, Buffalo and other large cities. Teams like Great Lakes Naval Training Station, Norfolk Navy Base, Norfolk Air Base, North Carolina Pre-Flight, Bainbridge Naval, Aberdeen Proving Grounds, Mitchell Field, Columbia Midshipman, Camp Warren and Camp Grant compiled splendid records against college, professional, defense plant and civilian opposition."[29]

In addition to achieving excellent records, many of these service teams did much to promote the game and served as a great example of the fighting forces. The Naval Training Station in Norfolk, Virginia, compiled a 31-2 record while averaging sixty-two points a game. "The Bluejackets displayed the fine caliber of their team work when, after losing two key men through injuries, they downed in succession Bainbridge N.T.C., Villanova, Norfolk Naval Air Station, and the Curtis

Bay (Md.) Coast Guard."[30] The team featured two future prominent NBA coaches, Red Auerbach and Red Holzman. Meanwhile, in Rockford, Illinois, the Camp Grant Medical Replacement Training Center earned a respectable 27-4 mark and was led by Mickey Rottner, who tallied 316 points, and Stan Szukala, who finished a close second with 291 points. At St. Mary's College in Moraga, California, the St. Mary's Navy Pre-Flight team dominated the competition on the West Coast. The annual *Converse Yearbook* highlighted its achievement: "The only undefeated major service team in the country, St. Mary's Pre-Flight annexed 21 wins, collecting 1,032 points to the opposition's 720. The Air Devils had too much stuff on the ball for the Pacific Coast collegiate and service teams they met, with [Hank] Luisetti heading the attack in every game he played. Averaging 18.5 points per game, Luisetti scored 32 points against the Coast Guard Sea Lions, and duplicated his feat against the Armed Guard quintet."[31] Back in Maryland the Aberdeen Proving Ground was led by Angelo Musi and Abe Novak, who paced the team to a 24-10 mark with wins over Philadelphia Coast Guard, Villanova University, Bainbridge Naval Station, and other collegiate and service teams on the East Coast. The Boston District Coast Guard won the New England Servicemen's Championship, while Kelly Field finished second in the San Antonio Army Service League and third in the Texas Amateur Basketball Tournament. The San Diego Marine Corps Base won the Army-Navy Pre-Season Service Tournament and was champion of the Eleventh Naval District. All in all, many of the service teams acquitted themselves well during the basketball season.

These service teams were also coached by college coaches or professional players, some of whom would go on to make a name for themselves in the years after the war. In addition to Great Lakes being coached by Tony Hinkle, Camp Luna in Las Vegas, New Mexico, was led by Cy Kaselman, a great outside shooter for the Philadelphia SPHAS teams of the 1930s. Hank Iba, the coach at Oklahoma A&M, coached the team at Fort Leavenworth in Kansas, and Harry Braun was in charge of the Glenview Naval Air Station in Glenview, Illinois. In 1943–44 Glenview was co-champion of the Chicago Area Service Men's League. Finally, March Field in California was coached by Frank Lubin, who starred on America's first Olympic basketball team in 1936.

Another recognizable individual who coached an armed services team was Everett Case, who oversaw the De Pauw Naval Pre-Flight program. Born on June 21, 1900, in Anderson, Indiana, a mere nine years after the game of basketball was invented, Case grew up playing basketball in a state that embraced the game as a religion. He eventually matriculated at the University of Wisconsin–Madison, where he played basketball and graduated in 1923. Soon thereafter he continued to pursue his passion and began a lifelong career as a basketball coach. He began his coaching career at the tender age of eighteen. His first stop was a high school in Frankfort, Indiana, and he led the school to four Indiana state championships (1925, 1929, 1936, and 1939). The school's gymnasium, Case Arena, was later named for him.

The onset of World War II impacted Case's career. In 1941 he enlisted in the navy and was commissioned as a senior-grade lieutenant. He reported to Annapolis for a four-week course. Upon completion he was assigned to Chicago for another five-week course, all the while on the way to St. Mary's College in California, where he joined the Naval Pre-Flight School. While at St. Mary's he served as athletic director and also director of basketball. He was also the athletic director at nearby Alameda Naval Air Station.

After two years at St. Mary's, Case returned to the Midwest to serve as the athletic director of the naval flight preparatory school at DePauw University. By this time he had risen to lieutenant commander. After his discharge in 1946, Case moved to Raleigh, North Carolina, where he assumed control of the basketball program at North Carolina State. In eighteen seasons, he led the Wolf Pack to a 377-134 record. His achievements included a third-place finish in the 1947 NIT and third place in the

FIG. 20. Everett Case oversaw the De Pauw Naval Pre-Flight Program before coaching North Carolina State University after World War II. Naismith Memorial Basketball Hall of Fame.

1950 NCAA tournaments. He was inducted into the Naismith Memorial Basketball Hall of Fame in 1982.

Case was one of many coaches and players involved with the V-5 Pre-Flight programs. Sponsored by the navy the V-5 program was part of a much larger system of V programs. Specifically, the V-5 program provided aviation training. As author Randy Robert notes,

> The goal of the V-programs was to educate and train junior officers to fight the war. Their goal was simple: use sports to train pilots. Along with a rigorous academic curriculum, which included mathematics, physics, celestial navigation, and aerology, and lessons in

naval nomenclature and navigation signals, they hardened their bodies. [Lieutenant Commander Thomas J.] Hamilton's plan called for the trainees to participate in a daily regimen of an hour and a half of running, swimming, chopping wood, calisthenics, and hard labor, in addition to another hour and a half instruction in team and combative sports. Finally, the plan called for the men to play two hours of team sports a day.[32]

The training program for naval aviators consisted of seven incremental steps: flight preparatory schools, war training service schools, pre-flight schools, primary air stations, intermediate air stations, operational air stations, and fleet air centers. Basketball was an integral part of this program. As noted by Lieutenant Commander Frank H. Wickhorst, "Like all the other sports, the court game is not carried on in a hit-or-miss manner. There is a progressive syllabus, which differs at each stage of training, and the entire course of basketball instruction becomes progressively more difficult as the cadets increase their knowledge of the sport in their training. It is handled like any academic subject, and the test of the student's ability to assimilate knowledge is out on the court in stern competition."[33]

Early in 1942 pre-flight programs opened at St. Mary's College in California, the University of North Carolina, the University of Iowa, and the University of Georgia. Other successful programs included the Corpus Christi Naval Air Station, the Olathe Clippers U.S. Naval Air Station, and the Pensacola Naval Air Training Center. In the summer of 1943 another V program began: the V-12 program. As Randy Roberts states, "The V-12 program effectively consolidated the V-1, V-7, and V-5 programs to funnel qualified students into reserve midshipmen's schools and produce commissioned officers. Thousands of college players entered the program. Some 372 colleges eventually participated in the Navy or the Army training scheme—241 Army and 131 Navy. The boom in government-funded students permitted many schools to remain open during the war, field varsity teams, and generate revenue from sports. Throughout the war, the schools with V-12 programs dominated the national rankings. Many of the finest coaches in the country enrolled in the V-5 and V-12 programs."[34] One such coach who eventually became involved in the V-12 program was Ben Carnevale.

Born in Raritan, New Jersey, on October 30, 1915, Ben Carnevale devoted his life to basketball. His interest began as a child while he accompanied his father to basketball games. "I was in junior high school," he recalled. "My father coached a team called the Trenton Moose and I guess I just picked up the interest from him."[35]

After a successful career at Somerville High School, Carnevale enrolled at New York University (NYU) to play under future Naismith Memorial Basketball Hall of Fame coach Howard Cann. An integral part of the team that won the 1935 national championship, he also played in the first National Invitational Tournament (NIT) in 1938. During his collegiate career, he was named to the All-Metropolitan and All-East teams.

After graduating from NYU Carnevale played briefly for two years as a professional with the Jersey Reds of the American Basketball League. While playing professionally he began his coaching career by serving as head coach of the Cranford (New Jersey) High School basketball team. From 1939 to 1942 he compiled a 75-20 record, and his teams reached the state tournament for three consecutive years.

With the onset of World War II, Carnevale enlisted in the navy. Serving as a gunnery officer Carnevale was engaged in fighting off the coast of North Africa. His ship was torpedoed, and he was cast adrift for five days in a boat at sea. After being rescued he arrived in Casablanca and was later flown back to the United States. He was then assigned to the Canal Zone, where he coached the navy team to the Canal Zone championship in 1943–44. He was also awarded a Purple Heart for his navy service.

After completing his tour Carnevale became the head basketball coach at the University of North Carolina and the athletic director of the navy V-12 program. In his first year, 1944–45, he led the Tar Heels to a 22-6 record and the championship of the Southern Conference. The following year he did even better, leading the team to a 29-5 record, the Southern Conference championship, and an appearance in the NCAA championship game against Oklahoma A&M coached by Henry Iba. Years later he reflected on that game: "I still recall that game vividly. We lost to Oklahoma A&M, 43–40. They had Bob Kurland, the first seven-foot center."[36]

With the war over in 1946, Carnevale moved to Annapolis, where he coached from 1947 to 1967 and compiled a 257-160 record. Hall of Famer Joe Lapchick, a contemporary of Carnevale's as both a player and a coach, noted, "As a coach with the material Ben had at Navy, he was one of the toughest guys in the country to beat."[37] Carnevale was inducted into the Naismith Memorial Basketball Hall of Fame in 1970.

Basketball was also used during World War II to boost morale and provide a diversion for those affected by combat. That is where Bernie Fliegel fit in. A native New Yorker, Fliegel starred as a kid for Clinton High School and later City College of New York (CCNY) under famed coach Nat Holman. He succeeded Moe Goldman as the next great CCNY center. After graduation he turned professional and played on various teams in the American Basketball League, including Wilmington and Brooklyn. With the onset of World War II, Fliegel found himself in a new role with the game of basketball. "I went into the service, but I had an enlarged heart, so I sat out a year," he later recalled in an interview.

> The next year, I went in. I played on a basketball team in the service. We beat the Navy [Great Lakes] team that had Bobby Davies from Seton Hall. I played on a team call the Five By Five. We had Bruce Hale, who was a great player from Santa Clara and later coached at University of Miami. He is Rick Barry's former father-in-law. We

also had Jake Ahearn and Dwight Eddlemann. Our team was located in Miami Beach.

I began my time in the service at Fort Dix in New Jersey. Mike Bloom was there. Nobody wanted to leave because you were not in harm's way of the fighting. They had an extra person and announced someone would have to go. Since I had twisted my knee and was out, I elected to go only if they would send me to a warm climate. The first stop was Miami Beach, and I stayed there for two years. The Long Island University sent their freshman team down, and they needed a team to play against. That is how we started the Five by Five. We played games in Tampa and then would come back. It was easy duty, and we played games.

For the first few months, I had a bad knee. I was in the aircraft specialization field. I was in Miami, and then I went to [Fort McClellan in] Clearwater, [Florida], and from there, I arrived in North Carolina at Fort McCullough. I was given a broom and put on KP duty. I ran into a friend, Captain Angie Monitto, who said I should call him. Every day I asked the sergeant if I could make a call, and he said to go back to work. After a few days Captain Monitto came to the office and asked why I had not called. I told him to speak to the sergeant. He said, "The general wants to see you." This was during the Battle of the Bulge and a lot of the men were having horrible nightmares of what they had witnessed, so the general wanted me to put together a basketball team to help raise the morale of the troops. I said I would if I could have a five-day furlough to visit my wife in Miami. Once I returned, I looked at a roster and found some players. One of them was Si Lobello from Long Island University. It turns out that he was shipped out two days later. He died in the first day in battle in Europe.

After that, I had a job in which I would go to the hotel and offer them to buy back their furniture that was stored away when the army came in and used hotels during the war. I did this for a year,

FIG. 21. A former standout player at Long Island University, Si Lobello died in his first day of action in Europe. Courtesy of Bill Himmelman.

and it was a cushy job. I traveled with the furniture man in Miami Beach in 1944, before I went to Clearwater and Fort McClellan. I was married in St. Petersburg in November 1944 and played at Largo High School gym the day after I was married.

When I was discharged from the Army, I was already married and had one child. The New York Knicks wanted me to play for them, but I could not afford to play. They offered me $6,000. I had just opened a law office. I thought I could make more money playing in the American Basketball League on the weekends. I was getting ninety dollars a game and playing three games each weekend.[38]

While the 1942–43 season was characterized by the integration of black players into a professional league, the 1943–44 campaign was noted for its inclusion of a Japanese American player at a major college program. Wat Misaka grew up playing basketball and eventually matriculated at the University of Utah. During the 1943–44 season the University of Utah finished with an 18-4 regular-season record. One of Misaka's teammates and the team's star player was Arnie Ferrin. The war affected teams and their composition as Ferrin noted,

> We didn't practice; didn't have a scouting report; no preparation. We just started playing. During timeouts you could not go to the bench. When you took a timeout, the players sat down on the floor and talked about what was happening and made the decision right there. You saw the coach before the game and at half-time. If he had a message for you during the game, he'd send in a substitute so you could take a timeout. It was wartime and if you played ball then, you were either 4-F, you were a freshman, or you were in medical, or dental, or engineering school. They were the only people still in school.[39]

Despite the lack of formal practice and scouting, Utah had a very good campaign.

Head coach Vadal Peterson, later a member of the Naismith Memorial Basketball Hall of Fame, summed up his team's competition and their style of play: "There were few collegiate teams in our area, so our competition was almost entirely against service teams before our trips to the Garden. Actually, we played only four all-civilian teams of collegiate nature. We met eight strictly service teams, often playing them twice. We met five college service teams, playing return games with

FIG. 22. A solid all-around player, Arnie Ferrin led the University of Utah to
the 1944 NCAA championship. Courtesy of Bill Himmelman.

several of them."[40] A balanced team, the Utes' style was described as
"one-handed shooting, fast-break style, unusual methods of foul shooting."[41] It all worked for Utah, which by the end of the season received
an invitation to play in both the NIT and the NCAA tournaments. At
that time it was not uncommon to receive an offer from both tournaments, and Utah selected the NIT, which was the more prestigious
tournament. Utah's opening-round match was against Adolph Rupp's

Kentucky squad. Although Kentucky came out with a 48–38 victory and the chance to move to the next round, Utah did not leave without a fight and made a strong impression in which "the Utes proved themselves a surprisingly good ball club, capable of keeping pace with the best of them until they wilted in the second half. This group of one-handed shooters, not quite as hard-driving an aggregation as Kentucky, but loaded with spirit, immediately won the fancy of the crowd and for a long time appeared capable of springing an upset."[42] Wat Misaka scored four points in the loss.

As the team left New York and headed by train back to Utah, team officials received a call from the NCAA asking them if it would like to fill for Arkansas, whose team had been involved in a car crash, forcing it to withdraw from the tournament. Utah stopped in Kansas City and played in the western regional of the NCAA bracket. In the first round the Utes dispatched Missouri, 45–35, before defeating Iowa, 40–31, to earn them a return trip to New York to face Dartmouth, the winner of the Eastern Regional. A hard-fought and close game throughout, Utah held a slim lead on Dartmouth as time wound down. With "three seconds before time ran out in the second half, Dick McGuire's desperate angle set shot hit the target and lifted Dartmouth into a 36–36 tie with Utah."[43] The teams entered the overtime deadlocked, and they went back and fought. With seconds remaining in the overtime, Utah's "Wilkinson followed the precedent set by McGuire, because with three seconds left in overtime the sandy-haired, baby-faced Ute let go with a set effort that paid off. It wasn't a perfect shot. The ball hung for a fraction of a second on the back of the rim and then fell through the hoop for a 42–40 upset triumph for the Western regional champions."[44] Utah was led by Ferrin's twenty-two points, while Misaka contributed four as "Little Walter Misaka's speed bothered the Indians."[45]

After defeating Dartmouth in a thrilling overtime game, Utah faced St. John's in the second annual Red Cross game, which pitted the NCAA and NIT champions. More than eighteen thousand fans filled Madison

Square Garden as the game raised more than $41,000 for the American Red Cross fund. Playing before its home crowd St. John's opened with a quick start and led 13–8 midway through the first period. It would be St. John's biggest lead of the game. At that point, Utah took over and a strong second period knotted the game at 19-all at halftime. As the second half started, Utah scored the first five points. After St. John's made a few shots, Utah again went on another run and scored seven points to open a 35–26 lead. "From then on St. John's was fighting a losing battle. The Redmen did narrow the deficit to two, 36–34, with five minutes to play, but then came [Arnie] Ferrin's personal sortie and the ball game."[46] Ferrin tallied seventeen points to lead all scorers. Meanwhile Misaka tallied five points as "the little Japanese-American freshman never seemed to tire and he was a leech on defense the entire night."[47] "I was one of the first few persons of color in pro ball," Misaka later noted. "There were a few blacks and no Asians at the university level. It was a white man's game."[48]

Misaka's success on the court overshadowed one of the nation's most shameful episodes during the war: the internment of Japanese Americans. On February 19, 1942, two months after Pearl Harbor and a month after his baseball "green light" letter, President Roosevelt issued Executive Order 9066, which permitted the internment of individuals of Japanese ancestry. War "relocation" camps sprung up in the country, mostly on the West Coast. More than one hundred thousand people of Japanese heritage were interned in these camps. After the war Misaka rejoined the University of Utah program, and in 1946–47 the Utes finished with a 16-5 record. They earned a trip to the NIT, and this time they won it, by defeating Kentucky, 49–45, for the championship. In the process Utah became the first school to win both the NIT and the NCAA tournaments. After his college career ended, Misaka received a telephone call telling him that he had been drafted by the New York Knicks. He played in three games for the Knicks in the 1947–48 season and scored a total of seven points. Misaka later stated, "I never really felt like a pioneer. I did not make too big a thing of it. I was more proud of being small and short and being able to play the game with the big boys."[49] He reflected on his departure from the Knicks:

> Ned Irish, the president of the Knicks, called me into his office, and told me that he had to let me go. He said that it would not be the way he would do it, but in those days, coaches had final say regarding contracts. [Knicks coach] Joe Lapchick never spoke with me. I don't recall talking to him. I didn't have any idea that there would be any more cuts. In those days, college players were as good as the pros, and I did not feel like I was trying for a spot on the team.
>
> [Globetrotter owner] Abe Saperstein told me "Anytime you come through Chicago, look me up." So on my way back, I looked him up and he offered me a job, but I wasn't interested in doing things like that.
>
> The highlight of my career was winning the NCAA and NIT championships. Back in those days, college basketball was the pinnacle of one's basketball experience. Pro ball was in its infancy. I do not have a lot of regrets. I had my day, as short as it was.[50]

While Misaka made his mark on college basketball, the professional game readied itself for another season. One team largely unaffected by the needs of the military and World War II in terms of personnel was the Fort Wayne Zollner Pistons. Now beginning their third season at the outset of the 1943–44 National Basketball League (NBL) campaign, the Zollner Pistons were entering their prime and set to become the top professional basketball team during the war years. The company was extremely productive and instrumental in supporting the war effort with its production of pistons for military vehicles. Because the players worked in the factory, they were largely exempt from being drafted since they were providing much needed assistance on the home front for war production. As a result their roster was less affected than those of other teams, and less player turnover led to better chemistry among

FIG. 23. Wat Misaka became the first Asian American to play in the Basketball Association of America when he joined the New York Knicks for three games in the 1947–48 season. Courtesy of Bill Himmelman.

the players. Better chemistry resulted in a team firing on all cylinders and competing at a high level. It showed in their play.

Prior to the start of the 1943–44 season, Curly Armstrong and Herm Schaefer enlisted in the navy and were sent to the Great Lakes Naval Training Station in North Chicago. Both players had been integral to the Pistons efforts from the moment the team joined the National

Basketball League in 1941–42. Armstrong's best year for the Pistons came in 1942–43, when he was named a first-team World Professional Basketball Tournament all-tournament member, was named the MVP for the 1943 tournament, was a first-team all-NBL member, and averaged 8.0 points per game in the regular season. A consistent player, Schaefer's best season occurred in 1941–42, when he was named second-team all-NBL, and averaged 8.6 points per game over twenty-four regular-season contests.

With their departure Carl Bennett faced a difficult task of replacing two key members of his squad at the height of World War II. Undaunted, Bennett landed arguably the best player on the market when he convinced Buddy Jeannette to join the Zollner Pistons. Bennett had some inside help in the form of Jerry Bush and John Pelkington, both of whom played with Jeannette in 1941–42 with the Detroit Eagles. In 1942–43 Bush and Pelkington joined Fort Wayne, while Jeannette signed with Sheboygan. Incidentally, the Pistons defeated the Red Skins in the quarterfinals of the World Professional Basketball Tournament that year. With a year under their belts in Fort Wayne, Bush and Pelkington convinced Jeannette to join them, most likely telling him that he was the missing piece to finally put the team over the top. Job security at the piston company probably did not hurt either. Convinced, Jeannette became the newest member of the team, and the Zollner Pistons soon realized that they had signed "probably the greatest 'clutch' player in the business," one who had given them great considerable trouble when he was an opposing player.[51]

After a standout college career at Washington and Lee University, Jeannette joined the Detroit Eagles and helped lead them to the 1941 World Professional Basketball Tournament championship. When he moved to Detroit and his monthly wage increased to $300, he recalled, "I said to my girl, 'Jesus, let's get married. Nobody makes that kind of money!' So what happens is, in Detroit I'm doing all the playing and the guys with the big names are getting $1500 a month."[52] Despite the

FIG. 24. Paul "Curly" Armstrong was named the MVP of the 1943 World Professional Basketball Tournament as a member of the Fort Wayne Zollner Pistons. Courtesy of Bill Himmelman.

pay difference Jeannette continued to play hard and soon made a name for himself with his performance. In 1941–42 and 1942–43, he made first-team World Professional Basketball Tournament all-tournament, and in 1942–43 was a second-team all-NBL selection. After playing for Detroit in 1941–42, he moved to Rochester, New York, where he worked in a defense plant and competed with the Rochester Eber-Seagrams, an independent team. One day in 1943 he received a call from Sheboygan asking if he would like to join the Red Skins, a team looking for a shot in the arm in the season's home stretch. As Jeannette tells the story,

> They wanted me to come out here and finish the season with them. They wanted me bad. I hemmed and hawed and finally said, "Well, I'll take $500 a game." They said, "Be here Saturday."
>
> The New York Central ran through Rochester, so on Friday night I'd catch the train at 10 o'clock and sleep into Chicago. I'd get up then and run over to the Milwaukee Line and grab a train into Sheboygan at noon. I'd play Saturday night and Sunday afternoon. Then I'd catch a train out of Sheboygan at 2 o'clock in the morning, change to the New York Central in Chicago, and sleep the whole way back to Rochester. Then I'd work the rest of the week.[53]

With Sheboygan he helped lead the Red Skins to the 1943 NBL championship over Fort Wayne, the only one that the team won. After the season he was weighing his options for the following year when he received a call from Bush and Pelkington. "At a time when guys were playing for $5 a game or $50 a game, the Zollner Pistons were getting eight or nine thousand at the end of the year. That was a pretty good piece of change. Zollner took us out of the nickel and dime league."[54] "Of all the moves I made, the one to Fort Wayne was the best."[55]

The move to Fort Wayne quickly positioned the Zollner Pistons as the team to beat in the league. After completing the previous season with four teams—Fort Wayne, Sheboygan, Oshkosh, and Chicago—NBL commissioner Leo Fischer figured that the 1943–44 campaign would be another difficult one to maneuver. Fort Wayne, Sheboygan, and Oshkosh all signed on for another season, thus offering some measure of stability to the league. With Chicago no longer playing after its historic season the year before, league officials quickly scoured the basketball landscape for another team to fill out the league roster. The Cleveland Chase Brassmen became the lucky fourth team. It marked the first time since 1938–39 that a team from Cleveland competed in the NBL. In that

FIG. 25. A solid all-around player, Buddy Jeannette won the World Professional Basketball Tournament title with the Detroit Eagles and later the Fort Wayne Zollner Pistons. Naismith Memorial Basketball Hall of Fame.

fateful campaign the Cleveland White Horses only played the season's first half, recording a 5-4 mark after absorbing the Warren Penns team earlier that season. After dropping out the city of Cleveland did not field another squad until the Chase Brassmen entered the fold to fill the void left by the Chicago Studebakers. The Chase Brassmen picked up where the White Horses left off. The Brassmen dropped twelve of their first thirteen games on their way to a dismal 3-15 mark. In many ways Cleveland was modeled after the Toledo Jim White Chevrolets from a few years ago in that the team's offense was based around one player. While Toledo had Chuck Chuckovits, Cleveland was led by Mel Riebe. A prolific scorer, Riebe led the NBL in 1943–44 with a 17.9 points per game average, which he managed to attain in eighteen games, 4 points more than his nearest competitor, Fort Wayne's Bobby McDermott, who averaged 13.9 points per game. For his scoring efforts he was a first-team member of the NBL and the World Professional Basketball Tournament all-tournament teams. Despite his scoring efforts he could not lift the Chase Brassmen from the league's basement. The one item of note for Cleveland was the inclusion of Wee Willie Smith, a center, previously with the New York Renaissance, who signed to play the last four games of the season. He averaged 6.0 points per game. Smith was the only person to integrate the league in 1943–44, a year after ten players over two teams made history by integrating professional basketball.

At the opposite end of the standings sat the Fort Wayne Zollner Pistons. Their roster, at eight deep, was far and away the most balanced in the league. The team included Blackie Towery, Dale Hamilton, Jerry Bush, John Pelkington, Paul Birch, Buddy Jeannette, Bobby McDermott, and Chick Reiser. Reiser was the other newcomer with Jeannette to the team, and he had been a mainstay for several years in the American Basketball League, including playing with the Jersey Reds. Blackie Towery and Dale Hamilton were the only two players who remained with the team since its inaugural NBL season in 1941–42. While Fort Wayne's roster was stable, Oshkosh's was anything but. Of all the professional teams during World War II, none suffered more than Oshkosh in terms of losing players to service. During the course of the season, Oshkosh lost Bob Carpenter, Lou Barle, Eddie Riska, Ralph Vaughn, and Herm Witasek to the military. By the end of the season, their roster was not recognizable to any basketball fan, composed mostly of local Wisconsin college talent. One player who joined them in time for the

World Professional Basketball Tournament was Ed Scheiwe, a former star at the University of Wisconsin. Scheiwe had recently received a medical discharge from the Coast Guard after being involved in the North African invasion. All the player movement took its toll on the All-Stars as the team finished a lackluster campaign with a 7-15 mark. With poor results from Oshkosh and Cleveland, the only question that remained was, could Sheboygan pose a threat to Fort Wayne? The answer was clearly no.

Fort Wayne charged out of the gate and never looked back. The only challenge for the team was determining which night the team would play its home games. "The home schedule differs from that of last year when all games were played on Tuesday nights. Because of transportation problems and the work of so many of the loop players are engaged in, no definite night could be established this year. Instead, the Pistons' league games will send them into action here on three Monday nights, two Sundays, one Saturday night (Christmas) and five Tuesday evenings."[56] It was also noted that Fort Wayne, Oshkosh, and Sheboygan would each play twenty-two league games, while newcomer Cleveland would play eighteen games. Fort Wayne jumped out to a quick 6-0 record by the end of December, comfortably in front of Sheboygan by four games. By early February Fort Wayne sported a gaudy 13-2 record, and the only suspense left was when the team would clinch the regular season title. At the midway point of February, Fort Wayne finally clinched and set its sights on the oncoming playoffs. Fort Wayne finished the regular season with an 18-4 mark, a full four games better than Sheboygan. It marked the second consecutive regular season title for Fort Wayne.

Despite the addition of Jeannette, the heart and soul of the team was Bobby McDermott. A native New Yorker, McDermott was one of the finest basketball players of the first half of the twentieth century. In fact, in 1946 he was named the Greatest Player of All Time by National Basketball League players and coaches. With only one year of high school ball under his belt at Flushing High School, McDermott turned professional and over a seventeen-year period came to dominate any team or league in which he played. Standing five feet eleven and weighing 175 pounds, McDermott began his professional career as a seventeen-year-old. He led the Brooklyn Visitations to the 1934–35 American Basketball League title over the Philadelphia SPHAS. He also played five years with the Originals Celtics, but it was during his time in the National Basketball League that he truly established himself. While with the Fort Wayne Zollner Pistons during the war years, he led the team to two NBL championships (1944 and 1945), was a five time all-NBL first team (1941 to 1946), was a three-time league MVP (1943 to 1945), once led the league in scoring (1943), four times finished second in scoring (1942, 1944 to 1946), and once led the league in free-throw percentage (1944). When his teams played in the World Professional Basketball Tournament, he was equally as dominant. He led the tournament in scoring in 1943 with fifty points in four games and was named MVP of the 1944 tournament. Despite the accolades and hardware that he amassed during his career, it was his deadly outside shooting, shooting with both hands, that left a lasting impression. Al Cervi, a formidable player in his own right, offered this recollection of McDermott

I played against him three years, and I made my credits playing him. He was my best rooter. He could run like hell but he couldn't jump. I could outjump him.

The first time I saw him I had just got out of service and joined Rochester. I had read about McDermott. We were in Fort Wayne, and in the dressing room Les Harrison told me, "Cervi, you've got McDermott." The other players looked at me and said, "Better you than me."

Before the game started he was putting on an exhibition. He made 10 for 10 our here, 15 for 15 here. The crowd is clapping. I'm clapping too and asking myself, "Doesn't the sonuvabitch ever miss?"

"You couldn't let him get the ball. I remember a game in the Chicago Amphitheatre, which had the longest court in the United States—112 feet. He scored three baskets from the midcourt line—that's 56 feet—on me that night and two flicked my fingers. Oh, he could shoot! If he shot 10 times from 30 feet, I'd guarantee he'd make eight in game conditions.[57]

Everyone who encountered McDermott formed the same opinion. Hillard Gates, who earned his own reputation as the radio voice of the Fort Wayne Zollner Pistons, remarked,

He was the greatest two-hand set-shooter I ever saw. Bobby had the greatest competitive spirit of them all. He was too aggressive. He was too excitable. But, I tell you, he had the talent to go with it. What made him so spectacular was that his shots, most of the time, were way out on the floor. Frequently in the North Side gym he would stand in the center of the floor and hit a shot—and at crucial times of the game! He had so much arch on his shot that the ball would seem to scrape the top of the ceiling of the North Side gym.[58]

Ed Stanczak, a former player, recalled how tough McDermott was to play against all those years. "Mac was just plain ornery. He'd get up close to you, spit in your face, then go around you. Players would be left there wiping their faces, and Mac was around them scoring another basket . . . . That's the way Mac played basketball."[59]

Throughout the team's regular-season dominance, it was McDermott who stood out from the rest. In twenty-two games that season, he averaged 13.9 points per game, which was good for second place. In a January 17, 1944, game versus Oshkosh, he led all scorers with eighteen points. Two weeks later against Cleveland, he tallied twenty points in a win. Against Oshkosh in early February, he netted sixteen in a win. Throughout the regular season he was consistent and often led the team in scoring. As the playoff neared, McDermott was reaching his

FIG. 26. Voted the top professional basketball player in the first half of the twentieth century, Bobby McDermott led the Fort Wayne Zollner Pistons to two National Basketball League titles and three World Professional Basketball Tournament championships. Naismith Memorial Basketball Hall of Fame.

peak. Much like the year before, all four teams made the playoffs. In the opening round Fort Wayne encountered little difficulty in sweeping Cleveland in two straight. Neither contest was close as Fort Wayne won 64–47 and 42–31. In the other semifinal match-up, Sheboygan defeated a much-depleted Oshkosh squad. That set up a rematch of the finals the previous season, in which Sheboygan won. Sheboygan was seeking to become the first team since Oshkosh to win consecutive league championships (1940–41 and 1941–42). Fort Wayne, meanwhile, was hoping to avenge last year's disappointing loss. For the first time since 1940–41, the finals were a best-of-five rather than a best-of-three series. Fort Wayne won the coin toss and elected to play the first two games on the road in Wisconsin, with the final three games to be held in Indiana. The move paid off immediately. In the first game Fort Wayne eked out a 55–53 win when Bobby McDermott and Jerry Bush each scored late baskets to lift the Zollner Pistons to a come-from-behind win. In Game Two the Zollner Pistons' defense was the story as they won 36–26 and held Sheboygan to a season-low six field goals on their home floor. Ahead 2-0 Fort Wayne looked to return home and wrap up the championship. With a raucous crowd and momentum on their side, the Zollner Pistons jumped out to an early lead and coasted to a 48–38 win. In only their third year in the league, Fort Wayne had finally won its first championship. It was the start of a great run over the next few seasons.

The challenges faced by Commissioner Leo Fischer of the National Basketball League were similar to those that Commissioner John J. O'Brien of the American Basketball League encountered for the 1943–44 season. When we last left the ABL, the league had completed the 1942–43 campaign with four teams, and the Philadelphia SPHAS had earned yet another championship, this time with a seven-game series win over the Trenton Tigers. As the 1943–44 season was set to commence, O'Brien's sole goal lay in making it through yet another season intact. Much like his counterpart Fischer, O'Brien could rely on a few teams to sign on for another campaign. The Philadelphia SPHAS, the Trenton Tigers, and the Brooklyn Indians all returned for another season. The Harrisburg Senators disbanded and were replaced by the New York Americans. The commissioner received good news when the Wilmington Blue Bombers, who had sat out last season after winning the title in 1941–42, resolved their home-court issues and rejoined the league. Thus the league would be starting with five teams. For the first time since 1941–42, the season would be split between a first half and a second half with the two winners of each half facing each other in the finals. After sporting a 2-9 record at the conclusion of the first half, the Brooklyn Indians withdrew, thus leaving four teams to play the second half of the season. Brooklyn would not field another team until the 1946–47 season, by which time the ABL had become a minor league to the newfound Basketball Association of America (BAA) and was strictly a weekend league. Due to the challenges of finding a home court and transportation, each team played a different number of games. Nonetheless, the teams were set to begin another ABL season.

In many ways this season was a continuation of the 1941–42 season, when Wilmington won the championship by capturing both halves of the regular season. In that campaign the SPHAS were seeking to become the first team to win three consecutive titles. It was not to be as newcomer Wilmington easily won the title. Wilmington did not have the opportunity to defend its title the following season, and in its place Philadelphia defeated Trenton to win its third title in four years. Now Wilmington sought to rightfully defend its championship while Philadelphia sought to win back-to-back titles.

By the middle of World War II, the war had taken its toll on Eddie Gottlieb's ability to field a competitive team. Many of his old guard players from the 1930s were retiring or getting on in years, and Gottlieb was forced to remake his roster while trying to stay competitive at the same time. No easy task. He looked to the influx of New York Jewish players to help as he added Jack "Dutch" Garfinkel, Ossie Schectman, and Irv Torgoff. Another player he would add was New York product Jerry Fleishman, who split his time between the team and serving in the U.S. Army. Stationed at Fort Jackson in Columbia, South Carolina, Fleishman remembered that Gottlieb "would fly [him] in on the weekends to play ball."[60] With all the uncertainty over filling out a new lineup each game night and developing a sense of cohesion among his players, the one player he could have used was Joel "Shikey" Gotthoffer.

As a youth growing up in the Bronx, New York, Gotthoffer gravitated to basketball immediately. In today's terms, he would be affectionately known as a gym rat. As Gotthoffer told an interviewer, "I can't recall when I didn't go to school dressed underneath with my basketball things so that at 3 o'clock I could stay in the playground and play basketball. The school had a gym, but when we played after school it was on the outdoor court. They had an indoor gym and they had playgrounds."[61] After a playing odyssey that characterized his college career, Gotthoffer was part of a trade that landed him with the SPHAS for the 1933–34 ABL season. Over the next ten years Gotthoffer was a mainstay, arguably the most consistent and well-rounded player in all basketball. As one fan who saw him often as a teenager in the 1930s remarked, "Shikey Gotthoffer was tough. He may have been the toughest. He was not a bully, but he played tough. He had a good body, he could run, and he played a hard-nosed game. He was one of the toughest guys I ever saw play in those days. He was a winner."[62] Gotthoffer's last full season as a professional was 1941–42. The following year he played in six games. As he tells it, his wartime commitments eventually affected his ability to play.

> During WWII, I was a supervisor at Wright Aeronautics in New York. I built engines for B-21s. When my local board called me, they told me I was going in as 1A. I made the request to go to officer school in the physical education area. I was sent to New Jersey, and I was questioned as to what I wanted to do. I told them I wanted to go into the health education program in Miami. They told me it was filled in Miami. They told me there was availability in the tanker destroyer unit. I told them I was not interested. I told them I would wait for an opening in Miami. My supervisor said that it is not the way we do it.
>
> I went back to work, and I received a 1A from my local board. I took it to the Colonel at Wrights Aeronautics. He tore it up. He told me to go back to work and forget about it. Two weeks later, I was called down to my local board. This guy had the hots for me. He thought I was avoiding him. He said they would not let me get away with anything. I said, "I wasn't trying to get away with anything. I took it to the Colonel and he tore it up, not I." He said, "You will not get away with it. You'll go in as a private." I was there until the end of the war. I was working double shifts. I didn't play any basketball. I had to sleep sometimes."[63]

FIG. 27. Joel "Shikey" Gotthoffer was a star player with the Philadelphia SPHAS during the 1930s in the American Basketball League. Naismith Memorial Basketball Hall of Fame.

Without Gotthoffer and with a retooled roster, Gottlieb's SPHAS struggled to find any consistency in the first half, finishing with a dismal 4-9 record. One team whose vocabulary did not include the word struggle was Wilmington. Despite not playing the previous season, the Wilmington Blue Bombers picked up where they left off. Starting strong out of the gate, Wilmington cruised to a 12–4 first-half mark, clearly outdistancing Philadelphia. Wilmington now had secured a spot in the championship round. The question for Wilmington was whether it would try to win the second half and claim its second title in three years or relax and get healthy for the finals. The team chose the second option, although Philadelphia had much to say about the outcome. The second half for Wilmington began with a home tilt versus the SPHAS, who sensed that a poor showing in the season's second half would effectively eliminate any chances of defending their championship. Philadelphia came out strong to start the game and after overcoming an early deficit stormed to a 52–36 win. To start the season's second half, Gottlieb added two new players he hoped would provide additional depth: Herm Knupple at center and Ossie Schectman, a guard. Playing nine players, eight of them scored at least one field goal as the team jumped out to a comfortable margin and an easy win. On February 19, 1944, the two teams met again, but this time in Philadelphia at the Broadwood Hotel. Wilmington coach Barney Sedran, an excellent player in his own right during the first quarter of the century and a future member of the Naismith Memorial Basketball Hall of Fame, sought to counteract the moves that Gottlieb had made last month by adding an additional player. Ben Kramer, a former member of the Washington Brewers in 1941–42, joined the team in time to face off against the SPHAS. A "rugged, swashbuckling type of player who excel[led] on the pivot play and [was] expected to help the Bombers in their second half drive," Kramer scored three points as Philadelphia again defeated Wilmington, 39–38.[64] During the regular season Philadelphia made their push and eventually clinched second half honors. Throughout the two teams kept jockeying for a personnel advantage. Even as late as the final week of the regular season, both teams added new players; Wilmington added Dan Christie, who had played his collegiate career at Manhattan College, while Philadelphia signed Art Hillhouse, another former Long Island University player and big man to bolster the front line. Philadelphia preserved and captured second half honors to set up a championship series versus Wilmington.

With the championship series set to begin, many of the prognosticators figured this series to be closely contested. Over the past few seasons, Wilmington and Philadelphia had developed a strong rivalry as the teams split their eight regular-season contests. With the teams evenly matched and fighting for basketball supremacy nearly thirty minutes apart, the contests often became heated. Ossie Schectman, who joined the SPHAS for the second-half stretch run, recounted one particular incident. "One incident I remember as a player occurred in Wilmington, Delaware. It was quite a rivalry between the SPHAS and Wilmington, although I don't know what created it. It was a Sunday afternoon in the Armory, and there was a skirmish on the court. The closest guys were wrestling with each other, and I stepped in to separate them. Some fan came out of the stands and punched me in the jaw. I had an impacted wisdom tooth and was taken to the hospital."[65]

The series opened in Philadelphia, and Wilmington jumped out to an early head start and easily defeated the SPHAS, 44–31. The next afternoon the teams headed south for an afternoon game in Wilmington. Looking to even the series, the SPHAS came out firing on all cylinders. John J. Brady captured the action the following day in the *Wilmington (DE) Morning News*: "The SPHAS triumphed due to their superior shooting from the field in which they outscored the Bombers, 15–13 in addition to making good on 12 of their 15 chances from the foul line as the Bombers collected nine out of 11."[66] Throughout the series the Bombers would have difficulty defending the outside shooting of the SPHAS. But it was newcomer Jerry Fleishman, who "broke loose with three straight field goals to practically end the Bombers' chances for victory."[67] The series now stood at a game apiece.

The war impacted the series in two ways. The first was the restrictions on travel, which necessitated that the series be played only on weekends. The other way the war affected the series was in player personnel. Prior to the start of Game Three, Barney Sedran signed Bob Dorn, former Temple University player and a member of the Manhattan Beach Coast Guard team. Sedran felt the need to sign Dorn because one his regular players, Matt Zunic, "was refused permission by Norfolk Naval Training Station authorities to play for the Bombers."[68] Dorn, a highly skilled six-foot-five center, was expected to compete with the big front line of the SPHAS. He had recently competed in a service tournament held in New York City at the Seventy-First Regiment Armory in which his Manhattan Beach Coast Guard won the tournament. Dorn earned outstanding player honors. But the Dorn signing was not all the personnel moves that were to affect the third game. Wilmington would be without Ed Sadowski and Angelo Musi. When not competing with Wilmington, Musi also played with the Aberdeen Proving Ground team since he was stationed there. Aberdeen was playing in the finals of the Cleveland Tournament, the one started by local businessman Max Rosenblum to counteract the World Professional Basketball Tournament. Aberdeen lost to the New York Renaissance as Musi scored ten points. Without Musi and also newcomer Ben Kramer, Wilmington was no match for the SPHAS, who won 50–44 to take a 2-1 series lead.

The personnel changes again continued before Game Four as Barney Sedran was forced to sign Bob Fitzgerald to replace Dorn. Dorn, the late signing the week before, was unable to "obtain a week-end pass from his Coast Guard station at Manhattan Beach."[69] The signing of Fitzgerald was consistent with Sedran's desire to bolster the team's front line versus Philadelphia. Fitzgerald was no stranger to the ABL wars of this past season as he began with the Brooklyn Indians and later went to the New York Americans after Brooklyn folded. Fitzgerald was considered one of the league's better big men, and he also played his service ball at Mitchell Field. Despite the addition of Fitzgerald and the return of Musi and Kramer, Wilmington still had no answer for Philadelphia, whose win gave it a commanding 3-1 series lead.

In 1936–37 the SPHAS found themselves down 3-1 to the Jersey Reds before they stormed back to win the next three games to claim the title. Up until this series it was the only time that a team had overcome a 3-1 series deficit to win the ABL championship. Wilmington would now become the second team to achieve this feat. Over the course of the next three games, Wilmington systematically chipped away at Philadelphia's advantage, which was its outside shooting and inside presence. With tenacious defense the Bombers took one game at a time and played relentless defense. The real surprise came in Games Six and Seven, in which the Bombers easily won 57–36 and 57–33, respectively. By the seventh game the Bombers had turned the tide with their own hot outside shooting led by Moe Frankel. As the *Wilmington (DE) Morning News* wrote the following day, "Frankel especially was outstanding. The Wilmington veteran just couldn't miss. He sent up shots from far and near, stole a pass and dribbled in for a lay-up, dropped a couple from the side court and on several other occasions sank long ones from the center of the court. As a result, he finished up with 17 points on eight baskets and a foul to take game scoring honors."[70] With the win Wilmington had now captured its second title in three years and wrested control of the league from perennial power Philadelphia. Looking back in 1944–45 on the championship season, Eddie Glennon, the team's publicity director, wrote, "Along came 1943–44 and Dynamic Barney had to rebuild. This he did with the same success that he had in 1941. The Bombers won the first half of the '43 schedule and were nosed out of the second half by the SPHAS, who they met in the playoffs. After winning the first game from Eddie Gottlieb's boys, three setbacks in a row followed and it looked like curtains for the boys of the First City of the First State. What happened is history—three in a row for the Bombers and the championship was retained by Wilmington."[71]

Although Wilmington represented the best of the East, Barney Sedran and company did not participate in the sixth annual World Professional Basketball Tournament. While Wilmington would be sitting at home, Fort Wayne set its sights on winning the elusive World Professional Basketball Tournament. Scheduled for March 20–22 and 24–25 with all games to be played at Chicago Stadium, the 1944 Tournament featured fourteen teams. The switch to Chicago Stadium was a big move; as Harry Wilson wrote, "The Tourney had grown in its sixth year to such an extent that the entire meet was moved into the Windy City's huge Chicago Stadium for the first time. The increased seating capacity was reflected by the fact that over 52,000 fans witnessed the games, an increase of over 8,000 from the best previous year."[72] The Wounded War Veterans' Fund was designated as the beneficiary of the tournament's proceeds.

In mid-February, more than one month before the start of the tournament, the *Chicago Herald American* noted that no fewer than thirty-seven teams were being considered for the field. With five years in the book, some changes were evident in the tournament program. In past seasons the program included not only a team photo and the roster but also a lengthy write-up of each team that provided the fans with some basic information about the teams since some of the contenders had never previously ventured to Chicago. For this year's tournament the organizers decided not to provide those write-ups. Instead, information was given about the previous champions, high scorer for each year, most valuable players, single-game scoring honors, and all-tournament teams. The coverage in the *Chicago Herald American* also changed. In addition to the preview articles and game write-ups, a new feature titled World Cage Briefs provided additional information and insight into some of the story lines leading up to the tournament. Topics included profiles of certain teams such as Indianapolis and

Pittsburgh; profiles of the soldiers competing; a brief history of the Globetrotters; and an article on Dutch Dehnert, the current coach of the Brooklyn Eagles. All in all, these features gave life to the tournament and its participants as the tournament entered its sixth year.

As usual teams based in the Midwest dominated the field. The Indianapolis Pure Oils made a return appearance after the team lost in the first round the previous season to the Fort Wayne Zollner Pistons, 56–52. The Pure Oils were very much representative of the Hoosier state, with only one of their twelve players not hailing from Indiana. That player was George Carrico who played collegiately at the University of Alabama. Despite a second consecutive appearance, the Pure Oils again lost a close first-round contest, this time to the Cleveland Chase Brassmen, 55–52. Another midwestern squad making a second trip to Chicago was the Akron Collegians. Once again Akron lost a first-round game, 52–38, to the Dayton Acme Aviators. Finally, the Detroit Sufferins entered, and their manager, Cincy Sachs, was slightly upset that his first-round match-up was against the vaunted New York Rens. As he told Harry Wilson, "What's the idea of giving us the champions in our first game? Those New York Rens, whom we meet on the March 20 card, will cop the title if they get by us. . . . I have seen them in action, and they are the best that Manager Bob Douglas has put in the meet since 1939 when they romped off with the championship."[73] Their stay was short-lived, a first-round exit courtesy of the New York Rens.

As usual the National Basketball League had a strong presence as all four teams entered the field. The Sheboygan Red Skins, runner-up to Fort Wayne for the league championship, accepted an invitation and earned a first-round bye. Sheboygan hoped to avenge a quarterfinal loss to Fort Wayne the previous year. As was his wont, Carl Roth, team manager, expressed optimism that his team could finally make a deep run in the tournament for the first time since 1939, when they reached the semifinals. As Roth explained to Leo Fischer, the tournament's publicity director, "Each season we've usually come into the world's championship tournament on the heels of our own National League playoffs. We have wound up the tough league competition and then jumped head-over-heels into this tournament without a chance to catch our breaths or get keyed up once more. Well, this year it looks as though we may have a short rest between league playoff and the world's championship. We'll be able to place a top-conditioned team on the Stadium floor. It will be a team in the best of shape—and ready to put up a terrific battle for that crown."[74] Despite some rest and a first-round bye, however, Sheboygan bowed out early in the first round with a 49–43 loss to the underappreciated Brooklyn Eagles.

Sheboygan's NBL counterparts, the Oshkosh All-Stars and the Cleveland Chase Brassmen, were hoping to stay in the tournament longer than the first round. Oshkosh finished a down year in the NBL, and not much was expected from the All-Stars come tournament time. Through the tournament's first five years, the All-Stars were the most consistent team and had compiled the best tournament record of any club. This year, though, Oshkosh was the thirteenth of fourteen teams selected, and that fact did not sit too well with Oshkosh's manager, Lon Darling, who told Leo Fischer, "I understand that we're the 13th team picked in the tournament. I guess that 13 means bad luck to the others who'll be there."[75] Despite an opening-game win versus newcomer Rochester, Oshkosh bowed out in the next round to the Harlem Globetrotters. After winning in 1942 and finishing runner up in 1943, Oshkosh's disappointing season came to a close.

With Cleveland in the field, all eyes were focused on high-scoring Mel Riebe. In his preview article of Cleveland, Leo Fischer extolled the great virtues and play of Riebe as one to watch in the upcoming games.

Riebe has easily been the sensation of pro cage ranks this year. In competition against the toughest sort of guarding, he has scored an average of 18 points a game, with 306 in 17 league contests. He's a stocky youngster just over six feet tall, and almost impossible to guard because of the versatility of his shooting. He tosses 'em overhand, underhand, from the left, from the right—in fact, from any spot or in any manner which fits the occasion. Mel broke into the limelight as a member of an amateur team in Cleveland last year when he appeared in a local tournament against the Fort Wayne Zollners and the New York Rens. He rang up 57 points against these two great pro aggregations. This year, when his team quit the simon-pure ranks to join the National Basketball League, he began the season with 20 against Sheboygan—a record of 77 points in three contests against a trio of the best guarding clubs in the business.[76]

In mentioning the local tournament, Fischer was referring to the 1943 Cleveland Tournament, in which Riebe, as a member of the Cleveland Chase Brassmen, faced the New York Renaissance and the Fort Wayne Zollner Pistons on consecutive nights. Although Cleveland lost both games, Riebe was the tournament's sensation, scoring thirty-six points against the Rens and twenty-three against the Pistons. The preview article by Fischer also mentioned that Wee Willie Smith would be playing with Cleveland. Alas, that was not the case. Smith played for the Rens, and as the *Chicago Defender* noted, he had "used up part of his vacation to play in the tournament. He [was] a street car conductor in Cleveland."[77] As for Cleveland it won its first-round game against Indianapolis but lost in the quarterfinals to Smith's Rens. Thus by the end of the quarterfinal round, three of the four NBL teams had bowed out.

Unlike the previous season this year's tournament did not integrate. The closest the tournament came to integrating was a preview article announcing that the Columbus, Ohio, Tubbys planned to participate and one of their players was William "Plunk" Ford, a former Harlem Globetrotter. When the brackets were finalized, Columbus was not among the fourteen on the board. Another preview article noted that Indianapolis would be featuring George Crowe, who played for them this year and also played Negro League baseball. However, in the Pure

Oils lone game, he did not appear. No reasons were provided. Usual stalwarts the New York Renaissance and the Harlem Globetrotters, however, both had high hopes entering the tournament as each came into town having won another mini-tournament the previous week. The Rens captured the Cleveland Tournament, while the Globetrotters won the Rochester Tournament. Both were primed and ready. The Rens, who were essentially the Washington Bears the previous year when they won, sought to continue their winning ways. They introduced a new center, Hank DeZonie, a rugged six-foot-six-and-a-half player from Clark University in Atlanta. The Globetrotters, meanwhile, added Piper Davis, but he did not see any action in the tournament. He also played shortstop for the Birmingham Black Barons of the Negro Baseball League. Abe Saperstein highly touted this year's version of the Globetrotters stating,

> This is the greatest Globetrotter team in its 17-year history. Its pass attack is even more dazzling and bewildering than ever. Our record, too, sounds almost fantastic. We established what I believe is a world record with 62 straight wins. . . . In all we have won 97 while dropping only 6. . . . That is a lot of games and a lot of wins. . . . While compiling this season's great record we broke the winning streak of the leading service teams on the West coast . . . such teams as Fort Lewis, March Field and Santa Anita Air Base . . . the first two, undefeated before meeting the Trotters.[78]

Both the Rens and the Globetrotters were in the same side of the bracket and eventually met in the consolation round. The Rens defeated Detroit and Cleveland before losing to eventual champion Fort Wayne in the semifinals. As for the Globetrotters, they faced a scare in the first round with Pittsburgh, winning by one point, 41–40, then defeating longtime rival Oshkosh, before bowing to the Brooklyn Eagles, the tournament's surprise team, in the semifinals. The quarterfinal match-up between Oshkosh and the Harlem Globetrotters devolved into a physical battle and an ejection and eventually led to the game being called, the only time in the tournament's history that a game was not officially completed. The *Chicago Herald American*, in its write-up of the game, noted, "The game was that between the Globetrotters and Oshkosh, and the score at the time was 41–31 in favor of the former. The two clubs have a bitter rivalry that dates back a number of years, and the intensity of their play wasn't the kind to cement cordial relations."[79] The game was a closely played affair as the Globetrotters held a 27–26 lead with ten minutes remaining "and from then on it was about as slambang an affair as anyone ever saw. Officials Nat Messenger and Steve Barak had matters pretty much under control, but as the clock neared the finish, the bad blood cropped out."[80] It was at that point that the game got out of control. "One fight broke out and was quelled. Play was resumed and again fists started swinging. Again things were quieted down, but once more tempers flared up and the boys began to mix. This time Managers Lon Darling and A. M. Saperstein agreed that it was time to call a halt. The score goes into the records as it was at the time."[81]

The *Chicago Defender* had a different interpretation of the game. It characterized the game as "about the worst display of sportsmanship ever witnessed in the history of the pro tournament [which] occurred Wednesday night as the Oshkosh team went down to defeat at the hands of the Globetrotters."[82] The second half became physical as "Oshkosh players resorted to all sorts of rough tactics. Zach Clayton was knocked unconscious twice but remained in the game. Two Oshkosh players put a flying football tackle on Roscoe Julien and Connie Mack Berry rushed from the bench in the closing minutes to go on the floor to take a poke at one of the Globetrotters. Two white spectators were arrested for going onto the playing floor to take part in the melee."[83] With five minutes to go, the game became out of hand, and the referees lost all control. "The last five minutes [were] a headache for the spectators, who were disgusted. The Oshkosh players, outclassed in the fourth period when the Globetrotters rang up 14 points to Oshkosh's five, used their fists, elbows, took swings at the Globetrotters as if the game was a battle royal such as is prohibited by most boxing commissions."[84] Whatever the differences in interpretation, the bad ending left both fans and players highly dissatisfied.

The Globetrotters' match-up against the Rens in the consolation game was just the third time in the tournament's six years that both teams faced each other. In the 1939 semifinals the Rens won 27–23 on their way to the first tournament championship. A year later the Globetrotters exacted revenge by winning 37–36 in the quarterfinals on their way to the championship. Unfortunately, a championship was not at stake for either team in 1944, just pride, and the Globetrotters won 37–29. Both teams came agonizingly close to earning another berth in the championship round.

With the war in full force, military teams also attracted the attention of the tournament organizers. Prior to the start of the tournament, it was noted that many of the teams, not just the military-based squads, would have active military players. As the *Chicago Herald American* observed, "A good many of them are expecting players in service to help out during the week's big carnival of caging, there being no objection to men on furloughs participating so long as they have been members of the quintets previous military call."[85] The Dayton Acme Aviators, who had played the previous year as the Dayton Bombers, entered. The surprise team of the 1943 tournament, they made it to the semifinals using only six players. They were led by four former Ohio State University players and claimed six victories over fourteen of the teams entered in the field. Their trip in 1944 was not nearly as successful; they beat Akron in the first round only to fall in a lopsided game to eventual champion Fort Wayne in the next.

It was the other military team, however, that garnered more of the attention and intrigue leading up to the beginning of play. The Twentieth Armored Division at Camp Campbell, Kentucky, became the first team to sign on. Writing his article announcing Camp Campbell as the first participant, Harry Wilson noted,

> Brig. Gen. Roderick R. Allen, commanding general of the 20th Armored Division, decided to accept the invitation to have his boys compete for the world's cage title for several reasons. Foremost was the fact that every member of the squad is due for a regular furlough and will not miss one iota of his military training as a result of participating. Another good reason is that the profits go to the Wounded Service Men's Fund. The general, who is one of the squad's staunchest friends, felt that the team record of losing only one game in 20 starts merited the recognition given the Camp Campbell team. Its solitary loss came at the beginning of the season before Dave Miley, Georgetown ace, and George Lacy, ex-Red Sox baseball catcher, joined the squad.[86]

That loss occurred in the team's second game. The team was led by Joe Niland, formerly of Canisius College. Despite the patriotism associated with Camp Campbell, the team lost in the first round to the Brooklyn Eagles.

The tournament did welcome three new teams from the East Coast, which represented a big shift from previous seasons. One was the Rochester (NY) Wings, coached by Les Harrison. This marked Harrison's first appearance, one that was largely forgettable in a 51–40 loss to Oshkosh in the first round. Harrison would be heard from in the coming years, and his contributions to Rochester basketball, the National Basketball League, and the early days of the Basketball Association of America and the National Basketball Association would be significant and eventually earn him a place in the Naismith Memorial Basketball Hall of Fame. Rochester was led by Chick Meehan, considered at that time to be the finest player to come out of Syracuse University, who was the "man with eyes in the back of his head" as one writer enthusiastically declared.[87] Another newcomer was the Pittsburgh Corbetts.

Sponsored by Sherriff Robert Corbett of Allegheny County, the team was led by Manny Hyatt, who descended from a prominent basketball lineage. The *Chicago Herald American* reported, "[Manny] Hyatt, by the way, is the third of an illustrious basketball family.... Most famed of the brothers is 'Chuck' Hyatt, the immortal star of Pitt University fame.... Art Hyatt was a member of the Detroit Eagles a few years back and Mansfield, currently starring with the Pittsburgh entry in the world title meet, is rated by many of the eastern experts as even better than his brothers."[88] Manny played his college ball at George Washington University and spent time as a professional with Elmira, New York, in the Eastern League. The Pittsburgh Corbetts sported an 18-3 record on the eve of the tournament. Largely unknown beyond the rust belt, Pittsburgh acquitted itself quite well in a tough one-point, first-round loss to the Harlem Globetrotters.

One of the other teams competing for the first time was the Brooklyn Eagles, who were coached by legendary player Dutch Dehnert, who had guided the Detroit Eagles to the 1941 tournament championship. Composed mostly of New York–area players, the team included Bob Tough of St. John's, Bob Synnott of St. Francis College in Brooklyn, Joe Bellis of New York University, and Al Frizell of Rutgers University. Another key player on the team was Jack "Dutch" Garfinkel. A New York City product, Garfinkel became one of the game's best point guards during the war years even if the term "point guard" had yet to be coined. Growing up in east New York, Garfinkel played all the time. As he recalled in an interview, "I played ball every chance I had. I loved it, and I made up my mind I wanted to be a basketball player."[89] He eventually matriculated at Thomas Jefferson High School and later St. John's University, where he led the Redmen to their first-ever NIT appearance. He played for the legendary Joe Lapchick, who was once a teammate of Henry "Dutch" Dehnert and Nat Holman on the Original Celtics. Lapchick once said of Garfinkel that he was "second only to Nat Holman as an all-around player."[90] As for his connection to Dutch

Dehnert, Garfinkel soon earned that same nickname himself. He later described his connection with Dehnert:

As a kid, I lived for basketball and followed it closely. One of my heroes was a player by the name of Henry "Dutch" Dehnert who, after a good college career, played for the Original Celtics along with Nat Holman, Davey Banks, and the other greats. Now this was the top pro team in the country and it received considerable press. One of their favorite offensive plays was to put Dehnert in the pivot with his back to the basket, and have two men, from either side, cut off him for a pass. This maneuver began to be called, "doing the Dutch" and the name was applied to Dehnert, who became well known as Dutch Dehnert. There was no three-second violation back then and Dehnert stayed under the basket for as long as he wished.

When I learned of this maneuver and how successful it was for the Celtics, I began to use it in my own schoolyard play. I played a lot of 3 on 3 in the schoolyard back then and I always liked the challenge of playing with the two worst players to see if we could win. I began to instruct them on "doing the Dutch" and it usually worked. Of course, I was the one in the pivot feeding off to my cutting teammates, which really helped me to become a very good passer. If I passed to the right cutting man, I could cut left myself, after the pass, and be in perfect position for rebounding a missed shot. Since I was so enthusiastic about this strategy, and I became adept at it, my friends, kiddingly at first, began to call me Dutch. The name stuck.[91]

Now known as Dutch Garfinkel, he finally earned his dream of being a professional basketball player. He joined the Baltimore Clippers of the ABL in 1940–41; as he later recalled, "I was paid $25 a game, and I had to pay all my expenses. I did not care. I was playing ball."[92] And playing ball he was. By 1943–44 he had signed on to play with the SPHAS for two seasons and part of a third. While a member of the SPHAS, Garfinkel was also part of the West Point Armored Detachment Team. "In

FIG. 28. After his college career at St. John's University was complete, Jack "Dutch" Garfinkel played professionally with Philadelphia, Brooklyn, and Baltimore. Courtesy of Bill Himmelman.

the army [Eddie] Gottlieb contacted me," he explained in an interview. "I spent two years at West Point as an enlisted man. I played for the SPHAS. I was there with Bernie Opper, and he played for Adolph Rupp. He was the only Jewish captain at Kentucky. I asked Gottlieb if we could sign Opper so he could also play for the SPHAS. After inspection four of us would leave to go to New York City. Bernie and I would go to the SPHAS, and the other fellows would travel to their teams. We ended up playing each other on the weekends. Afterwards we would drive back to West Point for inspection on Monday morning. I never slept in those days."[93]

Although he played for the SPHAS in 1943–44, Garfinkel also joined his hometown Brooklyn Eagles to participate in the World Professional Basketball Tournament. Their opening-round game against Camp Campbell was viewed by many as one of the best contests. "Both teams [Camp Campbell and Brooklyn] are made up of service men, the former representing the Twentieth Armored Division, while the latter wore the colors of that outfit a year ago."[94] Brooklyn was composed of "Bernie Opper, Dutch Garfinkel, Ken [Kevin 'Chuck'] Connors, Joe Bellis and Bob Tough. They [were] still in service, having saved up their furlough time for participation in the meet . . . delighted to have a chance to tackle their old club in the initial game."[95] The game started off close as Camp Campbell closed out the first half with a 20–15 lead. The third quarter saw momentum change as "Dutch Denhert's boys caught fire. Sparked by Mickey Rottner, a late addition to the Brooklyn ranks, they uncorked the most dazzling pass attack seen hereabouts in years."[96] By the end of the third frame, Brooklyn was out in front, 35–32. The Eagles kept the pressure on to win, 55–41. After its first-round win, Brooklyn fed off that momentum and defeated Sheboygan in the quarterfinals and then the Globetrotters in the semifinals, which set up a championship game against the Fort Wayne Zollner Pistons.

In the weeks leading up to the tournament, the Fort Wayne Zollner Pistons surprisingly received the least amount of press. Perhaps because they were the heavy favorites, not much hype was needed. Maybe they would let their play do the talking. After a first-round bye, Fort Wayne opened with an impressive win over Dayton, 59 to 34, and then a close victory against the New York Renaissance, 42 to 38. Next up for Fort Wayne were the Brooklyn Eagles, the tournament's surprise team. Fort Wayne was seeking its first tournament title. By halftime it had accomplished its goal. Nearly fifteen thousand fans packed Chicago Stadium and watched as "the Indiana contingent played what might be called the perfect game. Their passing was accurate, their shooting was deadly, their defense airtight."[97] With ten minutes elapsed the Zollners held a 12–9 margin. "Then they really began to click and by halftime had moved out to a 28–11 advantage."[98] Bobby McDermott had an answer every time Brooklyn looked to make a run, as "his sensational long shots" helped him net seven baskets for fourteen points.[99] His teammate John Pelkington led all scorers with nineteen points but was most effective under the boards. After the game Fort Wayne manager Carl Bennett spoke to reporters and gave his assessment of his team's brilliant play: "We knew we'd win if we forced the Eagles to play our game instead of theirs. That meant slowing 'em down and holding Tough (Bob) and Dutch Garfinkle [sic] from roaming without escort under the basket. That is where our height and experience paid dividends. And don't forget John Pelkington played a whale of a game and Bob McDermott's most valuable award election speaks for itself."[100]

As the *Fort Wayne News-Sentinel* wrote the following day,

Fort Wayne, long considered the center of basketball in many quarters, has a further claim on that high-sounding appellation. Its professional basketball team, the Zollner Pistons, climaxed a great campaign Saturday night by winning the titular battle of the sixth annual world's professional hardwood tourney at the Chicago Stadium. Nearly 15,000 fans saw the Pistons trim Brooklyn's Eagles so convincingly that they went away feeling that there was no doubt as to the outstanding pro team of 1944. The final score was 50–33 but even the 17-point margin did not tell just how badly outclassed did the Pistons have those driving soldier boys Dutch Dehnert had gathered together to compete in the meet.

Fans here who have seen the Pistons bear down on defense and click on offense in their late games can visualize just how they handled that Brooklyn five so handily Saturday night. Brooklyn had been getting better and better each game at Chicago and was the favorite for that title battle due to the heated demonstration it gave against the Harlem Globetrotters Friday. But the Pistons, realizing that they had to do it without their sparkplug, Bud Jeannette, whose ankle, sprained against the Rens failed to respond to treatment enough to permit him to play, laid their plans well. If ever a team followed a set pattern in a smart, efficient manner, the Pistons did for their payoff cash.

Their defense slowed down the Eagles' fast-breaking to a minimum and gave Dehnert's boys little to shoot at until the final decision was no longer in doubt. Their offense was almost perfect as they handled the ball carefully and then shot timely and accurate passes to each other for good shots. They had decided that they had the height and experience to win if they used them right. And how they did."[101]

For all the accolades given the players, the real success of the team rested with Fred Zollner. To a man everyone who ever worked or played with him believed he was instrumental not only in the team's success but also in keeping professional basketball afloat during the war years. George Yardley, a player for the Pistons in the 1950s and a future member of the Naismith Memorial Basketball Hall of Fame, stated, "He was, by far, the best owner to play for. His company was so successful, and that company was the financial backbone for our team. Therefore his team was the most stable in the league, and Fred paid the highest salaries in the league. So from a financial point of view, there was nobody better to play for."[102] Zollner was a passionate fan and that fact endeared him to his players. "I think Fred Zollner was the consummate professional team owner. He was a genuine fan for his basketball team," Dick Rosenthal, a former player, noted. "He had a very significant, important, and large piston manufacturing business that demanded most of his time and attention. Yet in the span I played with the club I can't remember Fred *not* attending the games. He was never too busy for his team. He was always there."[103]

During his time as owner Zollner was instrumental in introducing two important novelties that went a long way to cementing his relationship with his team. The first was creating a kitty that the players benefited from at the end of the year. "The rent for North Side gym was $175 a night. After that and other expenses were paid, the rest went into the kitty," Carl Bennett recalled. "I remember the first year, when we divided the kitty up. We gave each person $2,500, which was a pretty good chunk of change in those days. I think the players probably would have played for nothing. But the kitty was nice. And when we started winning, the kitty just got bigger and bigger."[104]

The other novelty introduced was a team airplane. In the decades to come, all professional teams would own their own charter planes, custom fitted, and be able to fly a team from city to city in luxury. When Zollner introduced a team plane, however, it was a novel idea. Carl Bennett remembered the story.

The funny thing about the plane was that Fred was not a flyer. I mean, he was a real "white-knuckler" when it came to flying. Early in 1952 we had a game in Rochester, New York, one night, then another game scheduled back in Fort Wayne right after that. So I asked Fred if we could charter a plan to get the team back quickly to rest for their second game.

"Well, if that's what's best, let's do it," Fred responded.

Well, when Fred gets an idea in his mind, he wants to do it and do it *now*. So he called me into his office the next day and said, "if we're going to fly in an airplane, we ought to fly our own. Where do you buy an airplane?" Can you believe it—just like that! Where do you buy an airplane? Well, the next thing I knew, Fred was on the phone with a guy on the West Coast and asked him how long it would take to get the plane. He told him, "About ten days or so."

"We'll take it," Fred said.

The guy must have fallen out of his chair. He said, "Mr. Zollner, wouldn't you like to at least come out and see the plane?"

"I don't know anything about planes," Fred responded. "You said it was good, didn't you? Well, that's good enough for me."[105]

Despite the airplane and the kitty shared by the players, Zollner's biggest contribution during the war years was to keep the league going. He often contributed financial resources to help other teams meet payroll or their other expenses. His generosity was often low key, in keeping with his personality. As Bennett remembered, "He never wanted anyone to know how he helped keep the basketball league going. He might help a particular team stay afloat for a period of time. Maybe he'd buy a player's contract for a large sum of money to help the other team meet its payroll. Or maybe he used his airplane to help transport *other* teams to games and cut down on their transportation costs. All this to say nothing of what he did for the community in Fort Wayne with his charity fund raisers and youth organizations."[106] In many ways he helped keep professional basketball operating during some difficult times. As Hilliard Gates recalled, "I liked him. He was always poised on winning. He wanted the best. Everything associated with his team had to be 'major league.'"[107] Zollner's determination was key as Dick Rosenthal recounted, "It took basketball owners with a great deal of business savvy and the sheer will of their own personality to manage to make enough money to meet the payroll. They simply did what had to be done to move professional basketball into the zenith it is today. And that's what Fred Zollner did for the Fort Wayne Pistons."[108]

Fort Wayne dominated the professional basketball landscape in 1944, and the team was just beginning a dynasty that would come to dominate the war years.

4

THE BIG MAN COMETH, 1944–1945

We opened the door to the idea that the big man could play the game, which in our day was, by Eastern standards, played by guys 5-foot-10, 5-foot-11, who were quick, and took the set shot and so forth. We opened the door for what the game is today. —BOB KURLAND

The photograph appeared on page 27 of the *New York Times* on March 29, 1945. It is about four inches high, and it shows Bob Kurland on the left and George Mikan on the right. In the middle is Cappy Lane, the timer for Madison Square Garden. Both Kurland and Mikan are placing their hands on Lane's head while their other hands rest against the exit sign above the door frame. All three are standing. Above the photo is the statement "Expect to Reach New Heights Tonight." The caption below the photo reads, "Bob Kurland (left) of the Oklahoma Aggies and George Mikan of De Paul University will be the rival centers in the Red Cross basketball game. Bob, who stands seven feet, and George, measuring six feet nine inches, are looking down on Cappy Lane, timer of Garden events."[1]

Kurland and Mikan were the featured participants in the third annual Red Cross Match featuring the winner of the NIT championship, DePaul University, versus the winner of the NCAA championship, Oklahoma A&M. The proceeds from the game benefited the Red Cross. In 1943 Wyoming defeated St. John's, and in 1944 the University of Utah bested St. John's. But this match-up was different. It featured college basketball's two biggest players and star attractions. The game was changing, and both Kurland and Mikan would be at the forefront of that change.

In the early days of basketball, the game was played largely with smaller players. Centers usually focused on two tasks. The first was to gain control of the ball off the center jump that followed each basket. The second was to rebound the ball. They were not expected to score heavily or be versatile in all facets of the game. In the mid-1920s the Original Celtics dominated professional basketball as they barnstormed across the country. Their center was Henry "Dutch" Dehnert, and he is often credited with popularizing pivot play. Arnie Risen, a center after World War II, who eventually was elected into the Naismith Memorial Basketball Hall of Fame, offered this perspective of the development of the center position and its early days: "If you go back to the early days of basketball, the big man was there for only one reason to get the jump ball. Then Dutch Dehnert came along with the old New York Celtics, and in their standard routine, he set up a high post and the others cut off it. Fans thought that kind of thing was exciting, so pivot play began. Until that time, everybody faced the basket. As a matter of fact, back in the thirties, the American [Basketball] League played with a rule that said you couldn't play with your back to the basket for more than three seconds."[2]

By the 1930s, though, the position was starting to change, and centers were required to do more, be more of a factor for their teams offensively and defensively. One of those early centers who started to transition the game was Moe Goldman, who played professionally for the Philadelphia SPHAS. In an interview he gave in the mid-1980s, he reflected on his own contributions to the game. "I was the first center man in those days who could run and shoot. The rest of the center men were tall, gangly, and couldn't run. All I had to do was fake and go. I could shoot if they stayed back. So I would say, without trying to be boastful, that I revolutionized the center position. I think I was the first center to be able to run and shoot, to dribble and pass, to do all those things."[3] Goldman did do all that and was instrumental in the SPHAS being the top professional team in the 1930s.

It was during World War II that the perception of the center began to change. Kurland and Mikan were instrumental in this because both players led their schools to postseason championships, faced each other at Madison Square Garden in New York, and developed a rivalry, the first time that one existed between two centers. Ray Meyer, who coached Mikan, offered this assessment,

> Back then, centers were basically like robots. Then, they had the jump ball at the center position, and the center mainly just did the jump ball and then stood under the basket. They weren't agile. The big centers were thought to be like posts out there. That's why they called them posts. Centers didn't move. I'd say George was the fore-runner of all big men being a rounded ballplayer. When big guys came in back then, they were either a defensive ballplayer or they stood around the basket. Don Otten mostly played the post, not much offense. Bob Kurland was a defensive ballplayer. He could score, but not like Mikan. Kurland couldn't run the floor like George. Mikan was a complete basketball player. He could do almost anything.[4]

While the game today is played above the rim, with seven footers who can shoot, run, defend, block shots, and dribble, that skill set did not exist in 1945. Most people had never seen such a tall person. Growing up in Oklahoma, Kurland was the tallest kid around, and being that tall was not always a blessing. "It was an embarrassing, difficult time, and I didn't like it," he remembered. "I was a big gangly kid, and height at that time was not looked upon in the same way as it is today. I had to carry my birth certificate when I went to the show, because the show was ten cents for a kid under twelve, and fifteen or twenty cents for a guy over twelve. I'd have to show them my birth certificate."[5] But Kurland gravitated to sports and took a particular interest in basketball.

Soon enough he joined the team at Oklahoma A&M led by its coach, Hank Iba. As Kurland recalled,

> He said, "You know, Bob, I like your attitude, I like your enthusiasm and your effort, but I've never coached a kid as big as you." He said, "I don't know whether you'll be a good basketball player or not, but I'll tell you what I'll do. If you come here, go to class, and stay eligible, I'll see that you get a college education." I was interested in the School of Engineering and Oklahoma A&M had one, so I said, "You got a deal." I went down there with a tin suitcase and got off the bus and all the kids gawked and said, "What the hell is this?"[6]

Kurland joined the team and worked hard to become a regular contributor. An interesting point from this era is that coaches like Iba had never coached big men before. It was a new endeavor for them as well. Iba and Kurland worked together, and before long Oklahoma A&M had become one of the country's best teams, winning the 1945 NCAA championship. "I have great admiration for men like Henry Iba and Ray Meyer, who were brave enough to take odd people or strange giants like myself and had the courage to put their careers on the line in trying to teach us how to play," Kurland reflected. "You can't measure our performance to today's performance or tomorrow's performance. That's foolish. But the thing I take pride in is, we opened the door for the big man and caused people to think."[7]

While Kurland was forging his way, George Mikan was doing the same in Illinois. He, too, faced many of the same challenges and perceptions of big men. Much like Kurland, Mikan found a willing partner in DePaul University coach Ray Meyer, who worked long, hard hours with Mikan to develop Mikan's coordination, footwork, and balance. It took time, but it paid off, and DePaul won the 1945 NIT championship. Meyer spent hours upon hours working with Mikan. As he noted years later,

FIG. 29. Bob Kurland led Oklahoma A&M to the 1945 NCAA championship and formed college basketball's best rivalry in the war years against George Mikan. Courtesy of Bill Himmelman.

When George first started playing ball at DePaul, he was a raw talent, but he was clumsy, awkward. He needed some work, and he and I set out to do it. The hours working with George were very enjoyable because it was watching a flower blooming. I could see him getting better everyday. I could see the agility. We had a little guy of about 5 feet, 4 inches named Billy Donato—very quick. And I made George guard him at the top of the free throw line. It was like an elephant chasing a fly for a long time, but you could see the improvement every day. Gradually, George was catching up with him. First, George would be blocking one shot from behind, and then Donato couldn't go by him that easily. Then, Donato had to work like hell to get by him. Sure, [speed was] a tremendous advantage, but those drills helped George to be quicker. Probably George's greatest asset is that he was a very intelligent ballplayer, he had the ability to make adjustments. You don't get that every day, where all you had to do was tell [a player something]. Some games, for instance, I'd say, "They're overplaying your right side, you're right side." I never had to tell him twice. He'd go immediately to his left hand and walk right by them. He could do things by being told.[8]

One aspect of the game that everyone—fans, players, coaches, referees, and administrators—had to confront was the effect of goaltending on the game. It was a part of the game, and Oklahoma A&M incorporated it into their game plan as Kurland noted,

We did it in an organized fashion. In my freshman year, in our last game against Oklahoma, Mr. Iba decided that we were going to goaltend. The rule said you couldn't hit the ball on the downward arc once it was inside the cylinder. Well, the OU game started and Mr. Iba said, "We're going to goaltend." We set up a defense where I was under the basket. Bruce Drake, who was coach then and later head of the Rules Committee for the Coaches' Association, just about had a hissy-fit when I knocked down the first ball, the second ball, the third, fourth, and fifth. They had beaten us the week before, but we beat their butts. The next year, that was our defense, my knocking the ball down. The rule was changed in my junior year because of that.[9]

Their victories in the NCAA and NIT championships in March 1945 led to the match-up everyone wanted to see. As Mikan remembered, "Oklahoma A and M had just won the NCAA tournament, and

FIG. 30. George Mikan led DePaul University to the 1945 NIT championship and later became one of the game's best centers. Courtesy of Bill Himmelman.

somebody got the idea that we ought to play seven-foot Bob Kurland and his Ags for the national title—with the Red Cross getting the proceeds. We were delighted at the opportunity to prove that we were the best team in the country."[10] The press certainly reflected the hype surrounding the game. William D. Richardson, writing for the *New York Times*, stated, "'The Battle of the Skyscrapers' is the way the circus people would bill tonight's grand finale of the 1944–45 basketball season—the Red Cross benefit game between DePaul, winner of the national invitation tourney, and Oklahoma A. and M., the N.C.A.A. champions, at Madison Square Garden. The prize will be the mythical national intercollegiate championship. It will bring together the two most talked-about centers in the country, seven-foot Bob (Foothills) Kurland of the Aggies and 6 foot 9 inch George (High-Ho) Mikan of the Blue Demons from Chicago."[11] Kurland and Mikan were evenly matched, and both were riding high entering the game. As Richardson wrote, "Each of whom was singled out as the outstanding performer in his respective tourney. Each one is his team's leading scorer—Mikan with 429 points to his credit in twenty games during the regular season and Kurland with 412 in twenty five."[12] The game figured to be close with a slight edge to Mikan. This marked the fourth time that Mikan and Kurland had squared off in their college careers; Mikan's team had won the first three contests. Before the game Kurland reflected on facing Mikan again. "We had the same game plan we always had. We didn't play Mikan any different than anybody else as far as the post was concerned. George and I were both pretty excited about the game. He had scored [a record 120] points winning the NIT and played a marvelous tournament. We had won the NCAA and were kind of underrated in terms of how good we really were."[13]

As the game approached, Iba and Kurland devised a strategy to limit Mikan's effectiveness. "The best defense against Mikan was to keep the ball out of his hands, from a direct pass, if you could. We used a sinking defense, where the offside would fall back and you had me alongside or in back of George, with one or two guys in front of him. It was like a rubber band: when the ball went to the other side of the court, the defense would spread out on that side," Kurland recalled. "Our offense was set up with screens and blocks, with me passing off rather than depending on me to score points. In my opinion, that's the kind of game that wins championships. If you're depending upon a particular individual and he's sick or having a bad night, you're in a mud hole, boy."[14]

The strategy worked as Mikan found himself in foul trouble rather quickly. As Kurland recounted, "He killed himself in that particular game. He was feeling his oats about being a great scorer—which he was—but I stood up against him and that's where he got his fouls. The shot he fouled out on was one I had practiced but never used before. He had his arms up, and I went under his arms and scooped the ball toward the basket. He came down across my arms and Pat Kennedy fouled him out. The game was over, for all practical purposes."[15] Fourteen minutes into the game, Mikan picked up his fifth personal foul and was disqualified. "At the time, De Paul held a 21–14 advantage, but the Chicagoans were to miss the 6-foot-9 inch center, who had scored 53 points in a national invitation tourney game and had achieved a 40-point average in that competition. Without him, Oklahoma's Bob Kurland, a seven-foot sparkplug, was left to control the rebounds and seal De Paul's fate. Before the final buzzer, four of the five starters for the losers had been banished on fouls."[16] Heavy fouling by both teams characterized the game as DePaul committed twenty-five fouls, while Oklahoma A&M was whistled for sixteen infractions. Oklahoma A&M won the game, 52–44, as Kurland scored fourteen points.

Everyone had his own opinion on how the game unfolded, including Mikan.

> It didn't work quite that way. . . . Kurland got 14 points and I got 9 before Pat Kennedy whistled me out at 13:50 of the first half. As a "Battle of the Century" it was a flop. But it taught me one big lesson: *never lose your head.* Coach Hank Iba and his Ags were a little too smart for me. Apparently, Iba had sent Kurland in with instructions to needle me, both physically and orally. Bob did just that. He was a skillful basketball player, of course, and he gauged his every move just to taunt me. And he wasn't bad with his tongue either. I lost my head. I jabbed deliberately at Kurland with my elbow, and when I nudged him in the pivot, it wasn't a mere nudge. It was a push. All

the time I was screaming at Pat Kennedy, the referee, "Look what he's doing to me!" and Pat would just walk away. Well, I lasted just fourteen minutes of the game. My five fouls came that quick.[17]

As Ray Meyer, DePaul's head coach, recalled, "We got off to a quick lead of 10 points, but Mikan picked up three early fouls. In those days, four fouls disqualified you. We knew we couldn't play without him. I called time out and told George not to commit a foul: 'Just hold your arms up on defense. There's no way they can beat us if you just stay in the game.'"[18] As Mikan reflected years later, "If I could play that Red Cross benefit game over, I wouldn't have lost my head. Kurland got to me with his strategy of verbal and physical abuse. It was designed to get me out of the game, and it worked."[19] But stay in the game he could not.

After their college careers ended, the two big men would go their different ways. Kurland joined Phillips 66 and worked at the company while playing on its team in amateur competition. Mikan would join the professional ranks and become professional basketball's best center in the 1950s. Bob Calihan, a contemporary of Mikan, had this assessment of him. "He was really the first good big man. There were other big men, but he was the first outstanding big man. He made the defenses double up on him. I think it was the first time I had seen double-teaming on a big man. I don't know that Mikan changed the game, but he was outstanding on rebounding and short hook shots. He was slow, and he'd have a time playing today. Of course, we'd *all* have a time playing today."[20] Both Kurland and Mikan were eventually elected into the Naismith Memorial Basketball Hall of Fame.

While George Mikan and Bob Kurland were regarded as the centers of the future, Leroy "Cowboy" Edwards was in the eyes of many still the best center in the game. Edwards played an important role in transitioning the center position from Joe Lapchick of the Original Celtics in the 1920s and 1930s to the postwar period dominated by Mikan and

Kurland. The 1944–45 season represented Edwards's ninth year with the Oshkosh All-Stars. A team that had dominated the National Basketball League since its inception, Oshkosh, more than any other team in the league, suffered the most in player shortages due to the war. After winning consecutive league titles in 1940–41 and 1941–42, the All-Stars fell on hard times as the call to service depleted Lon Darling's roster. In 1943 in-state rival Sheboygan finally won its only NBL title. In 1944 Fort Wayne emerged as the league's most dominant squad and won its first league championship. Oshkosh had finished the last two seasons with sub .500 records, and many wondered if it could stay afloat until the team could restock its roster.

One team not worried about any shortages on its roster was the Fort Wayne Zollner Pistons. Fresh off its league and World Professional Basketball Tournament wins the previous season, the Zollner Pistons began the season contemplating their end-of-the season victory party. The four teams who finished the 1943–44 campaign all regrouped for another year. Oshkosh, Fort Wayne, and Sheboygan were on board, while the Cleveland Chase Brassmen found a new sponsor, a trucking company, and were renamed the Cleveland Allmen Transfers. Two new teams joined the league, the Pittsburgh Raiders and the Chicago American Gears. The league now had six teams, the first time with at least six since 1941–42, when the league fielded seven. The teams were divided into an Eastern and a Western Division, the first time that had happened since 1939–40. The top two finishers in each division would advance to the playoffs. The Eastern Division consisted of Fort Wayne, Cleveland, and Pittsburgh, while the Western Division included Sheboygan, Chicago, and Oshkosh.

One of the two new teams was the Pittsburgh Raiders, who were essentially the Pittsburgh Corbetts from the previous season who competed in the World Professional Basketball Tournament. An independent team, their roster was comprised mostly of players from Pittsburgh and the East Coast. The other new entry to the league was

FIG. 31. Leroy "Cowboy" Edwards was a dominating center for the Oshkosh All-Stars during their time in the National Basketball League and was a key figure in transitioning the position during the 1930s. Courtesy of Bill Himmelman.

the Chicago American Gears. The Gears were the first team in Chicago since the Studebakers historic season in 1942–43. Dick Triptow, a key member of the Gears for several seasons and an original member, provided some background on how the Gears started.

Maurice A. White was owner and president of the American Gear & Manufacturing Company, a Chicago based company that manufactured gears and machine parts. His assembly lines were doing a tremendous business, meeting the Nation's war needs. Beyond being a businessman, however, White longed to field a basketball team that would bring the championship of professional basketball to Chicago. Entering a team in the National Basketball League was his first step toward this goal. White saw this as an opportunity to fulfill his vision of a Professional Basketball Championship in Chicago, and immediately got to work setting the stage for the Gears entrance into the NBL for the 1944–1945 season. He was familiar with the highly successful Fort Wayne Zollner Pistons basketball team that won the 1944 World Professional Basketball Championship sponsored by the Chicago Herald-American the previous spring. He was determined to pattern his program after that of the Zollners. White already had his own trade mark "White-Liner" imprinted over an outline of a spur gear. He, like Zollner, made a sincere attempt to employ all of his players year-round somewhere within the Gear organization, unless that individual was engaged in some other occupation that did not interfere with playing basketball.[21]

The Gears were led by Dick Triptow and Stan Patrick in their first season.

Making the transition from college at DePaul University to playing professional basketball with the Gears was an adjustment, as Triptow noted:

Moving into the pro ranks from college ball was quite a transition. Playing against seasoned pros, I found it necessary to make adjustments in my style of play. I was still a road runner with no slow speed but found playing twice as many games, playing longer games, often playing six nights in a row, and traveling more extensively, required that I slow down or I would not be able to come through in crucial spots when needed. When you got knocked down you had to pick yourself up and go right back in there. I remember playing against

Carlisle "Blackie" Towery of the Fort Wayne Zollner Pistons. He was 6'6" and weighed 230 pounds. His mother, an English teacher, named him Carlisle, after the famous Scottish author, Thomas Carlyle (1795–1881). During this game, I drove in on the right hand side of the court, for what I thought was an easy layup, when this long arm of Blackie's hit me across the throat and I went head over heels onto the hard wood. If he had a knife I would have been decapitated. I think the term used in those days was "clothes-lined."[22]

Triptow was not the only player adjusting to the new rhythms of professional basketball. Frank Otway, a bit player for the Gears that season, recalled how he joined the team prior to the start of the season.

I was in the Marine Corps, stationed in Chicago and attending the University of Chicago for a six or eight month course in Advanced Electronics. I saw an announcement in the paper about the Gears holding try-outs for their new Professional team and I decided to give it a shot. Jack Tierney was the coach and I was surprised and delighted to make the team. Our first two exhibitions were against the Harlem Globetrotters and a Service team, Fort Sheridan. I know we won the first game and think we won the second, but I'm not sure. We then made a trip to Sheboygan and Oshkosh to play our league openers and we lost them both. I remember playing against Mike Novak in Sheboygan, and "Cowboy" Edwards at Oshkosh and getting an accelerated education in playing pivot men in the N.B.L.!! I'm only 6'-4" and at that time, must have weighed about 200 lbs—give or take a little. Anyhow, the trip (as I recall), was to Rochester and came during the week, but the Marine Corp decided I had to stay in Chicago and go to school as I was supposed to—can you imagine that? Jack Tierney used this situation to take me aside and explain that I had to be available to play all their games or he would have to let me go. So I went.[23]

As for Fort Wayne, its roster was the league's deepest. It returned Bobby McDermott, John Pelkington, Buddy Jeannette, Jerry Bush, and Chick Reiser. The team lost old stalwarts Blackie Towery and Dale Hamilton to the military but replaced them by signing former Oshkosh player Charlie Shipp and Bob Synnott. Towery and Hamilton were original members of the Pistons' first year in the NBL in 1941–42. Shipp was no stranger to the Pistons as he made the last-second shot to defeat the Pistons as a member of the Oshkosh team in the 1943 World Professional Basketball Tournament. Prior to the start of league play, Fort Wayne traveled east and faced the American Basketball League champion Wilmington twice, the Baltimore Bullets, and Wilkes-Barre. Fort Wayne won all four games. As part of their East Coast preseason swing, the Zollner Pistons arrived in Philadelphia for a much-anticipated game against the SPHAS. The November 11, 1944, edition of the SPHAS Sparks, the program written and produced by announcer Dave Zinkoff, stated, "As we told you before, Fort Wayne is positively the best attraction in basketball today. They are really champions in every sense of the word and will present a lineup of stars that produced the most thrilling game ever seen against the SPHAS last season. Every man is a scoring threat, headlined by Bobby McDermott, and supported by Jerry Bush, Paul Birch, John Pelkington, Bud Jeannette, Chick Reiser and Stretch Towery. Tell all your friends about this game, and make your reservations NOW!"[24] In a close affair Fort Wayne held back Philadelphia 33–29 before an overflow crowd.

With the tour of the East Coast complete, the Pistons returned home to begin their league games. The question on most everyone's mind was, who would challenge the Pistons? The Eastern Division featured Cleveland and Pittsburgh, two teams that did not finish above .500 for the season. Pittsburgh completed its lone NBL season with an abysmal 7-23 mark. Cleveland would play one more NBL season before finally bowing out of professional basketball. In the Western Division Sheboygan fired longtime coach Carl Roth and replaced him with legendary

FIG. 32. Jerry Bush was a key member of Fort Wayne Zollner Pistons during the war years and helped lead them to multiple NBL and World Professional Basketball Tournament titles. Courtesy of Bill Himmelman.

player Dutch Dehnert, who had previously coached the Detroit Eagles to the 1941 World Professional Basketball Championship. For the past few years Sheboygan had been a championship contender, and it was assumed that trend would continue for the upcoming season. In its first season Chicago did well, finishing 14-16. In the coming years the Gears would more than make their mark on professional basketball.

Still affected by player shortages and turnover, Oshkosh ended the season with a 12-18 mark. This would be the first time since the NBL started in 1937 that Oshkosh did not make the playoffs.

For the third straight year, the regular season was a two-team race between Fort Wayne and Sheboygan. Sheboygan won the 1943 title, while Fort Wayne claimed the prize in 1944. Fort Wayne finished the 1944–45 regular season with a 25-5 record, the most wins ever in the regular season in the NBL. Sheboygan sported a 19-11 mark. Neither team was challenged in its own division. Fort Wayne jumped out to strong start, defeating Cleveland 51–34. The team cruised through the regular season, compiling a 25-5 mark. In one regular season contest Fort Wayne defeated Chicago by the unheard-of score 73–64. As Chicago's head coach Jack Tierney noted after the game to reporters, "As a player and coach I never thought I'd see the day when a team could score 64 points and lose a ball game such as we did against the Pistons."[25] Scoring was up; it was one impact that the war years had on the game of basketball. And Fort Wayne was a high scoring machine with a roster that had jelled for a few seasons. The team was experiencing the benefits of that as Fort Wayne was regularly scoring fifty or sixty points per game, tops in the league.

The Pistons clinched the regular-season title on February 18. The playoffs saw Fort Wayne quickly dispatch Cleveland in two games, while Sheboygan advanced past Chicago. In its match-up versus Cleveland, the Pistons felt that their advantage was their frontline. As the preview article in the *Fort Wayne News-Sentinel* stated, "Cleveland has been tough on the locals on more than one occasion. It has considerable scoring power in its forwards and guards, but mainly has been weak at center. With Ed Sadowski around to help out John Pelkington, the Pistons have plenty of size and an edge in the rebounding department."[26] That proved to be true in the first game as the Pistons racked up a 78–50 win. The advantage in the front line proved one of the keys as Pelkington tallied thirteen points while Sadowski scored ten. As Ben

Tenny reported the following day, "In running up the highest total they ever compiled in a loop tilt, the Pistons could have made it more had they so been inclined. That's how well they were going."[27] The second game proved more difficult, but the Pistons prevailed, as they "had to come up with some more deadly shooting from the field to make up for the steady procession of the Allmen to the charity line and the loss of three of their best men on fouls."[28] For the third straight year Fort Wayne and Sheboygan would face off against each other in the finals. For the second straight year the finals would be a best-of-five match-up.

The first two games were scheduled to be played in Sheboygan, and the Red Skins captured the first two to take a 2–0 series lead. In the first contest the Red Skins won 65–53; "playing a pivot attack that was too much for the Zollner defense the Redskins also shot well, hawked the ball and outsped the Pistons who never really got going."[29] Sheboygan led throughout and was paced by Ed Dancker, who scored a game-high twenty-four points. The second game again saw Dancker dominate Fort Wayne's front line. It was a closer game throughout as the Red Skins won 50–47. "The Pistons tightened their defense and actually outplayed Sheboygan in most departments, but their defense had no answer for Dancker's brilliant sniping on his favorite pivot and hookshots. He flipped 19 points in the first half and added 10 more in the third quarter to keep his team out in front."[30] The series then shifted to Fort Wayne and the home-court advantage paid off as the Pistons won three consecutive games to repeat as league champions. Bobby McDermott showed why he was considered the best player by scoring twenty-one points in Game Four and twenty-three in the series win. The Pistons also made adjustments on their coverage of Dancker, who scored fourteen points in the fourth game and only managed eight in the series clincher. As the *Fort Wayne Journal Gazette* wrote the following day in its game summary article, "The Pistons again showed their superiority over the Redskins in a game that followed pretty closely the pattern of the first two played on the local floor. They jumped away to an early lead, were threatened a couple of times along the way, and then finished breezing with plenty to spare."[31] Fort Wayne had earned the distinction of being the NBL's best team.

For the previous three seasons the American Basketball League (ABL) was characterized by a two-team race. Wilmington and Philadelphia dominated league play and the championship series. Wilmington won in 1941–42, while Philadelphia captured the title the following season as Wilmington sat out due to war issues that impacted the team's ability to find a regular home court. In 1943–44 Wilmington rejoined the league, and the Bombers and the SPHAS battled to an epic seven-game series, won by Wilmington after facing a three-games-to-one deficit. During this three-year period Wilmington had become the latest rivalry for the SPHAS. As the only team still playing in the league that began in 1933–34, the SPHAS continually faced a new, upstart team ready to knock them off the top perch. In the 1930s Philadelphia faced the Brooklyn Visitations and the Jersey Reds. Now it was Wilmington's turn. As the basketball clock turned toward the 1944–45 season, the question on everyone's mind was, would the two teams meet again in the postseason? Most preseason polls answered in the affirmative.

The 1943–44 campaign ended with four teams: Philadelphia, Wilmington, Trenton, and New York. With the 1944–45 season set for tip-off, Philadelphia, Wilmington, and Trenton all signed on with Commissioner John J. O'Brien. The New York Americans, who finished the previous season in last place with a 2-8 mark, were replaced by the New York Westchesters. During the season the Westchesters transferred to the New York Gothams. The name change did little to help the team; New York finished with an 11-15 mark. As was the case every year, Commissioner O'Brien and team owners faced the difficult task of wading through new applications. For many aspiring businessmen the challenges of World War II did not deter them from making a bid to field a professional basketball team. At an October 20, 1944, meeting at

FIG. 33. Ed Dancker, Sheboygan Red Skins' center, was an effective pivot player who led the team to the 1943 National Basketball League title. Courtesy of Bill Himmelman.

O'Brien's Wall Street office in New York, five applications were reviewed and voted on, a mere month before the start of the season.

The first application under review came from Mr. V. M. Conte, who applied to field a team in Washington DC. The league owners quickly approved this application, and Washington DC had its first team in the league since 1941–42, when the Washington Brewers finished out a dismal second half with a 5-7 last-place finish. Despite the high aspirations surrounding a new team in the nation's capital, the Washington Capitols fell to a 2-8 record before transferring to Paterson, New Jersey. The owners also considered an application for a team in Wilkes-Barre, Pennsylvania, but it was denied "in view of traveling restrictions."[32] Wilkes-Barre, though, would eventually be granted a team in 1947–48. The Barons, as they would come to be known, would quickly rise to the top and win back-to-back ABL titles in 1947–48 and 1948–49. Another application, this one for Paterson, New Jersey, was also rejected for the same reason, travel restrictions. This was more curious than Wilkes-Barre because Paterson was located in between New York and Philadelphia, where other teams existed. There was also a team from Trenton. Despite rejecting the bid the league owners did return to that application when Washington relocated to Paterson after ten games. In late December league officials were notified that "Mr. Conte, representing Washington, advised that efforts were being made by him to transfer the franchise of the Washington Capitols to Paterson, N.J., and that definite knowledge of this possible change would be made known by him to the league sometime after December 26 or December 27, 1944."[33] The change of scenery did not help as the Paterson Crescents finished with a 1-15 mark. Paterson would stay with the league until 1948–49, showing improvement each season. Another application, this one from Brooklyn, was tabled since a deposit had yet to be made.

The final application reviewed was one representing the city of Baltimore. Baltimore had not fielded a team since 1940–41, when the Baltimore Clippers finished with a 6-10 second-half finish, good for last place. These Baltimore Bullets were not the Clippers, and in short time they would replace Wilmington as the SPHAS' biggest rivalry. The Bullets would be the only ABL team to be offered a spot in the Basketball Association of America (BAA) after World War II. The team would eventually play in the National Basketball Association (NBA). Writing in the Wilmington Blue Bombers' program, Eddie Glennon offered this preview of the new Baltimore franchise: "Sam Behrends, owner of the Baltimore Bullets, will endeavor to give Monument City fans another winner. After having gone mad over the Orioles in baseball you can look for plenty of trouble from the Bullets who will be coached by Ben Kramer, who knows his abc's of the pro game."[34] With a few new teams joining the old stalwarts, the ABL was set to begin play for another year. A few wrinkles were added. The season would be one season, instead of two halves, for the first time since 1942–43. The top four teams would make the playoffs. Disregarding the poor showing of Washington/Paterson, the five remaining teams vied for four playoff spots.

Since 1933–34, when the ABL resumed after a two-year hiatus, the SPHAS had been the most dominant and recognizable team for the league. Although the team's heyday was in the 1930s, the SPHAS were still quite competitive during the war years. These were not Eddie Gottlieb's best teams, however. He faced a game-by-game struggle to field competitive teams, often securing at the last minute players who had been granted leave from their military bases. His best players who formed the core of his winning teams in the 1930s were retiring or were fulfilling military obligations. Shikey Gotthoffer, Gil Fitch, Red Rosan, Harry Litwack, Moe Goldman, and Cy Kaselman were no longer on Gottlieb's bench. Instead new players, mostly from New York, were recruited to continue the team's championship run. Now his team consisted of Irv Torgoff, Ossie Schectman, Butch Schwartz, Irv Davis, Dutch Garfinkel, Jerry Fleishman, Art Hillhouse, Irv Rothenberg, Len and Howie Rader, and Bernie Opper. All were great players, and all except Opper, hailed from New York. Long identified with the city of Philadelphia, the SPHAS were still Jewish but mainly a team with New York players. Only Inky Lautman, the longest tenured SPHA player, stayed with Gottlieb during the war years. With new players and the effects of operating a league during a world war, it was only natural that the SPHAS would not be as dominant or consistent as they were in the 1930s. The SPHAS won in 1940–41 but did not have the opportunity to defend their title as Wilmington won both halves in 1941–42 to secure the championship. The SPHAS did win in 1942–43 over Trenton as Wilmington sat out. When Wilmington returned in 1943–44, the two teams waged an epic championship series as the SPHAS lost a 3–1 series lead. For the SPHAS it was back and forth from season to season, series to series, and game to game. After the SPHAS lost a heartbreaking championship series, many wondered whether they could bounce back.

As the season began, the SPHAS split a home-and-home series with Wilmington, earning a small modicum of revenge. The team then won three in a row, lost two, won one, lost one, won two, lost one, won one, and lost one to earn an 8-6 mark. The team swung back and forth like a pendulum, never quite gaining enough momentum to generate a consistent winning streak. Starting with a home game on January 20 against Wilmington until the regular season ended on March 18 with a home contest against Paterson, the SPHAS compiled a league-best 14-2 mark to finish in first place with a 22-8 record. The team was finally clicking, and Gottlieb must have felt that this was the 1930s all over again. His team was playing consistent basketball, generating a long winning streak, and they were doing it by scoring points. In some cases scoring a lot of points. In the season's final sixteen games, the team scored more than forty points in eleven contests, including fifty points twice. The SPHAS won all eleven of those games. They won close games, blowouts, and overtime games. They won at home and on the road. It was the New York players who were having the biggest impact as Art Hillhouse and Irv Rothenberg each played in twenty-nine of the team's thirty regular-season games. Hillhouse averaged seven points per game. Irv Torgoff, meanwhile, played in twenty-one contests and averaged more than six points per game. This consistency, with Gottlieb being able to count on the same players from game to game, proved to be the biggest difference. It was that consistency that led the SPHAS back to the playoffs and a chance to avenge last season's disappointing loss.

With the top four teams making the playoffs, Trenton faced Balti-more while the SPHAS and old nemesis Wilmington were set to meet for the second consecutive year. The best-of-three first-round playoff series began in Philadelphia, where the SPHAS edged the Bombers, 49–44. As was the two teams' custom, the game was tight through-out, with each team tallying nineteen field goals. The *Wilmington (DE) Morning News* wrote that the "SPHAS clinch[ed] the victory of better work from the foul line where they outscored the Bombers, 11–6."[35] That difference of five free throws was the difference in the game. The other significant factor was the play of center Art Hillhouse, who "deflected many passes from Bomber receivers in addition to scoring four goals."[36] Hillhouse led all scorers with twelve points. Meanwhile, Wilmington was without the services of Moe Frankel, who was "with the Grumman Aircraft team playing in the Cleveland and Chicago pro tourneys. Chuck Connors, former Wilmington center, [was] with New-ark [NY], also playing in Western events."[37] The game's intensity reach a boiling point in the third period, "when [Jerry] Fleishman and Jackie Peters came to blows. They were quickly stopped by the interference of other players."[38] The SPHAS now led 1–0.

The series then shifted to Wilmington, to the State Armory at Tenth and DuPont Streets, and a little home cooking was all that the Bombers needed as they raced out to a 13–9 first period lead and never looked back. The second period was the SPHAS undoing as the Bombers thor-oughly outplayed the SPHAS in outscoring them 18–4. The third period was anticlimactic as Wilmington won going away, 48–29. Wilmington's fortune turned with guard Ben Goldfaden, "who played the entire game, scoring seven points, steadying the other Bombers and enjoying one of his memorable games. Scheduled to start at his favorite position, guard, the wiry veteran found himself matching jumps with the huge Hillhouse. Ben was up to the occasion, working a tap-off play with Szu-kala and Niemiera that reduced Hillhouse's advantage in height."[39] As the *Philadelphia Inquirer* noted, Goldfaden "curbed Hillhouse and the usually high-scoring SPHAS center was unable to break loose under the basket."[40] Hillhouse was held to five points. The SPHAS team as a whole was held to a mere nine field goals, a season low.

With the series knotted at a game apiece, the action shifted back to Philadelphia and the Broadwood Hotel. As everyone expected, the game was hard fought. Veteran Philadelphia sportswriter William J. Scheffer wrote the following day, "While the play could not be termed rough, four players went out via the five personal foul route, each team losing two men in the third period. The first to go was Ben Goldfaden, then followed Art Hillhouse for the SPHAS and at the time it appeared like a serious loss for the Gottlieb clan, but Inky Lautman did a commendable job at center. Cy Boardman and Ossie Schectman were the third and fourth players to be ousted."[41] The SPHAS jumped out to a 6–0 lead to start the game, but the Bombers slowly chipped away and tied the contest at 16 before a foul shot by Lautman gave the SPHAS a one-point lead at the conclusion of the first period. The second period was close, and Wilmington took its first lead of the game on a basket by Scotty McDonald (Scotty Hamilton playing under an assumed name) to break a 24–24 tie. It would be Wilmington's only lead as the SPHAS closed out the second frame with a 36–26 lead. Despite being outscored over the final fifteen minutes, the SPHAS held on for a 48–41 win.

Waiting for the SPHAS in the finals were the Baltimore Bullets, who had just completed their first season in the ABL. Despite being newcomers in the league, the Bullets finished with a 14-16 mark, good for fourth place. However, the Bullets lost five of six to the SPHAS, otherwise their record would have been 13-11, above .500. The Bullets had surprised the Trenton Tigers in the previous round, defeating the second seed, which had finished the regular season with a 21-9 mark. Robert Elmer, writing his preview article for the first game in the *Baltimore Sun*, noted positively, "After weathering the usual ups-and-downs of a first-year team, the Bullets have improved to the point where they are now playing about the best ball in the circuit. Finishing a good fourth, the

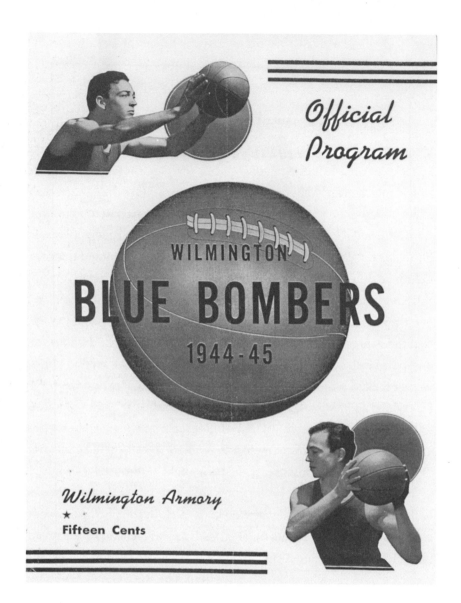

FIG. 34. In 1944–45 the Wilmington Blue Bombers finished the regular season with a 14-14 record and lost to the Philadelphia SPHAS in the American Basketball League playoffs. Author's collection.

locals scored a major upset by eliminating the second-place Trenton Tigers in the semi-final playoffs to gain the final round."[42] The Bullets were led by Red Paris and Moe Dubilier as well as "their leading scorer and top favorite, Whitey Scharnus, [who had] scintillated in the playoff series, especially in the handling of rebounds and securing the ball from the center jump."[43] The series opened in Baltimore, and the regular-season dominance by the SPHAS carried over as the SPHAS "simply ran away from the underdog Baltimore team, which never got closer than eleven points throughout the game. The SPHAS rolled up 15 straight points while holding the locals scoreless in the first eight minutes of play, and from there on it was no contest."[44] The SPHAS were led by Irv Rothenberg's sixteen points and Art Hillhouse's ten.

With the first game being played on April 5, baseball was set to begin another season, and league officials decided that "due to the lateness of the season, the championship series would be decided in three games instead of five."[45] With the benefit of the league's best record, the SPHAS would host the next two games in Philadelphia. With a chance to close out the series in the second game, the SPHAS jumped out to an 11–5 margin at the end of the first period. After scoring the game's first basket, Baltimore did not score another field goal in the opening period. The SPHAS continued to push the pace, racing out to a 23–11 lead. Former SPHAS great Red Rosan, now the coach of the Bullets, made two lineup changes that completely altered the outcome. First, he inserted himself into the lineup. Second, he replaced Red Paris with Stan Stutz. Stutz "was a speed marvel, cutting in fast and dribbling like a [Harry] Hough, so that the SPHAS were unable to stop him."[46] The Bullets used a furious attack to take a 29–27 lead entering the final frame. With momentum on its side Baltimore played like the veteran team; "moving the ball well, and patiently waiting for openings, the Bullets managed to hold the upper hand throughout the entire final period."[47] A 33–30 lead increased to 42–33, and the Bullets held on for a 47–46 win, evening the series.

The third and final game was played before the largest crowd of the season at the Broadwood Hotel. Riding the momentum of their Game Two win, the Bullets opened strong, surging to a quick 10–2 lead. A veteran team, the SPHAS clawed their way back for a 15–11 lead after the first period. From that point forward the SPHAS were in control and remained "in front from six to sixteen points the rest of the way."[48] The SPHAS led 33–19 entering the final frame. In that third period the Bullets had one final run in them, scoring ten straight points at one point, but it was too little too late. The SPHAS were led by Art Hillhouse, who "six times . . . sank the ball through the nets on one-handed overhead shots."[49] The SPHAS captured their seventh and final championship by defeating newcomer Baltimore. For the Bullets their first season was a great learning experience, and it would prove instrumental as they set their sights on the following season. Baltimore had now supplanted Wilmington as Philadelphia's biggest rival.

As the ABL and the NBL wrapped up their postseasons, the focus of the professional basketball world descended on Chicago with the annual World Professional Basketball Tournament. As was their custom, the SPHAS did not participate. However, fresh off their second consecutive National Basketball League championship, the Zollner Pistons set their sights on repeating in the World Professional Basketball Tournament. Only one team had won the tournament twice: the New York Renaissance in 1939 and again in 1943, reconstituted as the Washington Bears. But no team had yet won the tournament in consecutive years. The Detroit Eagles had an opportunity in 1942 when they faced Oshkosh for the second consecutive year in the finals; the Eagles had won in 1941. Instead, Oshkosh prevailed for its one and only tournament title. The Zollner Pistons were seeking to become that team to win consecutively. The seventh annual World Professional Basketball Tournament was scheduled to be played March 19–24 in Chicago Stadium, the same venue as the previous year. Each season the organizers had high hopes, and this year proved no different. In

1944 more than fifty-two thousand fans attended the games, a record, and as preparations were made for this year's tournament, the organizers hoped to exceed last year's number. Ticket sales and the annual hype machine that was the *Chicago Herald American* began six weeks before the first contest was played. The tournament would benefit the war effort; "as in past years, profits of the meet will go to purchase added comforts in hospitals in the Sixth Corps area."[50] With the war still being fought, its effects were part of the planning and preparations for the tournament. As Harry Wilson wrote in the *Chicago Herald American*, "Even though sports does not come under the ban placed on conventions and meetings, efforts to limit the amount of travel are being stressed."[51] "The field will be limited to 16 teams. In some cases, teams in the same area will play for the right to represent their section of the country."[52] "Although military demands again have cut into the personnel of the leading teams, the caliber of the entries in this year's meet will approximate the strength of the field in any of the previous tournaments. Most of the teams are composed entirely of war plant workers, while numerous players will be fresh out of college and taking their last fling in competition before entering the armed forces."[53] In the end fourteen teams would fill out the brackets this year, the same as the previous year.

The Zollner Pistons were considered the tournament's top team. The field was usually heavily peppered with teams from the National Basketball League, given the tournament's Midwest location. Five of the six NBL teams signed on to compete. The lone squad not in the field was the Sheboygan Red Skins due to the death of coach Dutch Dehnert's only son in the war. The Red Skins had acquitted themselves well during the league regular season, finishing with a 19-11 mark and good for first place in the Western Division. For the second straight year they lost in the championship round to the Fort Wayne Zollner Pistons, this time in five games. It was their third defeat in five years in the NBL championship series. This marked the first time since 1939, the first year of the tournament, that Sheboygan was not entered. The Red Skins often did not fare well in the tournament, making it to the semifinal round only once in 1939. Once they lost in the first round; the other four times they bowed out in the quarterfinals. Sheboygan would return in 1946 and 1947, only to lose in the quarterfinals both years. They would not participate in the tournament's final year, 1948. Although the National Basketball League was often heavily represented in the tournament each year, the teams generally did not do as well as one might have expected. In the six prior tournaments an NBL team won it twice: Oshkosh (1942) and Fort Wayne (1944).

One of the NBL teams in the field was the Cleveland Allmen Transfers, who finished the league season at 13-17, good for second place in the Eastern Division behind Fort Wayne. Cleveland was led by Mel Riebe; "unorthodox, heavy to the point of appearing out of shape and possessed of a galloping blood pressure, [he ranked] as one of the greatest shots in the game."[54] For the second consecutive year Riebe finished as the league's top scorer, tallying 607 points in thirty games for a 20.3 average. This bested runner-up Bobby McDermott's 20.2 points per game average. Much like McDermott, Riebe did not attend college, and after finishing high school, he played amateur ball in the Cleveland area before being discovered by the Cleveland Chase Brass team. Two years later he had become one of the game's best scorers. Dick Triptow, who played against Riebe in his first year in the NBL, remembered well how great a shooter Riebe was: "I don't believe Mel was ever given the credit due him for being such a great shot. He was the only player I can remember that banked everything off the backboard. He had an uncanny knack of throwing the ball up there with a one-handed push shot and his percentage off the board was amazing."[55]

Facing Cleveland in the first round was the Midland (Michigan) Dow Chemicals, one the nation's top amateur teams. The Dow Chemicals were no stranger to the tournament; "two years ago the Dow team [had] met Phillips 66 in a preliminary to the College All Star game at the Stadium. Officials of the Dow Chemical Company, sponsors of the nationally known amateur five, were so impressed with the Herald-American's cage extravaganza that they decided to send their team after the world title and the feature assignment in the 1945 All Star program."[56] Another factor in their decision to accept an invitation was "lack of outstanding amateur competition [which] also prompted the Dow officials to enter competition with the great pro lineups."[57] The Dow Chemicals were the only amateur team in the tournament, and "Dow officials . . . instructed Herald-American tournament officials to draw up a check in the amount of their minimum guarantee to the order of the Red Cross chapter at Midland, Mich. And any prize money won [would] be given to the Red Cross, too."[58] Excited to be playing in its first tournament, the team became the first to arrive and spent a few days practicing at the Town Club gymnasium, while working out three new college players, Ray Patterson, Bill Johnson, and Del Loranger, who would be joining them for the start of the tournament. The added practice and influx of new players paid immediate dividends as Dow claimed the first upset of the tournament by defeating Cleveland, 61–46. The newcomers earned their spot on the team immediately as "Ray Patterson of Wisconsin and Del Loranger of Western Michigan, ran Cleveland into the boards [that] night. Mel Riebe, Cleveland's sensational scorer, did heroic work for his losing team and totaled 24 points despite the very fine guarding by Loranger."[59] Midland's win earned it another game.

Next up for the Dow Chemicals were the Dayton Acmes. That year marked the fourth time and third consecutive year that a team from Dayton, Ohio, entered the competition. In 1940 the Dayton Sucher Wonders lost in the first round to the New York Rens. In 1943 the Dayton Dive Bombers became one of the tournament's surprises as they finished fourth, defeating the Chicago Ramblers and the Harlem Globetrotters before bowing to the Washington Bears and the Fort Wayne Zollner Pistons. A year later the Dayton Aviators advanced to the quarterfinal round before losing to the eventual champion, Fort Wayne. Comprised of Bob Colburn and Herb Brown, both former Ohio State players, and Rex Gardecki, a veteran player from the East Coast, the Acmes set their sights on the Long Island Grumman Hellcats.

For the first time since 1942, Long Island Grumman fielded a team. On December 1, 1944, the *Long Island Daily Press* announced that Grumman was supporting a new team: "The Hellcats will be mainly on the road this year and should be one of the greatest attractions in the pro cage ranks. During the two years that the Grumman club functioned, it won a total of 41 games out of 48 played against the best outfits in the country. Without exception, it should be the strongest independent outfit in this area."[60] Named the Hellcats, as opposed to the Flyers in 1942, it was the only integrated team in the tournament in 1945. The Hellcats featured former Rens Johnny Isaacs, Dolly King, and Pop Gates. Harry Wilson noted, "King is one of three famous Negro cagers with the Grumman club. 'Pop' Gates and Johnny Isaacs, both former members of the New York Rens, also help make planes at the Long Island war plant, and hope to aid in bringing the world's cage title to their country."[61] Other stars included Nat Frankel from New York University, Ossie Schectman of Long Island University, and George Glamack from the University of North Carolina. What was purported to be one of the more intriguing first-round games instead turned into a laugher as Dayton easily defeated Long Island, 43–27. William McNeil (actually Bruce Hale using an assumed name) paced Dayton with fourteen points. Unfortunately, Gates, Isaacs, and King only managed five points between the three of them. The one interesting side note was that Dolly King became the first black head coach of an integrated team in the tournament. Unfortunately, this accomplishment was not recognized by any of the major publications and media outlets covering the team or the tournament. Instead, it reflected more on the World Professional Basketball Tournament and its inclusion of all-black and integrated squads throughout its ten-year run.

The two surprise teams in the first round, the Dow Chemicals and Dayton, squared off against each other in the quarterfinal round. Dayton's defense in the first round limited Long Island to only twenty-seven points. In that game the Hellcats were held to ten field goals, and no player scored more than six points. Dayton's defense was sharp again at the outset as the Acmes "checked Dow Chemicals so well in the first half . . . that the strong amateur team from Midland, Mich., counted only 13 points and trailed at the intermission, 23–13."[62] The second half witnessed a different story as the Dow Chemicals started chipping away and evened up the game at 38–38 early in the final period. Riding the momentum and their own good play, the Dow Chemicals led 45–41 but saw their lead shrink to a slim 46–45. As described the following day in the *Chicago Herald American*,

> John Mahnken took over, then. Dribbling in close, he canned a push shot. Almost immediately Patterson potted one for Dows, but the inevitable Mr. McNeil came through with his 10th basket. By this time, of course, the crowd was wild with excitement but there was more to come. Danny Smick rebounded a long shot and put Dows ahead once more. That looked like the game but with 13 seconds to go Mahnken was hacked in the act of shooting. He went to the line with a record of three misses in five previous attempts but he slipped the tying and winning points through on a pair of clean shots. With three seconds to play, Chris Hansen added another point to the Dayton lead.[63]

Dayton held on for a 52–50 victory.

Dayton was not the tournament's only upstart team. The tournament's hometown Chicago American Gears made their first appearance in the *Herald American*–sponsored event. With excess revenue from its wartime production, the Chicago American Gears transitioned from the amateur to the professional ranks and joined the National Basketball League. They finished the regular season with a 14-16 record, second to Sheboygan in the Western Division. The *Herald-American* announced the Gears as the tournament's first team on February 18, 1945. Bolstering the team's credentials, writer Keith Brehm noted that the Gears had twice defeated eventual league champion Fort Wayne in the regular season, 52–50 and 57–55. Led by Stan Patrick, Dick Triptow, and Bill McDonald, the Gears caused havoc for many teams. At the forefront was Triptow, who "possessed of terrific speed and limitless energy, Triptow puts a collegiate spirit into the Gears' play. One of the league's better scorers, Triptow's greatest value to the Chicago team has been as a floor man, rebound specialist and feeder for the high scoring Patrick."[64] Patrick averaged 16.4 points, third in the league, while Triptow contributed 10 points per contest. Having the Gears in the field was a boon for the tournament organizers as reflected in Keith Brehm's article in the *Chicago Herald American*: "Entrance of the Gears into the tournament gives the Chicago fans a favorite. All 14 of the teams each year are great, but there is nothing like having a home team to rank among the best of them all."[65]

Facing the Gears in the first round was the Hartford (CT) Nutmegs. This was the first time in the history of the tournament that a team from Connecticut entered the field. A second team, the Bridgeport Newfield Steelers, would play in 1948, the tournament's last year, and encounter the same fate as their fellow Connecticut team in 1945: a first-round exit. The Nutmegs sported a 10-2 record, including two victories over the Rens. Don Kotter, a Long Island University product, anchored the Nutmegs' front line. Keith Brehm enumerated his virtues: "Kotter is one of the 'goal tenders' whose play brought about the college basketball rule pertaining to the downward flight of the ball. He is a great competitor and can absorb a lot of punishment under the boards. He leads the Nutmegs in scoring this season with 187 points in 12 games."[66] John Wright was also a key component on the team.

The first contest to open the tournament saw a tightly played affair for much of the game. "Hartford, led by John (Doc) Wright, matched the Gears point for point throughout the first half last night. Wright was tough under the baskets and made most of his nine field goals on rebound shots and driving pot shots. Four free throws added to his excellent shooting from the floor gave him a total of 22 points."[67] The Gears trailed at the half, 22–21, but slowly the tide turned as the Gears led 39–34 entering the final frame. The Gears kept the pressure on in the final period and emerged with a 58–47 win. Prior to the tournament, the Gears had signed George Ratkovicz, Kleggie Hermsen, and Price Brookfield. All three played key roles in the first-round win; according to fellow Gear, Dick Triptow, "The addition of Ratkovicz, Hermsen, and Brookfield to our roster in preparation for the first game of the Pro Tournament was a big factor in enabling us to defeat the Hartford Nutmegs 58–47. In a loosely played game, all 12 Gears played and contributed to the win."[68] Brookfield and Hermsen each scored seven points in the victory.

Next up for the Gears: Chicago's other team, the Harlem Globetrotters.

The Globetrotters entered the tournament as it did each year with high hopes and the express goal of winning the title. In the four years since their win in 1940, the Globetrotters had made it to the semifinals once and lost three times in the quarterfinals. Abe Saperstein wondered if this year would be different. Prior to the tournament Saperstein touted Babe Pressley, his best player: "If we had five Pressleys no team in America could ever beat us."[69] Despite playing with only six players, the Globetrotters hung tough and controlled much of the game. "Playing without Stan Patrick, who injured his arm Monday night, the Gear cause looked like a hopeless one when the Trotters took a 31–24 lead at the half and went into the final quarter out in front by 38–33."[70] The last period began with a quick comeback by the Gears, who cut the lead to one before the Globetrotters answered and regained their lead, 48–42. With less than four minutes to play, the lead was 49–45. Perhaps playing with only six players finally caught up with them or the Gears found another level of play inside them, but over the remaining four minutes, the Gears went on an 11–1 run to close out the game and keep their first-year hopes alive. Keith Brehm captured the excitement the following day in the newspaper:

> Triptow came through with a spectacular push shot off a fast break to make the count 49–47 with three minutes remaining. Then Price Brookfield took over. Awarded two free throws he canned the second after muffing the first. Seconds later he let fly a heaping push shot from the corner to put the Gears in front, 50–49. The crowd roared as the Gears sought to control the ball and ride out the remaining time. In a desperate effort to gain possession, the Globe Trotters jammed Bill McDonald to the floor. McDonald calmly slipped in his free throw to increase the Chicago lead. Two minutes remained, however. A free throw at the one minute mark was declined. Then out of a weaving group of players Brookfield broke loose for a clean lay-up shot at 30 seconds to go. That was all except for some neat ball handling by the Gears to kill off the last half minute.[71]

As Triptow recalled, "Price Brookfield, filling in for the injured Stan Patrick, had 12 points. Our other two acquisitions, Hermsen and Ratkovicz, combined for 18 points, while I added 13."[72] The Gears won, 53–49. Their sensational finish pushed them into the semifinals against upstart Dayton. Pressley had not played for the Globetrotters in that decisive game, and Saperstein could only wonder what might have been if he had.

The Gears and the Acmes, the surprises of the tournament, were two "teams which ha[d] captured the hearts of the big crowds."[73] "Tonight's second game brings together two teams whose fans still are trying to get back their breath," the *Chicago Herald American* declared. "Dayton twice has come from behind to win its way to the semifinal, and Wednesday night it lost and won the game back again in the last 15 seconds. Johnny Mahnken's two free throws decided the contest after a bad pass had permitted Midland Dows to take a one-point lead."[74] As for the Gears, the recent additions of Kleggie Hermsen and Price Brookfield before the tournament proved a key addition. "It was Brookfield who paved the way for the sensation win Wednesday night over the highly favored Harlem Globe Trotters. With three minutes remaining he made a free throw and two baskets to register all the points that turned what looked like sure defeat into a 53–49 win."[75]

With two teams riding the emotional wave of recent come-from-behind victories, the game figured to be a close and exciting affair. That was certainly the case in the first half as the Acmes held a slim 15–14 margin at the end of the first period, and a 33–24 lead at intermission. In the second half the wheels fell off for the Gears. The Acmes outscored them 21–9 to open a 54–33 lead. "The final period of play saw the Acmes pouring in shot after shot as their record total mounted."[76] The Acmes scored eighty points and established a few scoring records for the tournament. As the *Chicago Herald American* noted, "Dayton's 80 points set a new single game record for teams, bettering the 68 made by Fort Wayne. Their 33 field goals bettered the mark of 30 scored by the Rens against the Indianapolis Oilers in the first round of this tournament. The combined total of 131 points overshadowed the 126 made in the Rens-Indianapolis game."[77] On an individual level William McNeil had tallied sixty-two points for the first three games of the tournament and stood a chance of overtaking Chuck Chuckovits's tournament record set in 1941. For a team that won its first two games largely on the strength of its defense, it had now won because of its offense. Entering the finals the Acmes were firing on all cylinders.

Having survived their side of the bracket, Dayton readied to face the defending champions, the Fort Wayne Zollner Pistons. The Fort Wayne side of the bracket opened with the perennial fan favorite New York Rens facing the Indianapolis Oilers. Despite a tough semifinal loss the previous year to eventual champion Fort Wayne, the Rens were intent on making a deep run. Always a proponent of his team's chances, owner and coach Bob Douglas stated,

You know we won the first official world cage championship in the Herald-American's meet in Chicago in 1939 and the College All Star game was not inaugurated until 1940. We missed the opportunity of opposing an All-Star collegiate group in the Classic presented annually by the Herald-American and I have my heart set on winning this year's meet. We are working hard and intend to do it this year. My veterans 'Puggy' Bell, Zack Clayton and Hank DeZonie are having their most brilliant season. Benny Garrett and Eddie Wright, a couple of newcomers from the ranks of Eastern schools, have rounded out a finely balanced scoring quintet. What really makes me enthusiastic is that "Wee" Willie Smith, for years the outstanding center of the Rens, will be using his six-foot, seven-inch height to relieve DeZonie at the pivot spot. DeZonie measures only one-half inch less than Smith. Bell and Clayton by the way have been in every one of these tournaments. We haven't been out of the final round from the start back in 1939 and we don't intend to break that record this year.[78]

The Rens were pitted against the Indianapolis Oilers. The city of Indianapolis had become a fixture in the tournament in recent years. The Indianapolis Kautskys represented the city in 1941 and 1942, while the Indianapolis Pure Oils competed in 1943 and 1944. As the organizers noted prior to the start of the tournament, teams in the same city would need to compete against each other, and the winner would earn the right to advance to the tournament. This was the case with Indianapolis, as the city would "have a squad culled from the player lists of both Pure Oils and the Stars."[79] The team would play as the Oilers. Despite an aggregation of the best players from two teams, the Oilers simply could not keep pace with the Rens. The Rens started strong and built a 36–27 lead at halftime. Throughout the second half the Oilers made runs and were able to cut the lead to five points on several occasions but did not have enough firepower to make one final run. The 67–59

FIG. 35. Of all the players for the New York Renaissance, Clarence "Puggy" Bell was one of the most consistent. He was also one of the longest tenured players. Courtesy of Bill Himmelman.

score garnered the most attention as "the Rens and Indianapolis broke three single games scoring records. The Rens had high winning total with 67 points: Indianapolis high losing total with 59. The combined total of 126 points also was a record. Previous high total was 104 points set originally by the Globe Trotters and [Northern] Indiana Steelers in 1942."[80] As noted the increase in scoring was another outcome of basketball during World War II.

The Rens victory gave them little time to prepare for their next opponent, the Pittsburgh Raiders. The Raiders had joined the NBL for the first time and finished with a dismal 7-23 record, last in the Eastern Division. This was the second year that the city of Pittsburgh fielded a team in the tournament. In 1944 the Pittsburgh Corbetts lost in the first round, 41–40, to the Harlem Globetrotters. Their opponent this year was the Newark (NY) C-O Twos. The team was a fire equipment company and brought with them a solid roster of eastern stars such as Ed Sadowski, Kevin Connors, Bob Tough, Mike Bloom, Matt Goukas, Ace Abbott, and Sonny Hertzberg, all veterans of the tournament with other squads. John "Honey" Russell, the team's coach and a great player in the 1920s and 1930s, felt strongly about his team, stating, "Fans will recognize some of their favorites on our roster. I feel that I have a good team, a team which may bring the title back to the East."[81] Although Newark sported an all-star lineup of eastern stars, the no-name Raiders defeated Newark, 53–50. The *Chicago Herald American* summed it up the following day: "Actually Newark had about the most potent lineup in the tournament but suffered from lack of co-ordination. Such stars as Mike Bloom, Kevin Connors, Jack Garfinkel, Ace Abbott, and Bob Tough contributed fine individual performances but their play revealed lack of practice as a unit."[82]

Pittsburgh's impressive win placed the team in the next round versus the New York Rens. Pittsburgh's no-name team fought gallantly but succumbed to a team with more talent. The Rens win pitted them against the Zollner Pistons. After a first-round bye Fort Wayne faced NBL rival Oshkosh, which had beat Detroit in the opening round. Detroit had high hopes as supported by its head coach, Cincy Sachs: "I feel that we have a good team this year, one which could get hot and bring another world title to Detroit. In Kautz and McCall we have extra punch and hope to make it tough for any club we meet."[83] Despite his optimism the Detroit Mansfields lost to Oshkosh. Facing a team they had handled well in the NBL regular season, Fort Wayne showed why it was the best

FIG. 36. Ed Sadowski was a solid player in the National Basketball League and American Basketball League during the 1940s. Courtesy of Bill Himmelman.

team. "In the opening game Fort Wayne demonstrated why it is likely to become the first team in the history of the world tournament to retain its title."[84] The team led 37–21 at the half as "Fort Wayne connected on 13 of 29 shots attempted from the floor and clicked 11 out of 14 free those two periods."[85] Ben Tenny, writing in the *Fort Wayne News-Sentinel* the following day, outlined the dominance of the Pistons in defeating their league rival. "A brilliant first half carried the Pistons to what was an easier win over the strengthened and huge Oshkosh five than the final score indicates. Playing carefully and using plays against what they know was an Oshkosh weakness, defense, the Pistons literally took the Wisconsin five apart in the first half. It was big Jerry Bush, playing his best game of the year, who spearheaded this attack. Bush not only rebounded sensationally and did a nice defensive job, but he canned six out of nine shots, five in the first half, to help turn what loomed as a tough game into a runaway for the Pistons."[86]

Despite advancing to the semifinals for the second consecutive year against Fort Wayne, the Rens were no match for the Zollner Pistons. After jumping out to a quick 4–1 lead, the Rens felt the overwhelming force of the Zollner Pistons, who "unleashed their scoring thunder and ran 15 straight points to take a 16–4 lead. In this offensive splash Fort Wayne worked men free for three dribble in shots in which the shooters were unmolested."[87] Toward the end of the third period, the Rens found themselves down by two points, but the fourth period witnessed another onslaught by Fort Wayne. "Then Fort Wayne rolled again. Bud Jeannette and John Pelkington scored seven points apiece as the Zollners poured it on, and finally reached what was then a team scoring record for one tournament game—68 points."[88] Fort Wayne was led by McDermott with eighteen points, Jeannette with fourteen, and Pelkington with eleven.

The finals pitted the Fort Wayne Zollner Pistons, seeking to become consecutive championship winners, and the Dayton Acmes, the tournament's surprise team. Both teams featured high-octane offenses in the semifinals with Fort Wayne scoring sixty-eight points and Dayton tallying eighty. Would the finals be a high-scoring affair? From the outset Fort Wayne could not be denied "as a crowd of 15,119 sat in awe at the Chicago Stadium," as the Pistons "demonstrated their greatness once more by becoming the first team in cage history to win the world's championship for the second consecutive year. Victim of Fort Wayne's perfect exhibition of how the game should be played was a scrappy

FIG. 37. John Pelkington won the World Professional Basketball Tournament with Detroit and Fort Wayne during a solid professional career in the 1940s. Courtesy of Bill Himmelman.

Dayton O., quintet which lost, 78 to 52. The Ohioans never gave up, but every time it looked as though they had a chance, either Bobby McDermott or Bud Jeannette would come through—and spoil whatever hopes had begun to sprout."[89] Jeannette, who led the Pistons with eighteen points, was named the tournament's MVP, the third consecutive year that a Fort Wayne player earned that distinction. All five Fort Wayne

FIG. 38. The 1944–45 Fort Wayne Zollner Pistons were a deep team and featured Bobby McDermott and Buddy Jeannette, two future members of the Naismith Memorial Basketball Hall of Fame. Courtesy of Bill Himmelman.

starters earned either first or second all-tournament teams with Jeanette and McDermott named to the first team, and Reiser, Pelkington, and Bush on the second team. The tournament set a new attendance record as more than fifty-five thousand fans saw all the games. Pistons' beat writer Ben Tenny summed it up the best, when he wrote his recap of the finals: "The Pistons waded through Oshkosh, the New York Rens and Dayton's Acmes without too much trouble. None of the three meet foes was close at the finish and the Pistons were pulled up and coasting at the finish of all three of their tilts."[90]

After winning their second straight World Professional Basketball Tournament, the Pistons returned to Fort Wayne for a citywide celebration. As manager Carl Bennett recalled, "When we got home from the Chicago World Tournament, the mayor proclaimed 'Zollner Piston Day.' There was a big city celebration where they introduced the players to the fans, and that sort of thing. They were heroes. Bob McDermott was as big in Fort Wayne in his day as Michael Jordan is today. It was that kind of an atmosphere and that kind of a time for sports in the city. It was a special way of life in Fort Wayne."[91] Their win had stamped them as professional basketball's best team and certainly the best all-around team since the Philadelphia SPHAS in the 1930s. As author John Schleppi states, "The Ft. Wayne team was at an advantage, with their team nearly intact and the monetary resources to sign supporting players when needed, and they were a fine advertisement for professional basketball."[92] A dominant team in the war years, the Pistons would face a new challenge as the war came to a close.

5

LOOKING TOWARD THE
FUTURE, 1945–1946

Navy basketball helped me by giving me the experience of going against top athletes from all over the country, boosting my confidence, and convincing me that I could be a pro player. —RED HOLZMAN

On May 8, 1945, President Harry Truman walked into the Radio Room at the White House and announced to the nation that Germany had surrendered. A few months later he again addressed the nation when he proclaimed Japan's surrender by stating, "The thoughts and hopes of all America—indeed of all the civilized world—are centered tonight on the battleship Missouri. There on that small piece of American soil anchored in Tokyo Harbor the Japanese have just officially laid down their arms. They have signed terms of unconditional surrender."[1] War was officially over as thousands of Americans celebrated in the streets. The long, tough daily grind of sacrifice over the past five years—rationing and black outs—was officially over. Thousands of servicemen were returning daily and looking to reestablish their lives, the ones they had put on hold to serve their country. In sports, including basketball, these returning men wanted to resume their once-promising professional careers. The increase of potential players and a desire by the public to enjoy the new peacetime led professional sports leagues and teams to entertain high hopes for the upcoming season. An economic boom was under way, and sports were seeking to become one of the beneficiaries.

The National Basketball League had operated a lean business during the war years. The 1943–44 campaign was by far the toughest; only four teams completed that season. League officials felt encouraged by the political landscape and what appeared to be an eventual Allied victory when they decided to expand to six teams in 1944–45. It marked the largest number of teams since 1941–42. Now with the war over, the NBL decided to continue the expansion process and added an additional two teams to increase the total to eight. Fort Wayne, Cleveland, Sheboygan, Oshkosh, and Chicago all rejoined. The Pittsburgh franchise, which had finished the year before with a dismal 7-23 record, was transferred to Youngstown, Ohio. It was renamed the Youngstown Bears because a local Youngstown syndicate operated the franchise that season. Fort Wayne sold the contract of Paul Birch to Youngstown, who quickly assumed head coaching duties for the Bears. The Indianapolis Kautskys rejoined the league after a three-year hiatus. Finally, the Rochester Royals became the eighth franchise. With two new teams and one transferred franchise, the league reorganized itself. The Eastern Division consisted of Fort Wayne, Rochester, Youngstown, and Cleveland. The Western Division was Sheboygan, Oshkosh, Chicago, and Indianapolis. The league schedule was thirty-four games. The new NBL commissioner was Ward "Piggy" Lambert, the former coach at Purdue University and later a member of the Naismith Memorial Basketball Hall of Fame. For the first time in many seasons, the league sported a good distribution of franchises from Rochester, New York, all the way to Chicago, Illinois. It was becoming a bit more national in scope.

With a new season on the horizon, many of the teams boasted high hopes. Fort Wayne still figured to be the class of the league. The team had captured the previous two league titles, and its depth and balance separated it from its competition. As the team began preseason practice, the general consensus was that the Zollner Pistons were the team to beat yet again. The team was now coached by Bobby McDermott. Fort Wayne signed Bob Kinney, a former player at Rice University, to bolster an already strong lineup that featured Buddy Jeannette, Jerry Bush, Chick Reiser, Bobby McDermott, John Pelkington, Charlie Shipp, and Ed Sadowski. If that was not enough, the Pistons added players throughout the year to create one of the deepest teams ever in professional basketball. Early in the season Herm Schaefer, just out of the service, joined the team. In February, as the team prepared for the stretch run and the league playoffs, Bob Tough was signed away from the American Basketball League. And in March, on the eve of the World Professional Basketball Tournament, veteran Curly Armstrong was discharged and hoped to be part of another tournament title in Chicago. Fort Wayne figured to be a tough out. Despite its impressive lineup and past success, however, not everyone felt that the Zollner Pistons were unbeatable. As one rival city declared, "With this great array of talent, Fort Wayne is going to be hard to beat but all indications are that the Zollners are not going to have any cake walk this season."[2]

It was the addition of the Rochester Royals, though, that would have the biggest impact on the game. More than seventy-five years later, the Rochester Royals are still a fixture in professional basketball, now known as the Sacramento Kings of the NBA. Basketball had been played in Rochester on the professional, semiprofessional, and independent levels for several decades prior to the Royals. The man who became most associated with basketball in Rochester was Les Harrison. A child of Jewish immigrants, Harrison was born in 1904 and grew up in Rochester. He naturally gravitated toward basketball, the sport of choice for Jewish immigrants. By the 1920s he had found his way to the Rochester Ebers, an amateur and semiprofessional team in Rochester. The Ebers played from 1923–24 to 1935–36. In 1936 they became the Seagrams, and the Rochester Seagrams began playing professional ball starting in 1936–37. During World War II the newspaper endorsed a dry policy, and the Seagrams reverted back to the Ebers. Despite the name changes, the team continued to be operated by Les Harrison. In 1943–44 they were known as the Rochester Pros. Home games were played in St. Stanislaus Hall, the Armory, and Columbus Club Court. The Seagrams participated in the 1940 and 1941 World Professional Basketball Tournament, losing both times in the first round. In 1944 they traveled to Chicago and played as the Rochester Wings. During this time some of the best professional players were on the Rochester roster, which later became the Rochester Royals. Over time the Ebers, the Seagrams, and the Wings morphed into the Royals, and many of the Royals players had their start playing on one of these earlier squads. Among these players were Al Cervi, John Pelkington, Ed Sadowski, Buddy Jeannette, Sammy Kaplan, Gene Englund, and Sam Mink. Harrison had developed a strong team based in Central New York.

Seeking to capitalize on the popularity of the game in Rochester during the war years, Harrison, in conjunction with the leading newspaper in town, the *Rochester Democrat and Chronicle*, sponsored a basketball tournament on par with the ones in Cleveland, Buffalo, and Worcester. The Democrat and Chronicle Athletic Association tournament was held from 1941 to 1943. In its final year the proceeds benefited the local Red Cross chapter. The Rochester Seagrams played in 1941 and 1942, and the Rochester Ebers participated in 1943. The Seagrams captured the title in 1942. With the war over, Harrison set his sights on entering his franchise into the National Basketball League. As he later recalled, "In those days, the Rochester newspapers were dry and did not take liquor advertising. They said we're only going to let you use the name one year and then you have to be Ebers. So we used Seagram-Ebers for one year and then we dropped Seagrams and became Ebers. Eber Bros. and Seagram didn't want to go big-time and my brother and I mortgaged everything we had or could lay out hands on and we got a franchise in the National Basketball League, the only big league at the time. I think it cost us $25,000."[3]

FIG. 39. Les Harrison built the Rochester Royals into a top team in the National Basketball League, the Basketball Association of America, and the National Basketball Association. Courtesy of Bill Himmelman.

With a franchise in hand Harrison quickly set about assembling a strong squad. Like the other teams the Royals would benefit from the returning servicemen. "With star cage players being released from the service every day, all of the league clubs [would] be stronger than a year ago."[4] Harrison was confident that he would be able to assemble a competitive squad and land some of these players. Early in the season he addressed the local Rochester media: "I have submitted contracts to four outstanding ball players who expect to receive their discharge on or before Jan. 1. When I get these players—all of them former college All-Americans—we'll have a better all-around club than Fort Wayne. I've got their word that they'll play for me and I'm not going to let anyone beat me to the punch."[5] By early 1946 Harrison was in the process of developing a squad capable of challenging Fort Wayne for league honors. Included were such college stars as George Glamack, the Blind Bomber from the University of North Carolina; Bob Davies from Seton Hall University; John Mahnken from Georgetown; Red Holzman from City College of New York (CCNY); and Al Cervi. Coming off the bench were Otto Graham, later a great football star with the Cleveland Browns; Fuzzy Levane; and Chuck Connors, who would become the Rifleman on television. As Fuzzy Levane recalled, "I got a call from Les offering me $50 for practice and $110 to play against Sheboygan. Now I was from Brooklyn, and I had never heard of Sheboygan. I played seven or eight games at the end of the 1944–45 season and did very well."[6] Levane eventually became a regular for Harrison's squad. "We were millionaires! I was making five grand a year!" he recounted. "Before that I didn't know that you could get paid for what we were doing. I got married in 1945 and bought a house in Rochester and we stayed there until 1949."[7]

In a late season program for a home game versus the Indianapolis Kautskys, the Rochester Royals lineup read like an all-star roster. Indeed, Harrison had assembled a squad every bit as good as Fort Wayne. The program read

Otto Graham

No. 17; 6'; 190 lbs.; forward; Northwestern University 3 years; All-American 1943; College All-Stars 1943; Received most valuable player award 1943, College All-Stars-Washington Bears at Chicago.

William (Red) Holzman

5'11"; C.C.N.Y.; Capt. 1942; forward; 175 lbs.; 1942–1943 All-Madison Square Garden Team; 1942–1943 All-Metropolitan Team; 1944 Norfolk Naval Training Station Team; voted the most outstanding service team in the country.

Del Rice

No. 14; 6'2"; 190 lbs.; forward; Portsmouth, Ohio; member of Rochester Professional Basketball Team for 3 years; regular catcher for St. Louis Cardinals baseball team 1945.

Bernard Voorheis

No. 12; 5'9"; 165lbs.; forward; Cornell University.

Al Cervi

No. 15; 5'11"; 188 lbs.; forward; Rochester Professional Basketball Team 6 years; rated one of the greatest sandlot basketball players ever to don a uniform.

George Glamack

No. 20; 6'5"; 218 lbs.; center; North Carolina University 3 years; All-American 1940–41; College All-Stars 1941; Holder of Helms Foundation award for most outstanding collegiate basketball player 1941.

John Mahnken

No. 19; 6'8"; 220 lbs.; Georgetown University, 2 years; All-American 1943; College All-Stars 1943; was selected center on the All-World Professional Basketball Team at Chicago in March, 1945.

Al Negratti

No. 18; 6'3"; 205 lbs.; guard, Seton Hall College 4 years.

Thomas Rich

No. 11; 6'3"; 190 lbs.; Cornell University 3 years; Captain of Cornell University 2 years; Rochester Professional Basketball Team 7 years; selected All-Eastern forward 1937 and 1938.

Andrew (Fuzzy) Levane

6'3"; 190 lbs.; guard; St. John's University 3 years; voted the most valuable player in Madison Square Garden for 2 consecutive years; All-American Basketball Team member; member of All-Metropolitan Basketball Team.

Robert Davies

6'2"; 185 lbs.; guard; Seton Hall All-American; 1942 was selected as the most valuable college All-Star player, game against Oshkosh All-Stars at Chicago.

Jack "Dutch" Garfinkel

5'11"; 185 lbs.; guard; Captain St. John's University; All Metropolitan Team 1941–42; All-American.[8]

Harrison built his team around guards and forwards, and in 1945–46 he had three of the best in Al Cervi, Bob Davies, and Red Holzman. Al Cervi was arguably the best player in Royals history. As George Beahon, columnist for the *Rochester Democrat and Chronicle*, described him, "Pound for pound best offensive and defensive player, as a combination, to play for the Royals."[9] Cervi started playing professional basketball straight out of high school. He played for the Buffalo Bisons of the NBL and also the Rochester Eber Seagrams in 1937–38. A year later he was voted MVP of the Bisons team. Ralph Hubbell, the broadcaster for Bisons' games, noted, "He was the fastest man going to the basket with the basketball."[10] Like many of his contemporaries, Cervi lost time from his career while serving in World War II. In 1940–41 he joined the U.S Army Air Force and a year later was stationed in Niagara Falls. He was eventually transferred to Texas. Upon his discharge he reunited with Harrison and joined the Royals. As a player he was fierce and competitive, and he made an impression on everyone who saw him play. Fuzzy Levane, a teammate of Cervi, remembered the type of player Cervi was. "He was dynamite. He was very strong and could drive. There was no jump shot then, only a set shot, but he was strong and very competitive. He had an up-and-under shot, a layup. He'd be hit going in but he'd make the shot. He was very tough defensively; he used to shake up Bobby McDermott, who was the best set shooter with the smoothest shot and was the greatest offensive player of that era."[11] Les Harrison, his coach, recalled, "I named him 'digger' because he was one of the best competitors I ever saw. He showed by example. There was nothing too hard for Al to handle. I knew he would instill a positive, fighting spirit into the team. He was a great leader. That's why I named him my captain."[12] Bob Davies, one of his teammates, offered this recollection: "I didn't believe he was real the first time I saw him. I had never heard of him. Nobody ever showed his competitiveness and zeal on the floor like Al did. It was just an attitude that was so visible all the time. When I played with Al I played with a super star."[13]

Joining Cervi was Bob Davies, who would become one of the game's best guards, an innovator before the likes of Bob Cousy. Born in 1920 in Harrisburg, Pennsylvania, Davies, the "Harrisburg Houdini," excelled at basketball at John Harris High School, where he was a three-time letter winner, All Conference (1937), and the second leading scorer in Central Pennsylvania (1937). He enrolled at Franklin & Marshall for one year, then left and matriculated at Seton Hall University. As a ball player he found himself while at Seton Hall. He helped lead the team to forty-three consecutive victories, was a two-time All-American (1940 and 1941), scored 661 points in his college career, and was the MVP

FIG. 40. A hard-nosed player, Al Cervi was the heart and soul of the Rochester Royals, who won the 1945–46 National Basketball League championship. Courtesy of Bill Himmelman.

of the 1942 College All-Star Game held in Chicago and sponsored by the *Chicago Herald American*. During his time with the Pirates, the team compiled a 55-5 record, including an undefeated season, 19-0, as a sophomore. During World War II he served in the navy and spent time playing at Great Lakes Naval Training Station under the guidance of coach Tony Hinkle. He was also stationed in Brooklyn, New York, and the good location afforded him the opportunity to play in the American Basketball League for the Brooklyn Indians and the New York Gothams over two seasons. When the war ended, he signed with the Rochester Royals. Davies spent ten years with the Royals in the NBL, the BAA, and the NBA, where he earned many honors and became one of Rochester's most accomplished players. He is often credited with originating the behind-the-back dribble. Levane remembered playing with Davies. "Bobby Davies was a great offensive player. He was a flashy player; he would dribble, pass the ball behind his back, but defensively, he couldn't play my grandmother. We used to have to cover for him all the time. Davies always liked to go to the ball. He took chances, but could fly. All around offensive player with great fast break. He had the outside shot and could drive to the basket."[14] Like Cervi and Harrison, he eventually was elected into the Naismith Memorial Basketball Hall of Fame.

The other newcomer was William Holzman, who would forever be Red Holzman. A native New Yorker, Holzman grew up playing what would eventually be called the city game. He starred at Franklin Lane High School (later the gym was named in his honor). He began his college career at the University of Baltimore in 1938–39. After one year he transferred to City College of New York (CCNY) to play under another famed New York player, Nat Holman. During his two years at CCNY (1940–41 to 1941–42), Holman earned All-Metropolitan and All-American honors while averaging 10.9 and 12.5 points per game in his two seasons respectively. He left for the service and played three years for the Norfolk (VA) Naval Training Station. In 1942–43 he scored 305 points, and in 1943–44 he tallied 258. He joined the Rochester Royals for the 1945–46 season and averaged 10.7 points per game in thirty-four games as the team won the NBL championship. He was named to the NBL All-Star First Team in 1946. Later he became known as the coach of the two-time NBA champion New York Knicks and was inducted into the Naismith Memorial Basketball Hall of Fame as a coach. Holzman later reflected on playing basketball during his military service.

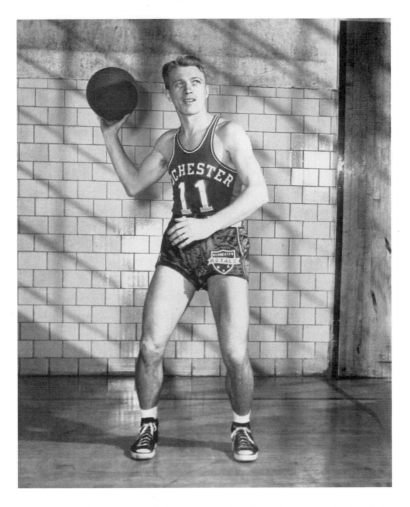

FIG. 41. A standout player with Seton Hall University, Bob Davies helped lead the Rochester Royals to the 1945–46 National Basketball League championship. Naismith Memorial Basketball Hall of Fame.

In the summer of 1942 I put on a new uniform. I enlisted in the United States Navy. My life and that of millions of others was affected by World War II. My parents weren't too happy that I had joined up, but instead of being drafted I gave myself a choice. I had heard good things about the Navy. I was stationed at Norfolk Naval Base and placed in the morale unit, which drilled and exercised troops and maintained recreational facilities. In our time off we also played basketball against other service and college teams. Those service teams had tremendous athletes. Norfolk's baseball team had Phil Rizzuto, Vince DiMaggio, Freddie Hutchinson, Pee Wee Reese, Hugh Casey. All our games took place before enthusiastic, packed houses and the style of play was very physical. When I had first arrived at Norfolk, I was a seaman first class—the only sailor playing with chief petty officers. After a while I became a chief too. Our coach, Gary Bodie, was an old chief warrant officer. He knew how to motivate. "Get your ass moving," he'd yell, "or you'll be on a ship to the Pacific tomorrow." We moved our asses. Our Norfolk team was real good. One year we won 31 of 33 games we played.[15]

After his stint in the service was complete, Holzman joined Harrison and the Royals. With his team finally intact Harrison set about making a good first impression in the National Basketball League. One of the advantages for the Royals was its home court, Edgerton Sports Arena. As one former opponent remembered,

> Three Hall of Famers, Bob Davies, Red Holzman and Al Cervi played on the Royals and were coached by Les Harrison and Eddie Malano-wicz. This arena was another difficult place to play. The exit doors at either end were no further than 10 feet from the end of the court. You might go driving in for a shot and come down and go right out the doorway into a snow bank. The visiting team had to exit the court at the half and also at the end of the game at the end court, which paralleled the stands. You did not know what you were going to get hit with as you came off the floor.[16]

The home court advantage would play a big role for Rochester later in the season.

Although it was starting to feel more national in scope, the league

FIG. 42. After his military career Red Holzman joined the Rochester Royals. He later coached the New York Knicks to two NBA championships. Courtesy of Bill Himmelman.

still had challenges related to arenas and the home courts for each franchise. These varied widely for each franchise, which impacted the finances for the teams and league but also still gave the perception of a ragtag outfit that characterized the 1930s. For Youngstown this would the first of two seasons in the NBL, and in both years the team would finish near the bottom of its division. Despite the team's poor play, the

Bears had a strong local following. As the *Chicago Herald American* wrote, "Youngstown is primarily a community quintet, and its gym with a seating capacity of more than 4,000 has been jammed to the rafters for every game—even when it looked as though the Bears weren't going to win this season."[17] The team played its games in the Youngstown South Field House. Dick Triptow, who played there as a member of the Chicago American Gears, offered this recollection: "The Youngstown Bears were coached by Paul Birch, former great with the Celtics and the Fort Wayne Zollners. The Bears had baseballer, Frank Baumholtz, former Chicago Cubs, playing backcourt for them, along with Press Maravich, father of the great 'Pistol' Pete. This was one of the four great field houses in which we played."[18] Youngstown struggled throughout the season and was led by Frankie Baumholtz and Moe Becker. The team would play one more year in the NBL before ending its big league dreams.

Youngstown was not the only team to struggle mightily that season. Cleveland experienced its fair share of adversity. Playing without two-time league scoring leader Mel Riebe, who was stationed at Great Lakes Naval Training Station, the Cleveland Allmen Transfers struggled to find any semblance of offense. Riebe played in only five regular-season games but did lead the team with a 14.4 average. Without Riebe Cleveland was led by Mike Bytzura and Tom Wukovitz. Due to its poor record the team often played before an empty house at Cleveland Auditorium, and that compounded its problems. Dick Triptow remembered playing in Cleveland as a visitor: "The Auditorium was actually that, a big hall with bleachers set up on the sides to accommodate the fans and a huge balcony circling the playing floor. You could just feel the emptiness when you were suited up and on the floor. This is the one court that did not have glass boards and maybe that was the reason Mel Riebe led the League in scoring for two years."[19] Playing before empty crowds and without their leading scorer in Riebe, Cleveland fell to a dismal 4-29 mark and last place in the Eastern Division. This would be its last year in the NBL.

The Eastern Division quickly became a two-team race between Fort Wayne and Rochester. Both teams started strong out of the gate. Fort Wayne won fourteen of its first sixteen games, while Rochester won eleven of its first twelve. Fort Wayne traveled to Toronto to play the Rochester Royals in the first professional basketball game in Canada. The date was January 16, 1946, and the game was held in Maple Leaf Gardens, where twelve thousand fans saw the game. As Carl Bennett, Fort Wayne's manager, recalled years later, "Most of them had never seen professional basketball before. They were all hockey fans. I'm not sure they knew exactly what they were watching. We'd make some spectacular plays, and they'd just sit there on their hands or clap politely. I've never heard 12,000 fans be so quiet before."[20] The Pistons won 60–53. For the remainder of the regular season, the race for first place was a tale of two stories. Fort Wayne was plagued by inconsistency. In some games the team flashed its trademark brilliance, using its depth and experience to ward off any challenges from upstart teams. In other games, the Pistons looked lethargic and lacked the necessary aggressiveness, as if they had trouble getting motivated for each game. Rochester, meanwhile, was searching for its identity. The team did not have its full complement of players. Al Cervi missed two weeks with a back injury. Harrison, seeking to improve his team's inside presence, signed six-foot-five Bob Fitzgerald in February shortly after Fitzgerald was discharged from the military. Fitzgerald had played for Harrison the previous season and quickly signed on for the remainder of this one. John Mahnken missed time waiting to be formally discharged. Throughout this continual flux of roster uncertainty, Harrison mixed and matched his lineup, looking for the best combination for starters and reserves. For Rochester it was a team that had yet to find its groove, even though it was winning games. In the last eight regular season games, Fort Wayne went 4-4, including back-to-back losses to Rochester. Fort Wayne still won the regular season title with a two-game lead over Rochester.

As the regular season concluded, Harrison sounded optimistic about his team's chances in the oncoming playoffs.

Sure, I'm looking at the brighter side. Right now, with Bob Davies, Al Cervi and Red Holzman at their peak, I believe this team is ready for the best in the game. A lot of fans thought the club had hit the skids after we lost to Oshkosh, Sheboygan and Chicago. I'll have to admit it did look pretty dark at times, with Fuzzy (Levane) still hobbling around with an injured leg and Cervi playing with an aching back. Why, we didn't even have Mahnken (Johnny Mahnken, 6-foot 8-inch center-forward who recently was discharged from service) and Negratti [sic]. Al Negratti [sic], who played on the crack Wright Field five with Mahnken for some of those important games in the west. Believe me, if Malanowicz (Royals' coach) and I could have kept the squad together for a full season . . . well I think we could have clinched the Eastern Division pennant. We'll finish second, only a few games behind Fort Wayne, a team that has been at full strength most of the season. And don't forget, gentlemen, that same club won the world's professional basketball championship last season. We had a 4–2 margin on them in the league this year.[21]

In the Western Division the two Wisconsin teams, Sheboygan and Oshkosh, fought for the division title. For Oshkosh this was the first time in years that its roster resembled the personnel from prewar levels, as the description in the Royals' 1945–46 program indicates: "Oshkosh, perennial National League champion, before Fort Wayne came into power, is another club that promises to regain pre-war strength this season. Bob Carpenter, former Texas A. and M. All-American, and all-National League center before entering the Navy, is again back with the all-stars as is Eddie Riska, ex-Notre Dame ace who was also an all-league choice before signing up with Uncle Sam. Gene Englund, Wisconsin's all-American center and an Oshkosh star before he, too, went marching away to fight the Japs, is expecting to rejoin Oshkosh before Christmas."[22] The team was joined by two rookies who made an immediate impact: Bob Feerick from Santa Clara and Wisconsin's Fred Rehm. Sheboygan, meanwhile, had a lineup similar to its roster in past seasons. Joining Ed Dancker on the front line was Mike Novak, "an all-American at Loyola during his collegiate days, [who was] still with Sheboygan and at the peak of his career."[23] Along with Dancker and Novak, Sheboygan had largely the same team, except for longtime member Rube Lautenschlager, who would play only three games that season and none in the playoffs. The Red Skins had been a mainstay in the league but always the perennial bridesmaids. Sheboygan had won the league title in 1943 but in the two subsequent years had lost in the finals to the Fort Wayne Zollner Pistons. With a solid nucleus the Red Skins were hoping to break out of that funk and win one more title.

The second division of the Western Conference featured the Chicago American Gears and the Indianapolis Kautskys. This marked Chicago's second year in the NBL. The previous season it had finished 14-16, good for second place in the Western Division behind Sheboygan. Only two starters remained from the year before, Stan Patrick and Dick Triptow. Nick Hashu, who played on the Gears in 1945–46, recalled, "I remember Stan Patrick with good coordination and quick hands. He would go up for a shot and at the same time slap his thigh and he would the foul (in his favor). Officials could not detect this—except for Nate Messenger, and he would say, 'You can't fool me.'"[24] Patrick and Triptow formed a solid duo. New additions included Bob Neu, former University of Detroit star Bob Calihan, and George Ratkovicz. The influx of new talent helped but could not significantly improve the Gears. None of their players was in the top ten in league scoring. They were a quick, feisty group of players that lacked a true center in the middle. This became apparent when they faced Oshkosh with Cowboy Edwards and Gene Englund, and Sheboygan with Ed Dancker and Mike Novak. Chicago simply could not compete with these two teams in the middle. Those big men were fixtures of the league and professional wars for the past decade, and their experience and cunning ability to use their bodies to score, defend, and rebound became too much for the inexperienced Gears to handle. As a result the team finished 17-17 and in third place in the Western Division. Chicago did not make the playoffs. However, the team would make some noise in the upcoming World Professional Basketball Tournament.

The other team in the bottom half of the Western Division was the Indianapolis Kautskys. After a three-year hiatus the Kautskys returned, but their team was a far cry from its earlier incarnation. When we last saw the Kautskys, they had finished the 1941–42 season with a 12-11 record, in fourth place out of seven teams. The team was now coached by Nat Hickey, a former standout with the Original Celtics in the 1930s. He played in thirteen contests that season, but his play or experience could not help elevate that of his players. Part of Hickey's challenge was that his roster had little talent. His starters included Roy Hurley, Woody Norris, Ernie Andres, and Jerry Steiner, none of whom was a household name. The team played their home games at Butler Field House. Triptow, who played there as an opponent, remembered those trips from Chicago to Indianapolis: "Butler Field House was the home court for Butler University, as well as the Kautskys, who were coached by Nat Hickey-1945–1946, and Ernie Andres-1946–1947. This is where the Indiana State High School Basketball Tournament was held each year and where Tony Hinkle, the legendary coach of Butler University, fielded his Butler Bull Dogs. It was one of the NBL's better arenas, and a great place to play. Jerry Steiner, Butler's exceptional guard, who later coached the Bulldogs after his playing days were over and Bob Gerber, the fine Toledo University center, were their mainstays."[25]

Early in 1946 the Kautskys bolstered their lineup by adding a big man who would eventually earn his way into the Naismith Memorial Basketball Hall of Fame. Arnie Risen starred at Ohio State and was considered the best big man in the Big Ten Conference. However, college eligibility rules prevented Risen from finishing his college career, so he immediately turned professional. He quickly became an integral member of the team. As Frank Kautsky's son, Dan, a seventeen-year-old who helped his father at the store, remembered, "My dad offered to pay Risen $75 a game. I thought to myself, 'My, goodness. Pop must have really lost his marbles. How's he going to pay someone that kind of money?' Reserve seats were only $1.50 in those days, balcony seats were 65 cents. We just didn't charge very much. I didn't know how we were going to afford to pay Arnie and keep the rest of the team on the payroll."[26] Bob Dietz, a former Kautsky player, recalled that first game Risen played against the Fort Wayne Zollner Pistons: "Pelkington and Sadowski were about as tall as Risen, but they outweighed him by 100 pounds. By the second half, I think Arnie was running down the floor with his nose hanging about six inches above the ground. It wasn't pretty. Fort Wayne beat us, and Arnie learned quickly after that. He became a heckuva player for us."[27] In eighteen games that season, he averaged 12.2 points but could not help his team avoid the cellar as they finished 10-22. It would take another year before Indianapolis could jell as a team and make a serious run in the Western Division.

As early March rolled around, the playoff matches were set, and the Eastern Division featured Fort Wayne and newcomer Rochester, while the Western Division was a Wisconsin battle—Oshkosh versus Sheboygan. Both playoff series proved to be tough-fought battles. In the Western Division Sheboygan outlasted its longtime rival, Oshkosh, in a hard-fought five-game series. In the Eastern Division Fort Wayne and Rochester readied themselves for what was expected to be a classic series. The first two games were scheduled for Fort Wayne, and in Game One Fort Wayne came out strong to start the contest and put the game out of reach early. "The Royals were never in the ball game after the first four minutes of play. They trailed by as high as 13 points at several stages and up until the closing moments of the first half, when two fouls and a basket by [George] Glamack whittled the Hoosiers' margin to eight, the visiting forces were unable to close the

FIG. 43. A former standout at Ohio State University, Arnie Risen joined the Indianapolis Kautskys for the 1945–46 NBL season before embarking on a Hall of Fame career as a center. Courtesy of Bill Himmelman.

gap to better than 10 points."[28] As Ben Tenny wrote in the *Fort Wayne News-Sentinel*, "The Pistons were really ready for that opener and gave their backers a look at one of their most effective performances of the season. This was the Pistons team that fans here have grown to admire. It played an aggressive, tight defense that harried the Royals on every shot and gave them few easy ones. As a result, the Royals' usual accuracy from the field was way off, with Rochester hitting only 12 times in 77 attempts for a miserable .156 mark."[29] Rochester could not contain Ed Sadowski, who tallied a game-high twenty-one points to lead Fort Wayne.

With Game Two on the horizon, Fort Wayne sought to take a commanding two-games-to-none lead. Rochester was hoping for a split before heading home, where it had earned the best home record of any of the teams all season. With a game under its belt, Rochester turned the tide and over the next three games systematically defeated Fort Wayne to earn a trip to the NBL finals. In Game Two the Royals made a lineup change that negated the impact of Sadowski. As the *Rochester Democrat and Chronicle* observed, "It was obvious from the outset last night that a revamped Royal lineup which saw John Mahnken and Al Negratti replace George Glamack and Bob Fitzgerald was not going to let the champions roar away to a commanding lead and sew up the game in the first 10 minutes as they did in the first skirmish."[30] Sadowski, who had a huge performance in the first game, "was out of the game before the first period ended last night. Guarded by Al Negratti, big Ed was in constant trouble, being removed from the game after he had committed his third personal foul."[31] With Sadowski out of the lineup, the Royals pushed ahead, 30–29, at the half. In the second half Sadowski "was charged with a fourth personal early in the second half and was forced to guard big Bob Fitzgerald so loosely in the closing period that the lanky Royal lefthander dribbled away from him for two clutch baskets that broke the champions' back at the outset of the fourth period."[32] Sadowski still led the Pistons with fourteen points, but his effectiveness was limited. Glamack countered with thirteen points, while Davies and Holzman each tallied eleven points in the series-tying win.

The series shifted for the next two games to Rochester, and with 3,800 fans packing the Edgerton Sports Arena, the Royals relied on their speed and quickness to flummox the Pistons. After a terribly slow start in Game Three, the Royals, "breaking with such sizzling speed," simply outclassed the Zollners.[33] "The second period, so fast that at times Referees [Pat] Kennedy and [Chuck] Solodare had difficulty keeping up with the pace as the Arena forces moved the ball at a withering clip, saw the Royals gain the upper hand, 14–13 midway in the period, then roar away to a 26–21 advantage at halftime as George Glamack, Johnny Mahnken and Bob Davies hit consistently from the field."[34] The Royals played a balanced game; "it was the precision-like teamwork of the entire Royal five which broke the backs of the Zollners, the scoring being fairly evenly distributed among six men."[35] Glamack paced the Royals with 14 points while Cervi had 12, Davies 9, Holzman 8, and Negratti 7 points. Riding the momentum of their Game Three triumph, the Royals picked up where they left off and ran the Pistons out of the building to the tune of a 70–54 win. Glamack and Davies again the led the way, each scoring a game-high 23 points "as the feature-footed Arena forces outplayed their weary and foot-sore adversaries from Indiana."[36] As the *Fort Wayne News-Sentinel* wrote, "The Pistons had no answer in George Glamack's sensational pivot shooting and also failed to stop Bob Davies again."[37] The speed of the Royals was simply too much for the veteran Pistons to handle. While Cervi had a solid series offensively, it was his defense against his personal rival, Bobby McDermott, that made the difference. He held McDermott to 24 points in four games for a 6.0 per game average. The Royals claimed seven of ten contests from the Pistons during the season.

With the Royals' impressive win over the two-time league champions, the championship series must have felt like a letdown for the team. Facing them was Sheboygan, perennial runner up in the NBL. With the first two games scheduled for Rochester, the Royals figured to continue riding the wave of momentum and establish themselves early in the series. Against Fort Wayne the Royals needed to make an adjustment guarding center Ed Sadowski. The Royals faced a similar challenge with Sheboygan's big man, Ed Dancker. "The Royals' ability to bottle Big Ed Dancker, the Redskins' pivot powerhouse in the second half represented the margin between victory and defeat. Dancker, hitting spectacularly with his long-armed turn-around buckets, pitched in 13 points in the first half but collected only three in the final stanza. He spent a greater share of the fourth period on the bench after a fourth personal foul had been charged against him."[38] Holzman led the way with seventeen points, while Glamack tallied thirteen. Glamack was known as the Blind Bomber, although not everyone was convinced that he was vision impaired. As Levane recalled, "That guy always said he couldn't see, but every time he passed the ball, he'd give you a wink. He was a hook shot artist, and he had that back board shot. He shot with both hands, left or right. George's hook shot was longer than Mikan's. He hooked towards the baseline because he liked to play the [angle of] the boards."[39] Glamack was instrumental in the Royals play all season and throughout their playoff run.

Much like their performance in the final two games against Fort Wayne, the Royals' speed proved too much for Sheboygan. Game Two started out as a close contest, but when play resumed after halftime, the Royals shifted to warp speed while Sheboygan was still stuck in neutral. Elliot Cushing observed, "The score, 61–54, hardly represents the Royals' margin of superiority, especially in the final 15 minutes when Sheboygan, electing to play a running game in an attempt to match the White Shirts' blazing speed, literally collapsing under the terrible pressure applied by the Harrisonmen in that decisive third period."[40] This time Davies led the way with twenty-two points as Glamack chipped in with eleven and Cervi ten. The series then shifted to Sheboygan, but the change of scenery did little for the home team. The Royals were on a mission and turned in arguably their best performance with a 66–48 thrashing of the Red Skins to claim their one and only NBL championship. Once again their speed and the third period proved all that the Royals needed. "Spurting with even more fury than they displayed in winning the first two games at home, the Rochester speed burners set such a blazing second-half pace that the 'Skins were literally run under the boards."[41] The Royals outscored the Red Skins 20–6 in the decisive third period. Holman led the way with sixteen points followed by Cervi and Mahnken (each with thirteen points) and Davies (twelve points).

With a full and healthy roster as the playoffs approached, the Royals jelled as a team at the right moment. Their speed proved the decisive factor in defeating Fort Wayne first and then Sheboygan to win the title. The team was balanced, and each game saw a different player step up and lead the team in scoring. The accolades started to pour in immediately after the Royals won. Johnny Murphy, who once starred at the University of Rochester, stated, "In my entire 30 years associated with basketball, I never saw a club with better spirit than this one. This team simply refused to be beaten; it was quick, smart, and simply ran the opposition out of breath."[42] Nat Messenger, one of the referees for the series, was even more impressed: "Those guys were a bunch of wildcats out there tonight. I thought the Illinois Whiz Kids were fast, but Davies, Cervi, Holman and Mahnken would have left those kids standing still. There is no offensive like the fast break when you have the men who can make it tick—and this Rochester bunch was tailored to order for the lightning break."[43] The Royals celebrated all the way back on the train, and when they arrived at 10:52 a.m. at the New York Central Station they were greeted by twenty loyal supporters. Over the next ten seasons the Royals would develop a special bond with the city of Rochester.

Much like the Rochester Royals in the National Basketball League, the Baltimore Bullets of the American Basketball League would prove to be the one franchise in the league that looked toward the future and had a firm place in the postwar professional basketball landscape. In their first season in the ABL, in 1944–45, the Bullets fared better than initial expectations. The team finished the regular season at 14-16, then pulled the surprise upset in the playoffs by knocking off second-seed Trenton in the semifinals. Their win pared them against the Philadelphia SPHAS

FIG. 44. The Rochester Royals won the 1945–46 National Basketball League championship by defeating the Sheboygan Red Skins in three games. Naismith Memorial Basketball Hall of Fame.

for the championship. The Bullets lost in three games, but their lone win in Game Two was a 47–46 squeaker on the road at the Broadwood Hotel, one of the more difficult places to play for an opposing team. They played tough and hard throughout the season and playoffs, a trait that let them entertain positive thoughts for the upcoming season. With their first year in the books, the Bullets looked forward to the 1945–46 campaign. All six teams who had finished the previous year readied themselves for another season. This marked the first time in the history of the ABL that the same teams competed in two consecutive seasons. Along with Baltimore, Philadelphia, Trenton, Wilmington, New York, and Paterson all prepared for another year. The season would be one season—no first or second halves—and the top four teams would earn postseason berths. The number of games each team played increased to thirty-four or thirty-five, depending on the schedule. The stability of the six teams and the increase in games bode well for the league as the war concluded.

Fresh off their runner-up finish the previous season, the Bullets quickly positioned themselves as one of the league's contenders, setting the pace for the season. Baltimore's chief rival, Philadelphia, started the season slowly, sporting a pedestrian 6-5 record as the New Year approached. For the second straight year the SPHAS had trouble gaining momentum over the season's first few weeks. Two days before Christmas the SPHAS traveled to New York to face the New York Gothams, one of the surprise teams in the league. The Gothams would finish the season in third place with an 18-16 record and lose in the playoffs to Baltimore. Eddie Gottlieb needed an infusion of talent to shake the team out of its early-season lethargy. With the war over and thousands of service men returning daily, Gottlieb scoured the newspapers and contacted all his sources, looking to find new players to add to his team. One of the players he homed his sights on was Ralph Kaplowitz.

When we last saw Kaplowitz, he had been drafted and had forgone his senior year at New York University. He was being trained as a pilot and eventually was sent to the Pacific theater as a fighter pilot who flew thirteen missions. August 6, 1945, started as any other day for Kaplowitz, who "was leading a flight of four, escorting a B-24 over the island Kyushu. He recalled,

> I was flying back and forth over the island, taking pictures for the eventual invasion of Japan. Meanwhile, at the briefing that morning, they told us to stay away from the west side. As I was flying, I looked over to the west and saw terrific clouds, which I thought must be thunderstorms in the area. When I got back to the base, they said over the loudspeaker that a bomb was just dropped on a Japanese

island that was twenty thousand times more powerful than anything we had. At that point, I realized what it was and I said to myself that the war is over and I am still alive. Thank God.[44]

Soon enough Kaplowitz flew home and was discharged at Mitchell Field in New York.

He was home only a short time with his wife and young daughter when his phone starting ringing. It was Gottlieb, and he was looking for Kaplowitz to join his team. Gottlieb invited him to attend the SPHAS game against the Gothams. Not one to mince words or wait, Gottlieb made his move.

"I am ready to play you tonight," Gottlieb said to Kaplowitz. "No, I want to hear what you have to say," Kaplowitz replied. "I would like you to play for me. I will pay you $150 a week whether you play two games or three games," Gottlieb replied. "And we shook hands on the deal," as Kaplowitz recalled in a 2007 interview. "He had a very good reputation as an owner and manager, and I felt we did not need a contract. His word was good from what I heard from other people so I was content."[45]

With that Kaplowitz joined the team and resumed his basketball career. The SPHAS did defeat the Gothams that evening, 59–54, to up their record to 7-5. Kaplowitz's first game was against the Trenton Tigers on December 29, and the SPHAS crushed their old rival, 86–61, as he scored fifteen points. The eighty-six points were the most the SPHAS would score all season. The addition of Kaplowitz proved an immediate burst of energy for the team as the SPHAS won seven of eight and pushed themselves into a two-way battle with Baltimore. As Kaplowitz remembered, "I played a half season with the SPHAS. I joined them in December 1945 and the season ended in March 1946. I played half a year. I did rather well."[46] He did do well and was a factor, but after a few weeks, the initial burst of energy that the team enjoyed from the addition of Kaplowitz soon evaporated as the SPHAS lost four in a row to drop to 15-10. Over the next eight games, the season's home stretch, the SPHAS compiled a 5-3 mark to boost their record to 20-13. In that span the SPHAS once defeated the Bullets and won a tough 74–73 overtime contest against Paterson. On March 13, as the regular season was winding down, the SPHAS headed south to face the Bullets in Baltimore. The SPHAS sported a 20-13 mark, while the Bullets owned a 21-12 record. A win by Baltimore would ensure the regular season title and the top seed in the oncoming playoffs. A Philadelphia victory would place the two teams in a first-place tie, forcing a one-game playoff to determine the regular season champion.

Gottlieb understood the importance of home-court advantage in the playoffs, and he had his team "loaded and primed for their best performance."[47] The SPHAS jumped out to early leads and coasted to a 70–46 win, one of their largest margins of victory all season. The seventy points marked the ninth time the team scored at least seventy points in a contest, winning all nine games. Jerry Fleishman and Ossie Schectman combined for thirty-nine points to lead the SPHAS. The win forced a one-game playoff, only the second time this occurred in league history, to be played at the Broadwood Hotel three nights later. At the end of the 1934–35 season, the SPHAS and the Brooklyn Visitations finished the second half tied and needed a best-of-three playoff series to determine who would face the New York Jewels in the championship. Brooklyn won two games to one.

The March 16 one-game playoff marked the third time in ten days that the SPHAS and the Bullets faced each other. In their brief time in the league, the Bullets had built a strong following in Baltimore and had established themselves as one of the league's best squads. Capitalizing on a renewed interest in basketball, Baltimore hosted its one and only invitational tournament in March 1946. Sponsored by Eddie Leonard, a local sportsman, and Jack Embree, president of the Bullets, the four-team field featured the Indianapolis Kautskys, for years a midwestern power, the Detroit Mansfields, the SPHAS, and host Baltimore. The

Baltimore Tournament was patterned after similar tournaments in Worcester, Rochester, and Buffalo.

A carnival atmosphere permeated the two-day affair as prizes "were awarded for everything from the best looking married player, presented to the Bullets' Stan Stutz, to the tourney's most valuable player, won by Ralph Kaplowitz, and the best all-around player by big Mike Bloom."[48] A foul-shooting contest was held, and Bob Roth of Detroit won by scoring a perfect 10 for 10. After the SPHAS first-round win over the Kautskys, SPHAS player Virgil Vaughn "was presented a plaque by blond Bettye Mills, as the best looking player in the tourney, and the pair drew a tumultuous applause when Miss Mills planted a kiss on the 6-foot soldier."[49]

Notwithstanding the festival atmosphere, the four teams staged a highly competitive tournament won by the host Bullets. As for the SPHAS, they played exceptionally well and were five minutes from winning it all. In their first game the SPHAS and the Kautskys flashed, exhibiting "fine shooting form, great passing, and a bitterly contested struggle. The score was tied no less than nine times, and the lead changed hands on 12 different occasions."[50] Ralph Kaplowitz scored a game-high twenty-five points as future Naismith Memorial Basketball Hall of Fame member Arnie Risen chipped in with fifteen points for Indianapolis. The SPHAS defeated the Kautskys 71–63, setting themselves up for another tough contest against their league rival in the finals. In control for most of the night, the SPHAS held a five-point lead with five minutes remaining before the Bullets ended the game on a 12–2 run to claim a 51–46 win. "The late stages developed into a rodeo, the players racing up and down the floor like wild steeds."[51] The close win and competitive games were indicative of the previous regular-season match-ups between the two squads. It would also be an omen for the future.

Baltimore and Philadelphia knew each other well, and the one-game playoff lived up to the hype. Much like the team's performance in the last regular-season contest three days prior, Gottlieb had his team "playing brilliant basketball, and more than primed to successfully defend its title."[52] The first two periods were tightly played with neither team able to open a sizable margin. As the game entered the final frame, the prevailing sense was that the game would go down to the wire, with the outcome based most likely on the team who had possession last. As the *Baltimore Sun* noted the following day, "The teams engaged in a crushing point-for-point battle which saw the score change hands nine times in the last period and tied on four different occasions at 49, 54, 55, and 61."[53] With the score tied at 55 with only a few minutes remaining, the excitement level reached its zenith. Baltimore surged ahead 58–55 on foul shots by Ace Abbott and Stan Stutz. Philadelphia responded as Jerry Fleishman and Ralph Kaplowitz each sank a foul shot to close the margin to 58–57. Baltimore's Jackie Peters, fresh into the game, "launched a long set shot for a 60–57 margin."[54] Stutz followed up with a foul shot to increase the lead to 61–57. Down four Philadelphia tied the score on a basket by Kaplowitz and two foul shots by Art Hillhouse. Tied at 61–61 Baltimore took possession of the ball off the center jump and looked to play for the last shot. As recounted the following day by the *Baltimore Sun*, "The Bullets got possession of the ball off the center jump, waiting for an opening, and then Stutz came through with his Frank Merriwell toss from the middle of the floor to give the Bullets the title."[55] Stutz's improbable shot from four feet beyond half court gave the Bullets the regular season title and the home-court advantage throughout the playoffs.

Stunned by the last-second defeat, the SPHAS needed to regroup fast in the first round of the playoffs if they wanted any chance of revenge against Baltimore in the championship series. For the third consecutive year Philadelphia and Wilmington faced off in the playoffs. Similar to their performance in the previous season, the SPHAS swept past the Blue Bombers in two games. This Wilmington team was far different from the one that had challenged the SPHAS a few years ago. The roster

FIG. 45. Baltimore's Stan Stutz hit an incredible shot over the Philadelphia SPHAS to give the Bullets the 1945–46 American Basketball League regular season title. Courtesy of Bill Himmelman.

had turned over, but the Bombers still posed a challenge. In the first game played in Wilmington, the SPHAS needed a late scoring push from Jerry Fleishman, Bernie Opper, and Ralph Kaplowitz to pull out a 69–65 win. Trailing as they headed into the final frame, the SPHAS outscored the Bombers 27–21 to pull out the win. The second game was played at the Broadwood Hotel, and the SPHAS hot shooting from the outside carried over. SPHAS beat writer William J. Scheffer wrote the following day, "The SPHAS' spectacular shooting, particularly in the early part of the game, provoked thrill upon thrill for the capacity throng. While there was only a three-point difference at the end, the SPHAS were infinitely superior from the floor, outscoring the Bombers 33 goals to 23. It was only the consistent foul tossing that kept the Bombers in the game."[56] Art Hillhouse's twenty-one points paced the SPHAS, who advanced to the finals for the fourth straight year and who were seeking their third title in that time.

In two short years the Baltimore Bullets had quickly become the SPHAS's newest rival. After quickly dispatching the New York Gothams in two games, the Bullets sought to avenge last year's championship loss. The best-of-five championship series opened in Philadelphia as the SPHAS continued their strong offensive play in recent weeks, with "Ralph Kaplowitz's all-around play in stopping Stutz Modzelewski and the brilliant long-distance shooting of Ossie Schectman enable[ing] the SPHAS to spank the Baltimore Bullets at the Broadwood Court last night, 63–48." The opening frame was close, and the SPHAS took a 15–14 lead entering the second period. At that point the recent travel schedule for the Bullets caught up with them. Earlier in the week the Bullets had traveled to the World Professional Basketball Tournament in Chicago and won their first two games. After their two wins in Chicago, Baltimore quickly headed back east to play the first game of the championship series. The *Baltimore Sun* reported, "Playing their third game in four days, following their two victories in the annual world pro cage tourney in Chicago, the Bullets failed to give the SPHAS much of a contest."[57] Without their legs the Bullets stood no chance in the first game. Baltimore's participation in the World Professional Basketball Tournament would continue to be a factor in the scheduling of the championship series. As the *Baltimore Sun* noted, "Following tomorrow night's second game of the series in Baltimore, the Bullets will return

FIG. 46. A former standout for Long Island University, Art Hillhouse was an effective center for the Philadelphia SPHAS in the 1945–46 season. Courtesy of Bill Himmelman.

to Chicago for their semi-final tournament game against the defending champion Fort Wayne Zollner Pistons."[58]

When the second game shifted to Baltimore, the entire complexion of the series changed. With a day to recover after the first game, the Bullets resumed their winning ways. Over the next three games, the Bullets simply dismantled the SPHAS, winning by an average of eighteen points. In Game Two the Bullets jumped out to an early lead and never looked back.

> Clicking from the outside and under the boards with neatly executed cut plays, the Bullets raced out to an 18–4 lead in the first ten minutes of play, with Hagan Andersen [*sic*], Mike Bloom and Jake [*sic*] Ahearn accounting for the bulk of the scoring. At the five minute mark, the SPHAS finally untracked themselves to run off a string of ten straight points, closing out the first period at 18–14. The Bullets were in no disposition to let up, and exploded with their biggest second period of the year. With Ace Abbott, Johnny Norlander and Moe Dubilier joining Ahearn, Bloom, and Stutz in the basket assault, the Bullets poured thirty points through the webbing while holding the SPHAS to a season's low of seven.[59]

In that fateful second period for the SPHAS, in which they were out-scored 30–7, the team "actually had but 11 shots at the hoop throughout the entire second stanza."[60] As the *Philadelphia Inquirer* wrote the following day, "With the entire team figuring in the scoring, the Bullets were in command from the outset, and at one time enjoyed a 27-point advantage."[61] Ace Abbott led the Bullets with twelve points.

The theme of one bad quarter would become a recurring nightmare for the SPHAS for the remainder of the series. In the third game the Bullets jumped out to a 25–7 lead after the first period. The SPHAS simply could not recover. As the *Baltimore Sun* recounted the following day, "The Baltimoreans were hitting the net with amazing consistency and their man-to-man defense prevented the SPHAS from getting set for balanced shots either from the outside or underneath the hoops."[62] The tremendous Baltimore offensive explosion coupled with the inept Philadelphia scoring was recounted the following day in the *Philadelphia Inquirer*: "Baltimore goals came thick and fast and the SPHAS' efforts were feeble, scoring only two field goals in the first session and the Bullets had a lead of 25–7. This was the biggest lead any team had obtained over the SPHAS in the 13-year history of the American Basketball League contests played at the Broadwood."[63] This time Jake Ahearn led Baltimore with fifteen points.

The fourth game was much the same as Baltimore's balanced scoring proved too much for the defensively challenged SPHAS. Baltimore beat writer Robert Elmer captured the game the following day: "Well versed in each other's style of play, the Bullets performed exceptionally well as a unit, and appropriately their three mainstays, Bloom, Hagan Andersen, and Stutz, shared high-scoring honors at 12 points apiece."[64] The Bullets extended their lead to seventeen points with less than four minutes remaining and ran out the clock for their first championship.

A strong season for the ABL came to a close and with that the league's time as an important player in the professional basketball landscape. The following season the ABL would become an unofficial minor league to the emerging Basketball Association of America (BAA). Philadelphia, Paterson, Trenton, Wilmington, and Baltimore all played the following season in the ABL. They were again joined by the New York Gothams, who relocated as the Brooklyn Gothams. The 1946–47 season would be Baltimore's last in the ABL and the minor leagues. As the 1947–48 BAA season unfolded, Baltimore was added to the roster of teams. Coached by Buddy Jeannette, the Bullets defeated the Philadelphia Warriors, led by Eddie Gottlieb, to win the championship. The Bullets folded during the 1954–55 NBA season. As for the SPHAS, this marked the end of a glorious run as a top team. Since joining the ABL for the 1933–34 season, the SPHAS had become synonymous with the league and arguably the best professional basketball team in the country. In thirteen seasons (1933–46) the SPHAS reached the finals nine times and won seven championships. In claiming those titles they defeated all comers including the Trenton Moose, the Brooklyn Visitations, the Jersey Reds, the Brooklyn Celtics, the Trenton Tigers, and now the Baltimore Bullets. The SPHAS would play three more years in the ABL before joining the Harlem Globetrotters as a touring team during the 1950s.

FIG. 47. Hagan Andersen was a key contributor for the Baltimore Bullets as they outlasted the Philadelphia SPHAS in four games to win the 1945–46 American Basketball League title. Courtesy of Bill Himmelman.

Since its inception in 1939, the World Professional Basketball Tournament had hosted many of the finest professional, independent, and barnstorming teams in the country. Conspicuously absent most years was the champion of the American Basketball League. Except for 1941, when the SPHAS played in their one and only tournament, no ABL team was represented until 1946, when the Baltimore Bullets accepted an invitation to play. ABL commissioner John J. O'Brien spoke for many in the league when he wrote in a 1945 letter:

> We have never recognized it as such for the reason that it is of one week's duration and specially recruited clubs have been secured for participation therein, some with established reputations and others drawn together only for this tournament, so that it is nothing more than an outstanding professional competition with the ultimate winner having no particular claim to territorial supremacy than would be true of many other tournaments promoted in other parts of the country; such as Cleveland, Rochester, and Worcester, Mass.[65]

Notwithstanding the opinions of the commissioner, the Bullets were an upstart team looking to insert themselves into the conversation of the best professional teams. They became one of the few eastern teams to head to Chicago to test their mettle against the best. In 1947 Baltimore again participated in the tournament, and in 1948 Wilkes-Barre accepted an invitation. The play of Baltimore in the tournament elicited strong reviews, particularly among the Chicago press.

The 1946 World Professional Basketball Tournament was the first to be played since the war had come to an end. Now entering its eighth year, the tournament more than exceeded all expectations since its inception in 1939. As always high hopes preceded the tournament, and a few changes were announced prior to the event. The tournament was scheduled for the end of March and early April, but there would be a day off between games. As the *Chicago Herald American* reported, "In addition to the opening night, March 25, games will be played on March 27, March 29, April 3, April 5 and April 6. On the last two nights, the two finalists will meet in the first two of their three-game series to determine the championship—an innovation in this year's play. If a third game is necessary it will be played April 8."[66] These two changes proved popular with the players as noted by the

Chicago Herald American: "Teams have complained that one game does not eliminate the element of luck, and the new arrangement is the result. The other novelty is the staggered schedule, due to a desire to rest the clubs and also permit the hockey playoffs between cage thrillers."[67] Chicago Stadium, the host venue, faced a busy schedule during that period. In addition to the tournament the facility was also hosting Chicago Blackhawks games, a high school basketball contest, and the Chicago Relays track meet. Following the precedent established the previous year, if two teams from the same geographic region were seeking to participate "elimination contests [would] be held in various sections to decide upon the entry if there [was] some question as to the better club."[68] The two-time defending champion, the Fort Wayne Zollner Pistons, was the first team to sign on. Fort Wayne sought to become the first three-time champion. As in the past two years, fourteen teams were scheduled to compete. Due to its Midwest location, the National Basketball League was always well represented in the tournament. Of the eight teams competing in the league, six of them were set to participate in the tournament. In addition to Fort Wayne, Cleveland, Oshkosh, Sheboygan, Indianapolis, and Chicago all accepted the organizer's invitation. Curiously, the Rochester Royals, the NBL champions, chose not to compete. Youngstown, after a lackluster 13-20 league mark, was set to compete but withdrew days before its scheduled game because of a team member's death. The other team that did not participate was the Harlem Globetrotters, who had been a mainstay in the tournament for the past seven years. Instead, the Globetrotters and the Royals were traveling and playing games against each other in a series of exhibition matches. Sheboygan and Fort Wayne earned first round byes. As was the case in recent years, the tournament would benefit the Wounded Veterans Fund.

In the articles promoting the tournament in the months leading to its start, the *Chicago Herald American* focused on two aspects regarding player personnel. The first was the fact that many returning servicemen would be participating. The second was the noted college players who would be competing. In an article on March 18, 1946, a week before the start of the tournament, Keith Brehm wrote, "More than 75 per cent of the player personnel in the eighth annual world championship basketball tournament will be composed of veterans, discharged from service or on leave."[69] Brehm went on to highlight two teams in particular: the Chicago American Gears and the Oshkosh All-Stars. "But during the league play, the Gears were constantly strengthened by return of servicemen as the season rolled on. Nine of the dozen American Gear players are men out of service this year. They are Bob Calihan, Charlie Butler, Jim Olsen and Price Brookfield of the navy, and Stan Szukala, Bob Neu, Bill Hapac, Bob Rensberger and George Ratkovicz [sic] of the army."[70] As for Oshkosh the team had "nine servicemen in the lineup," including "Bob Carpenter, Eddie Riska, Bob Sullivan, Gene Englund and Fred Rehm of the navy, Ed Erban of the marines, and Warner Engdahl, Bob Feerick and Erv Prasse [sic] of the army."[71] The return of servicemen bolstered the teams' lineups, creating more depth across the league.

The Sheboygan half of the bracket featured three interesting games: Chicago American Gears versus the Pittsburgh Raiders; Oshkosh All-Stars versus the Detroit Mansfields; and the Toledo Jeeps versus the New York Renaissance (Rens). The most interesting first-round game, the one that drew the most publicity and intrigue, was the Chicago American Gears versus the Pittsburgh Raiders. Pittsburgh played only one season in the NBL, in 1944–45, in which it finished 7-23 and last in the Eastern Division, a full eighteen games behind eventual champion Fort Wayne. Pittsburgh did not join the league in 1945–46, instead playing as an independent team on the East Coast. The team did play in the 1944 and 1945 tournaments. Known as the Pittsburgh Corbetts in 1944, the team lost a close first-round game, 41–40, to the Harlem Globetrotters. A year later, in 1945, the Raiders, as they were now known, won their opening game, 53–50, over the Newark (NY) C-O

Two's before bowing out to the New York Renaissance (Rens), 61–52, in the quarterfinals. Pittsburgh featured a few familiar names from the previous season, including Manny Hyatt, Joe Urso, and Fred Crum. One of the players on the team was Zigmund "Red" Mihalik, who later would become a well-regarded referee in the Basketball Association of America and the National Basketball Association and was inducted into the Naismith Memorial Basketball Hall of Fame. In his lone tournament game Mihalik scored two points. For the 1945–46 basketball season, Keith Brehm reported, the "Pittsburgh team has won 20 of 24 against some of the best quintets in the country. The Raiders, who are sponsored by Congressman Robert J. Corbett, have played free-lance ball this season while on an inactive status in the National Basketball League, and their opponents included such teams as Oshkosh, Dayton, Columbus, Brooklyn, Buffalo, Baltimore and Washington."[72] Pittsburgh's hopes were to repeat its surprising first-round upset from the previous year.

Little did Pittsburgh know when it signed up for the tournament that its first-round game would be the professional debut of George Mikan. On the eve of the World Professional Basketball Tournament, Maurice White, the Gears owner, landed arguably the best college player when he signed Mikan to play for his Chicago American Gears. Mikan's signing created the most buzz in the eight-year history of the tournament and significantly increased publicity and ticket sales. His signing ushered in the third and final phase of the tournament's history. The tournament can be thought of as having three distinct periods. The first was from 1939 to 1943, when three of the first five winners were all-black teams. The second period featured the dominance of Fort Wayne from 1944 to 1946, when it won three consecutive tournament titles. And the final period was 1946–48 and the emergence of Mikan. Mikan would leave his mark on the tournament and become the best professional basketball player in the 1950s.

His signing of a five-year contract worth $60,000 was unheard of for basketball players in 1946. In its announcement of the record signing, the *Chicago Herald American* stated, "Mikan's contract calls for interval payments totaling $60,000 for five years, a record salary for a professional basketball player, and comparable to those paid in baseball and pro football. The salary is for Big George's basketball services exclusively. He has one more year of law at DePaul, after which he is expected to join the American Gear 7 Manufacturing legal department."[73] As Dick Triptow, a member of the Gears recalled,

> A meeting was set up with Mikan and Maurice White, owner of the American Gears basketball team, to talk over White's offer of $5,000 for his signature. It was rumored that Rochester and Dow Chemical had come up with a $6,000 offer for his signature. Mikan seemed to be leaning towards the Gears, since he was planning on getting his law degree at DePaul. Mikan's decision to sign with the Gears may have even been influenced by the fact that former members of the DePaul basketball teams, Bob Neu, Stan Szukala and I, were already in the fold, along with his former coach, Ray Meyer, who was acting in an advisory capacity. When White finally announced on March 16, 1946, that George Mikan had signed with the Gears, it was like gold being discovered in California![74]

One of the reasons Mikan might have signed with the Gears was that his college coach, Ray Meyer, was an advisory coach with the team. As Meyer recalled,

> I was deeply involved in coaching DePaul basketball when I was approached to coach the American Gears. I realized that DePaul came first and the Gears would come second. My agreement with Maurice White was that I would get $50 or $75 for every time I showed up at practice or a game. (I can't remember the exact figure.) It was a day-to-day agreement for I knew I couldn't make all the games or practices. In order to have a stand-in, Swede Roos was the man who

would sub for me in my absence. It was an offer I couldn't refuse. There were four former DePaul basketball players on the team and I had two of them in college. (Bob Neu, Stan Szukala, Dick Triptow and George Mikan.) I was looking forward to this opportunity to be a part of this Gears team.

The Gears were practicing daily at the Cicero Stadium. When I finished practicing the DePaul basketball team I would drive out to the Cicero Stadium. Mr. White had the players lounging around waiting for me. I felt sorry for them and I would only go a half hour to an hour and let them go. The team had a load of talent and they played very well together. I really enjoyed working with them for I had good inside players in Neu and Mikan and two very good guards in Szukala and Triptow. Triptow gave us great quickness for he could fly up and down the court. Szukala was a great all around basketball player. Neu could fake and draw fouls under the basket and going to the basket. Mikan was a real force, he dominated the game. Calihan was another forward who had a great left-handed shot.[75]

As Dick Triptow recounted,

It was difficult for Meyer to run practices for the Gears similar to what I endured when I played for him at DePaul. The Gear practice sessions were more oriented towards preparing us for the next game, since we had already done most of our running during the day prior to Meyer's appearance. A typical DePaul practice ordinarily lasted three hours. When practice was over and before we were allowed to shower, each player had to shoot at least 50 free throws, with no one leaving until 10 free throws were made in a row. On the days when Meyer was scheduled to conduct practice, after working with his DePaul University basketball team, we had to wait until he arrived for the special practice he would set up for each session. Those long days found us visiting the ice cream parlor, steps away from Cicero Stadium.[76]

The announcement of Mikan's signing immediately drew strong support not just from his soon-to-be teammates such as Triptow but also from the Gears Company itself. John Boord, the company's attorney, noted, "Believe me, we want George in our legal department. He's a mighty smart boy. We can use him."[77] Despite Boord's excitement Mikan's focus for the immediate future was on the basketball court. Soon after signing him, White issued a statement to the press expressing his high hopes that the addition of Mikan would propel the team to the next level. As White optimistically declared, "We've had a good basketball team all year long. Position for position we wouldn't trade any of our forwards or guards. Now, with Mikan at center, I feel we have the best basketball team in the nation. We ought to win the world title. I don't want George to feel that we are placing too big a load on his shoulders. We should win, sure, but I am satisfied that all my basketball players give their all at all times."[78] White was not the only person excited to have Mikan on the team. After Mikan's first practice with the Gears, his teammates addressed reporters seeking comment on the new big man. George Ratkovich stated, "We'll get plenty of rebounds now, and the load won't fall on one man."[79] Rebounding was also the theme sounded by guard Bob Neu: "It's a strange feeling to line up on the side of the free throw line, knowing that if the shot is missed, Big George will be in there for a couple of bats."[80] Even coach Ray Meyer was optimistic: "We'll be the best conditioned team that ever hit the world tournament and anybody who plays us better be prepared to run."[81]

With only a week before the start of the tournament, the Gears needed to find a way to quickly integrate Mikan into the lineup, have him meet his new teammates, and give him time to understand the offensive and defensive plays. In order to ease Mikan into the lineup, the Gears set up two exhibition matches. The first was against the Anderson Chiefs, while the second was versus the Detroit Mansfields. Both Anderson and Detroit would be playing in the upcoming tournament, and this would provide a good test for Mikan on the improved caliber of play he would be facing as a professional. Mikan was scheduled to play in both games, and then he would be "in New York with his coach, Ray Meyer, to receive an award as the No. 1 player of the year from the New York basketball writers."[82]

First up was the Anderson Chiefs. As Mikan recalled,

I joined the Gears right away for the remainder of the 1945–46 season. They set up a special scrimmage to help me get accustomed to its style of play, and then it was off to our first game, a practice game against the Anderson (Indiana) Chiefs. In my first outing as a member of the Gears, I scored 17 points on the way to a 68–60 win for the team, but I landed on the bench by the third quarter, called out on fouls. I had encountered the same kind of vocal and physical barrage I used to deal with when playing against Oklahoma A&M's Bob Kurland, except on a pro level, and unfortunately it had the same result. Back then, joining the pro ranks was not as prestigious as it is today. I was a college boy with a substantial reputation, but I was coming into a professional game that had always been popularized by a bunch of tough, road-weary, street-wise working stiffs who were anything but All-American boys. Since I'd reached the pinnacle in college, I naively figured that I would have my own way in the pros, also. I found out, however, that I may have graduated, but my education was not complete.[83]

In his next game against Detroit played at Cicero Stadium in Chicago, he scored twenty points as the Gears won their second consecutive game with Mikan in the lineup.

The signing of Mikan and the expectations associated with the Gears and his impending play in the tournament spilled over to the promotion surrounding the tournament. On March 23, 1946, two days prior to the start of the tournament, an advertisement in the *Chicago Herald American* stated, "Mikan—and the Rest!"[84] It would be a familiar refrain that Mikan would encounter throughout his professional career. Although Mikan garnered most of the attention, the Gears were a good, solid team, having completed the league regular season at 17-17, good for third place in the Western Division. As Keith Brehm, the *Chicago Herald American* writer assigned to cover the tournament, wrote in his preview article, "Besides Mikan, the Gears, host team in this spectacular meet, will present Dick Triptow, all-world tournament choice last year; Bob Calihan, hottest scorer in the National Basketball League in the last month of play; Bob Neu, Stan Szukala, George Ratkovich and others familiar to Chicago fans, including Price Brookfield, who played an important role in the Gears' third-place triumph of 1945."[85] The Gears would need to rely on their entire team to pull out a victory over Pittsburgh.

The Chicago-Pittsburgh game was the second tilt on the opening night of the tournament. It was an exciting game from start to finish as "the Chicago victory was one to leave the crowd limp with exhaustion at the finish. Pittsburgh, displaying a sharpshooting aggregation as good as anything ever seen around here, held a 33–32 lead over George Mikan and his associates at half-time—only to fade before an amazing Chicago rally which tied the count in 3½ minutes of the second half. After that it was point for point until the closing minutes, when Chicago's pressure finally broke through the scrappy Pittsburghers for the winning margin."[86] In his tournament debut Mikan scored a game-high seventeen points before fouling out. In Chicago's 69–58 win Stan Patrick set a tournament record when he tallied nine free throws in coming off the bench. With Mikan's debut a success, the Gears next foe was the Sheboygan Red Skins.

With a first-round bye Sheboygan was rested and ready for the new-look Gears. Despite its NBL championship loss to the Rochester Royals, Sheboygan felt confident heading to Chicago. Coached by Dutch Dehnert the team had good reason to be optimistic. As Leo Fischer noted in the *Chicago Herald American*, "The Red Skins are coming here with as colorful an aggregation as ever has competed in the spectacular affair. It's a squad which combines scoring skill, stalwart guarding and scintillating speed."[87] Adding to the team's success this year was Mickey Rottner, who had "returned from overseas service a month ago," and Al Grenert, who had "joined the team at the start of the season after his discharge from the Marines."[88] The anchor for Sheboygan was in the middle with Ed Dancker. Fischer observed, "Dancker, who looks like a cinch to be on the circuit's all-star squad for the third straight year, is finishing his tenth season with Sheboygan and is captain of the team. Standing 6 feet 7 inches in height, he is among the league's top scorers and a demon on snaring rebounds. He is one of the few stars in the pro loop without college experience, having jumped into the league from independent Milwaukee ranks."[89] Dancker was voted to the NBL first team three times (1943, 1944, and 1946) and twice to the second team (1942, 1945). He also finished second in MVP balloting in 1946 to Fort Wayne's Bob McDermott. His experience and toughness would prove a good challenge for Mikan in the next game.

Regarded as a pre-tournament favorite, Sheboygan added to its already strong lineup when it signed All-American Fred Lewis, who had just finished his college career. More than sixteen thousand fans crammed inside Chicago Stadium to witness a spectacular game as evidenced the following day in which "along came the classic between Chicago and Sheboygan which for sheer drama probably topped anything seen around [there] in years."[90] With the home crowd behind them, the Gears jumped out to a quick 12–6 lead as the entire team was involved offensively from the outset. The lead slowly evaporated as the veteran Red Skins withstood the early Gears momentum to take a 27–23 lead in the half. Sheboygan picked up where it left off to start the third period, as it extended its margin to 39–30, its largest of the game. At this point momentum shifted, this time for Chicago. Behind the play of Mikan, Triptow, Patrick, and Szukala, the Gears made a run of their own and by the end of the third period had reduced the deficit to three points, 41–38. Two minutes into the final period, the score was knotted at 44–44 when Bob Calihan picked up the scoring for Chicago. The *Chicago Herald American* provided a recap of the game's hard-fought finale.

> After that it was a battle royal. With three minutes left, Sheboygan led 48–47. Then Patrick caged one, but Novak sank a free throw and it was knotted again with 1:45 to play. Patrick's one-hander gave the Gears a two-point edge and then came the fireworks. Fred Lewis made a free throw to bring Sheboygan within a point. A double-foul (one a technical on Chicago) gave each team a chance. Patrick missed first and it was up to Lewis to tie the count. But he missed, too. Now only 23 seconds remained. Calihan and Mickey Rottner tangled, and a foul was called on each. Bob Neu replaced Calihan, since it was his fifth foul, and calmly sank the shot. So did Rottner. Then the two teams scrambled wildly in the remaining seconds. Sheboygan missing one which would have won as the crowd gasped. Mikan grabbed the rebound, froze to the sphere—and the game was over.[91]

Mikan led the team with 14 points as the Gears held on for a 52–51 win.

The Gears entered the semifinal round for the second year in a row. Their opponent would be the Oshkosh All-Stars. A rejuvenated Oshkosh had an easy time in its half of the bracket. The All-Stars' opening match was against the Detroit Mansfields, whom coincidently they defeated in the first round of the 1945 tournament. Detroit was one of the last two teams to earn a berth in the tournament. Under the guidance of head coach Cincy Sachs, the Mansfields prepared for the tournament by "strengthening up for the big show by adding several new men. Among them are three men who scintillated on service teams—Chester Gabriel, 6–1, Carl Campbell, 6–4, and Sam Leiberman, 6–8."[92] Despite the excitement that Detroit evoked with the additions of new players, it was Oshkosh who had the most to be excited about regarding player personnel. During the early years of the tournament, Oshkosh boasted the league's strongest lineup and was a regular contender in the games in Chicago. Oshkosh won in 1942 and was a three-time runner-up (1939, 1941, and 1943). However, no team was more affected by the call for service than the All-Stars, who lost key players for nearly three seasons. As a result the team was a shell of itself and lost in the quarterfinals in 1944 and 1945. Now with the war over returning players boosted the prospects of Oshkosh as Bob Carpenter, Gene Englund, Eddie Riska, and Warner Engdahl all rejoined the team. As Keith Brehm noted in his preview article of Oshkosh after it was announced that the Wisconsin team would be playing,

> Its lineup resembles those with which it dominated the pro sport for so many years, with numerous stalwarts back from service in Uncle Sam's ranks. Chief among them is Bob Carpenter, the elongated forward who returned to the Oshkosh lineup this season after four years in the navy. Eddie Riska has been the hero of many important Oshkosh games. The former Notre Dame star played with the Stars when they won the world title in 1942. He played service basketball at Great Lakes for one season and returned to the Oshkosh lineup this season. Warner Engdahl of Superior, Wis., returned to the Oshkosh lineup late this season after 44 months of service.[93]

With the return of key contributors plus the addition of first-year player Bob Feerick, Oshkosh set its sights on making up for lost time.

Oshkosh jumped out of the gate quickly and built a ten-point margin, 32–23 at the half. In the second half the All-Stars simply wore down the Mansfields and won going away 60–32. Carpenter led the All-Stars with twelve points, while Gene Englund chipped in with eleven points. Next up for Oshkosh were the New York Rens, an old rivalry that dated back for more than a decade. In 1939 the Rens had defeated Oshkosh to win the first World Professional Basketball Tournament. In 1943 the Washington Bears had defeated Oshkosh to win the title. This game figured to be a close affair. Like the All-Stars the Rens had an easy time in their first-round match-up by defeating the Toledo Jeeps, 82–39. The Rens entered the tournament on a strong note, having won sixty-one of sixty-five contests to date during the basketball season. With a team composed of veteran stalwarts like Dolly King, Pop Gates, Sonny Wood, Puggy Bell, and Hank DeZonie, manager Bob Douglas had every reason to believe that this year's team would make a strong showing. With his usual optimism Douglas declared before the start of the tournament, "I believe this is the best team I've ever had. Definitely we expect to make the grade this year. Between our veterans and the young fellows back from service, we're back to our prewar class."[94] Douglas was excited to add Len Pearson, Lou Badger, and Benny Garrett, all of whom were returning from military service. Only Garrett would actually compete for the Rens. The Rens first-round opponent was scheduled to be the Youngstown Bears, but a day prior to the game, Youngstown withdrew as "early yesterday morning Pierre (Huck) Hartman, one of the great centers of professional basketball and a standout performer with the Youngstown, O., team in the National Basketball League, died in a Youngstown hospital after a brief illness."[95] Hartman's death from pneumonia shocked his teammates, who decided to withdraw. Replacing the Bears at the last minute were the Toledo Jeeps, managed by Sid Goldberg, who had helped integrate the National Basketball League in December 1942 with the Toledo Jim White Chevrolets. On the Jeeps was Chuck Chuckovits, a star in the early years of the tournament, who still held the tournament scoring record with eighty-three points in four games. With little time to prepare the Rens ran rampant over the Jeeps and won 82–39. Their eighty-two points exceeded the eighty scored the previous year by Dayton. It also spoke to the increase in scoring, which was becoming one of the positive outcomes of basketball during World War II. As Leo Fischer wrote prior to the tournament, "The scores are interesting by comparison with current figures, for they indicate how vastly point-making has increased in these days of racehorse basketball. The tournament this year will average almost double."[96] The *Chicago Herald American* devoted one preview article to the scorers who would be competing in the tournament. It noted, "Last year 11 team scoring records fell as the 14 tournament games produced an average score of 61–49, but the individual marks held, except for a couple of free throw records which went to Bruce Hale of Dayton and Bobby McDermott of Fort Wayne. Hale slipped in 19 of his 21 free throws in four games for one record and McDermott converted eight out of nine in a single game for another mark."[97] It also noted that Sonny Boswell, Chuck Chuckovits, and Bob Tough, all of whom held scoring records from previous tournaments, would be playing this year. Scoring would continue to increase in the 1946 tournament.

Even though both the Rens and the All-Stars coasted in their first-round match-ups, the prevailing wisdom was that the game would be a close affair. As was typical with these two foes, the game was a low-scoring affair. Each team tallied seventeen field goals, but Oshkosh made six more free throws, and that proved to be difference as the All-Stars won, 50–44. The All-Stars had four players in double figures and were led by Bob Carpenter's fourteen points. Clint Wager scored twelve points, and Cowboy Edwards and Fred Rehm each contributed ten points to Oshkosh's win. Pop Gates led all scorers with fifteen. Another disappointing run in the tournament ended too early for the Rens, while a rejuvenated Oshkosh returned to the semifinal round for the first time since 1943.

While the top half of the bracket was off to a strong showing, the Fort Wayne side of the bracket proved to be equally entertaining. The first round featured three compelling contests: the Baltimore Bullets versus the Dayton Mickeys; the Cleveland Allmen Transfers against the Anderson Chiefs; and the Midland Dows against the Indianapolis Kautskys. For the first time since 1941, the American Basketball League was represented by one of its top teams, the Baltimore Bullets. In only their second season in the ABL, the Bullets were fast becoming one of the league's top teams. In early March the Bullets found themselves in a dogfight with the Philadelphia SPHAS for top honors in the regular season. Despite their focus on winning the league title, the Bullets accepted an invitation to play in the tournament. Coached by Red Rosan, formerly a great player with the SPHAS in the 1930s, the Bullets featured a well-balanced lineup with Stan Stutz, Mike Bloom in the middle, Hagan Andersen, Jake Ahearn, and Moe Dubilier. Although the tournament naturally had a midwestern bent, the Bullets were poised to become the first eastern team since the Washington Bears in 1943 to win the tournament. Bill Dyer, the team's general manager, optimistically noted, "Although we naturally are prejudiced, we believe right now we have one of the best ball clubs in the country."[98]

Facing Baltimore were the Dayton Bombers, who sometimes went by the name Dayton Mickeys. They were named for the Mickey McCrossen Tavern, their sponsor. The Bombers had largely the same team as last year, when they competed as the Dayton Acmes and went all the way to the finals, where they lost to the Fort Wayne Zollner Pistons. Dayton was led the previous year by Bruce Hale, who scored seventy-seven points while playing under the assumed name William McNeil so as not to affect his college and military career amateur status. Dayton played the season as an independent squad and defeated the likes of Fort Wayne and Sheboygan. After their early-season loss to Dayton, Red Skins coach Dutch Dehnert declared, "That's one of the best clubs I've seen this year."[99] The Baltimore-Dayton contest proved to be one of the best games of the first rounds. Baltimore jumped out to an 18–12 lead before Dayton pulled away for a 33–30 halftime lead. The teams played a back-and-forth third period and were deadlocked at 44 entering the final frame. The fourth quarter equaled the third period for its tight affair as both teams "carried their struggle clear to the end before reaching a decision. The clock showed only 15 seconds remaining when Hagan Andersen of the easterners sank a shot for the winning margin after Dayton had missed on a free-throw which would have sent the battle into extra time."[100] Baltimore won 61–58 as Mike Bloom and

Stan Stutz each paced the Bullets with fifteen points. Bruce Hale led Dayton with nineteen points.

With a win under their belt, the Bullets began to focus on their next foe, the Anderson Chiefs. While the Gears proved to be the most interesting team in the top bracket, Anderson quickly became the fan favorite in the lower bracket. For much of the 1945–46 basketball season, the Anderson Chiefs played as a semiprofessional club in Indiana facing the Kautskys and the Zollner Pistons, among other professional teams in the state. Anderson was a small town in Indiana, but the town quickly supported the club in large measure due to the colorful personality of its owner, Isaac "Ike" Duffey. Duffey owned a meat-processing plant in Anderson and always harbored big ideas. One of those ideas was to operate a professional basketball team and compete against the best teams. As his nephew Martin Duffey remembered, "Uncle Ike was always gregarious. He wasn't a family man per se. He had no children of his own. But he was a great uncle. He always had this big smile on his face. You could tell he really liked to be around people. He captured the activity of everything around him. Ike always had a head for business. He was a real salesman—a wheeler dealer. He sure liked doing business."[101]

The Chiefs biggest rivals were local—the Kautskys and the Zollner Pistons. The team played in the Anderson High School gym, known affectionately by the locals as the Wigwam. "During the games, Uncle Ike would let me sit on the bench as the team's waterboy. I got to take the towels to the players, give them water, etc.," Martin Duffey recalled decades later. "The competition was always pretty fierce, especially when we'd play the Kautskys in Indianapolis or the Pistons in Fort Wayne. I remember that we sold out Butler Fieldhouse in Indianapolis when we'd play the Kautskys."[102] One of the team's top players was Ed Stanczak, a star at Fort Wayne Central Catholic High School, who did not attend college. As Stanczak recalled, "That first year we played the Renaissance and the Globetrotters and other good touring teams. Ike would bring those clubs into the Wigwam, and the fans loved it. We routinely scored more than 100 points a game. Back then we were 'run-and-gun'—a real fast-break team. It was really something to see."[103]

After high school Stanczak played independent ball in Indiana. As he recalled,

I got paid $25 a game. I thought that was big money back in those days. I only played there about a month when Gabby Cronk approached me. He told me that Mr. Ike Duffy was starting a team in Anderson. It impressed me because they were hoping to become a member of the NBL. And Duffey offered to pay me $100 a game. Well, that's all I needed to hear. I joined immediately. Some say I was overaggressive. I was just showing them that I wasn't going to be pushed around. There was even one time when a referee came over to me before the game started and blew the whistle at me. I said, "What'd I do? I just walked onto the floor." And he said, "I just want to settle you down. I want you to know that I'm watching you."[104]

Anderson entered the tournament as one of the last two teams, but that did not faze Duffey, who brought his showmanship and flair for the dramatic to Chicago by "bringing a special train-load of rooters from the Hoosier town to see if they [couldn't] whoop it up for their pro quintet to emulate the example of the Anderson prep representative, which won the coveted high school title in Indiana a week ago."[105] The Chiefs faced the Cleveland Allmen Transfers in the first round. Cleveland was making its third consecutive appearance in the tournament and was led by the high-scoring Mel Riebe. Riebe spent the season playing for Great Lakes Naval Training Station and scored a remarkable 564 points in thirty games. Back in time for the tournament, Riebe tallied 9 points, but the Transfers were no match for the Chiefs, who easily defeated the Cleveland club, 59–46. The Chiefs "display[ed] a fast-breaking club with plenty of defense."[106] Anderson was led by Stanczak, who paced all scorers with 21 points. Both teams featured integrated squads, for

Anderson had signed Sonny Boswell, formerly of the Chicago Studebakers, which integrated the NBL in 1942–43; Boswell still co-held the tournament's single-game scoring record with 32 points. Also playing on the Cleveland squad was Willie Smith, a longtime center for the New York Renaissance, as the tournament continued to champion the integration of the game. Boswell scored 2 points, while Smith tallied 7 points.

With a win Anderson faced Baltimore. In the first of four quarterfinal matches played, the Anderson-Baltimore game became one of the tournament's best. The game seesawed back and forth with neither club able to extend a large margin. Baltimore held a slim 30–27 lead nearing halftime. In the second half "the Hoosiers tied the count no less than four times in the last two periods, [but] they just couldn't get over the hump. As it was, it took some long shots by Mike Bloom to sew up the game, with Anderson never more than 2 points off the pace until almost the final seconds."[107] Baltimore held on for a 67–65 win as Mike Bloom and Hagan Andersen each scored seventeen points for Baltimore. Meanwhile, Ed Lewinski's twenty points and Sonny Boswell's fourteen led Anderson.

The Bullets now headed back to Baltimore to face the Philadelphia SPHAS in the ABL championship series. Although Anderson lost, its good showing left a positive taste with fans and the team. As Stanczak reflected, "We were a Cinderella team in the tournament. [The tournament] had all these big-name NBL teams and the national touring teams. And we were this little team from Anderson, Indiana. Nobody'd ever heard of us."[108] "I think after the tournament Mr. Duffey just wanted to keep getting better and better. So he started recruiting some big-name talent to come to Anderson to play. Basketball had become a very serious venture to him."[109] Anderson would join the NBL for the 1946–47 and 1947–48 seasons as the Anderson Duffey Packers. They would also play in the 1947 and 1948 World Professional Basketball Tournaments.

Baltimore had now advanced to the semifinals, where it faced the two-time defending champion, the Fort Wayne Zollner Pistons. Fort Wayne continued to be the class act of the tournaments and was the odds-on-favorite to win the title again. After a first-round bye the Zollner Pistons faced the Midland Dows, a surprise team from 1945 that "had spirit and speed and swept into the quarterfinals."[110] The Dow Chemicals compiled a 34-5 record as an amateur team. Midland opened the tournament against the Indianapolis Kautskys, who made their return to the NBL after a three-year hiatus. Midland lost in the quarterfinals of the 1945 tournament to the Dayton Bombers, 52–50, while Indianapolis's last tournament appearance was in 1942, when the team lost to the Long Island Grumman Flyers. Indianapolis finished the NBL regular season with a 10-22 mark, last in the Western Division. Its subpar season continued in the tournament as it fell to Midland, 72–59. The game "resolved itself into an individual duel between two of the greatest centers in the business—'Slim' Wintermute of Midland and Arnold Risen of Indianapolis. Wintermute, a former all-American from Oregon State, finished with 23 points to 20 for Risen, who won honors at Ohio State, but the former had a more balanced ensemble."[111] Ten Midland players scored as the Dows tallied thirty field goals.

Next up for Midland was two-time defending champion Fort Wayne. The contest was the second of four quarterfinal match-ups on March 29. Fort Wayne figured to have this game under control, but it was anything but. As recounted the following day in the *Chicago Herald American*, "Fort Wayne, defending champion, had the narrowest kind of escape from elimination at the hands of a fighting Midland outfit which refused to concede defeat even when trailing by 17 points in the second half. The Dows came up with a rally that had the crowd standing on the seats and with 1:30 remaining, missed a set-up shot that would have put them ahead, 64–63. Then Jerry Bush sneaked off for a sleeper as the game ended to sew up the affair."[112] Instead, Fort Wayne pulled out a 65–62 victory, led by Bobby McDermott's fourteen points; Chick

Reiser's thirteen, and Buddy Jeannette's twelve. Both teams sported nearly identical statistics. Fort Wayne tallied twenty-three field goals and nineteen free throws, while Midland had twenty-two field goals and eighteen free throws. Even the fouls committed were nearly even; Fort Wayne tallied twenty-three to Midland's twenty-one. For Fort Wayne the experience paid off as it advanced to the semifinals for the fourth consecutive year.

The semifinals were now set, and they included the Chicago American Gears versus the Oshkosh All-Stars and the Baltimore Bullets against the two-time defending champion, the Fort Wayne Zollner Pistons. Three of the four teams were NBL squads, the first time that had occurred in tournament history. The first semifinal pitted Mikan, the center of the future, against Cowboy Edwards, the game's best big man over the past decade. After holding his own against Sheboygan's Ed Dancker in the quarterfinals, Mikan figured to be in for a tough assignment versus Edwards.

As Mikan recalled,

In one of my first games, we were playing the Oshkosh (Wisconsin) All-Stars, who had Leroy (Cowboy) Edwards out of Kentucky, the league's top center at the time. Edwards was 6 feet, 9 inches, 280 pounds and strong as a bull with a temperament to match. Ray [Meyer] said to me, "George whatever you do to him, stay away from him. Give him a lot of room."

"Geez," I thought, "I'm just coming out of college. I'm in the best shape of my life. I weigh a strapping 190 pounds. Bullshit, I can handle him."

The first play of the game I was going to guard Edwards close, so I was up against him, determined to hold him out of the lane. He reached down with his left arm and grabbed me above my knee and squeezed it. It just petrified me, and I couldn't move. He turned around and hit a hook shot.

On our second trip down to the Gears' defensive end, I still hadn't learned my lesson. I was on Edwards, and I tried to hold him out—you could hear my gym shoes squeaking as I strained to hold any position. Cowboy threw a nice little elbow and hit me right in my midsection. He knocked me over and made another hook shot.[113]

After his second encounter with Edwards, all Mikan could do was listen to his coach and give Edwards plenty of room, which he did. Ironically, moving away from Edwards actually helped Mikan as Edwards kept missing his shots, not used to having the pushing and shoving with Mikan under the basket. It threw his rhythm off.

The contest indeed was physical as "the game was one of the roughest in tournament annals, breaking all records for points, fouls, free throws and other miscellaneous items except that for individual scoring. Even that would have been tossed into the discard, too, had not George Mikan been forced to bow out on fouls with 25 points to his credit after seven minutes of the second half had been played."[114] Oshkosh jumped out to a quick lead as rookie Bob Feerick paced the All-Stars to a 19–11 lead. The Gears clawed their way back and took a 50–44 lead heading into the final period. But Oshkosh slowly chipped away and grabbed its first lead of the final period, 61–60. The score was tied at 62 with a few minutes remaining, but Oshkosh executed better down the stretch as Clint Wager hit a free throw, and Fred Rehm and Bob Carpenter each scored a basket, enabling Oshkosh to hold on for a 72–66 win. Mikan led all scorers with twenty-five points, while Edwards was held to just four points. The Gears committed thirty fouls, while the All-Stars had twenty-nine. For the second straight year the Gears lost to the eventual runner-up. In 1945 the Dayton Bombers had beaten them in the quarterfinal round. For Mikan the tournament was a learning experience facing two seasoned big men in Dancker and Edwards. As Price Brookfield, his Gears' teammate, acknowledged, "When we played Sheboygan and Ed Dancker, or Oshkosh and Cowboy

Edwards, that bunch beat on George that first year. They had him so upset at times that he came to me and I talked to him. I said, 'George, you either have to give it back to them or quit the game. They'll keep doing it. If you give it back to them, they'll stop.' That's what happened. He started giving it back to them and they quit."[115]

Oshkosh returned to the finals for the first time since 1943, and the return of its lineup to prewar levels of player personnel made the difference. This marked the fifth time in eight years that Oshkosh was playing for the title. Oshkosh would face league rival Fort Wayne, which squeaked out a tough 50–49 semifinal win over the Baltimore Bullets. The Zollner Pistons had not played exceptionally well in either of their two previous wins; "in their first tilt with Midland, the Pistons almost lost to Baltimore's closing rush. Another last-quarter fadeout nearly cost the defending champions."[116] After jumping out to an early lead, Fort Wayne saw its advantage dwindle over the ensuing periods, and Baltimore tied the score at 48 with ninety seconds remaining on a shot by Mike Bloom. Fort Wayne found its way as "John Pelkington then tipped in a rebound shot that proved the life saver. Modzelewski made one of two free throws and Andersen hit from way out with 40 seconds to go. But the Pistons successfully stalled it out with Bud Jeannette and Bob McDermott doing some great dribbling to keep control."[117] Fort Wayne held on and now earned an opportunity to capture its third consecutive championship.

Oshkosh and Fort Wayne would play a best-of-three finals, the first time this arrangement had been made for the tournament. The third place pitted the Gears versus the Bullets, also in a best-of-three series. The Gears won in two straight to claim third place for the second consecutive year. For his outstanding play in the tournament, scoring one hundred points in five games, Mikan was voted Most Valuable Player of the tournament. He set records with thirty-five field goals, thirty free throws, and a single-game record of thirteen free throws. As opponents would witness in the coming years, Mikan was just getting started.

Capitalizing on their recent momentum, Oshkosh seized control of the first game early and led 53–43 entering the final period. Bobby McDermott would not let the Pistons lose without a fight. Slowly, the Pistons clawed back and with a minute remaining, trailed by four at 61–57. McDermott and Paul Armstrong each made a foul shot to close the gap to 61–59, and "there the score remained while those last 30 seconds produced a scramble which had everyone up on the seats screaming."[118] Oshkosh managed to hold on as four All-Stars scored in double figures, led by Bob Carpenter's nineteen points. McDermott paced Fort Wayne with seventeen points, the only Piston to score in double figures. The Pistons' poor play in the past several weeks was discussed in Ben Tenny's championship preview article for the *Fort Wayne News-Sentinel*: "The Pistons also hope they can avoid any more of those inexplicable letdowns that have featured their play in the late moments of games in the last few weeks. Some figure the team went stale after too much basketball in the first three months of the season. That may be true. But the real truth is that letdowns like those cost them in the Rochester playoff set and almost cost them in their two tourney games thus far."[119] For the Pistons to hoist the championship trophy one more time, they would need to snap out of the late-season funk and resort to the type of early-season play that most closely reflected the talent level on their team.

Down a game and facing elimination, the Pistons regrouped, and their depth and balance proved the difference as they won the next two games, the first by nine points and the second by sixteen to claim their third consecutive title. For the past three years the strength of the Fort Wayne roster was its depth. With a lineup featuring Pelkington, Tough, Sadowski, Reiser, McDermott, Kinney, Bush, Jeannette, Shipp, and Armstrong, it was difficult for any opponent to counter the waves of players that Carl Bennett could put on the floor. Prior to the start of Game Two, Bennett shook up his lineup with the hopes of jump-starting his team. "They juggled their lineup for Saturday, starting with

Bob Tough, John Pelkington, Ed Sadowski, Bob McDermott and Chick Reiser. That one really clicked and the second class of the series would have been a runaway but for some sensational pivot shooting by the old veteran, Leroy (Cowboy) Edwards. He was plenty hot, hitting some uncanny heaves and Oshkosh would have taken a real drubbing but for his ability to toss that ball up there somehow and see it fall through."[120] While the new lineup proved important, it was the play of McDermott, arguably basketball's best player during the war years, who willed his team to victory. In Game Two he led the Pistons with thirteen points, and in the clincher he again carried his team with twenty points. Fort Wayne convincingly won both games as it "went out to bedazzle the towering Wisconsin five with some of that old precision basketball."[121] For Oshkosh it was the one that got away, although Cowboy Edwards, after scoring only twelve points in the first contest, erupted for twenty-four points in both of the final two contests. Despite his heroic efforts, however, it would not be enough to overcome a balanced and determined Fort Wayne team.

Shortly after the Pistons' win, the accolades started to pour in. "Already the Zollners have stamped themselves as one of the greatest cage organizations of all time and their player-coach Bobby McDermott, last year was acclaimed the greatest professional basketball player in history. Adding further glories to the illustrious record of this great team would be but 'gilding the lily,'" noted one Chicago sportswriter. "Fort Wayne's basketball dynasty is controlled by three men: owner Fred Zollner who sponsors the world's championship men's softball team in addition to the basketball champions; Carl Bennett team manager; and Coach McDermott. These three administer the business of the team and plot the strategy of the court champions."[122]

In their three-year dominance of the tournament, the Zollner Pistons accumulated many tournament accolades. In 1944 Bobby McDermott was named tournament MVP, while Buddy Jeannette garnered that distinction in 1945. In 1944 McDermott and Blackie Towery were named

FIG. 48. The Fort Wayne Zollner Pistons won their third straight World Professional Basketball Tournament in 1946 by besting Oshkosh in three games. Courtesy of Bill Himmelman.

to the all-tournament first team, while Jerry Bush was named to the second team. John Pelkington and Buddy Jeannette were honorable mentions. A year later Jeannette and McDermott were first-team members, while Pelkington, Bush, and Chick Reiser garnered second-team honors. And in 1946, their third title, Bush and McDermott were first-team members. Fort Wayne had dominated the war years in both the National Basketball League and the World Professional Basketball Tournament. Now that the war was over, a new professional league would alter the balance of power and shake up the basketball landscape.

EPILOGUE

Basketball Arrives

The first superstar the league ever had. He [Joe Fulks] had the great-est assortment of shots I've ever seen, with a terrific ability to make them even with players hanging all over him. —EDDIE GOTTLIEB, COACH, PHILADELPHIA WARRIORS

Shortly after the conclusion of the 1945–46 basketball season, the game's landscape changed considerably. On June 6, 1946, a meeting was called at the Hotel Commodore in New York, where hockey league and arena owners gathered to form the Basketball Association of America (BAA), a new professional basketball league. These owners filled their arenas with hockey and ice shows and other events, but the arenas were still empty on too many nights. They decided that basketball would be a good solution, so they formed the BAA. With the war now ended, professional basketball had become an attractive option for these owners, for the success of the college doubleheaders, service bas-ketball, and the World Professional Basketball Tournament all showed that professional basketball was gaining a foothold in popularity and over time could be profitable. The owners who met for that first meet-ing included Walter Brown, Peter Tyrell, John Harris, James Norris, Lou Pieri, Emory Jones, Arthur Morse, Al Sutphin, and Mike Uline.

The BAA experienced the typical growing pains associated with inaugural campaigns. Eleven teams began the season with a sixty-game schedule. The Eastern Division consisted of the Washington Capitols, the Philadelphia Warriors, the New York Knickerbockers, the Providence Steamrollers, the Boston Celtics, and the Toronto Huskies. The Western Division was comprised of the Chicago Stags, the St. Louis Bombers, the Cleveland Rebels, the Detroit Falcons, and the Pittsburgh Ironmen. Many stories emerged during that first year of the BAA, but the biggest sensation was the emergence and play of Joe Fulks. Born in western Kentucky in 1921, Fulks played basketball as a child with a ball filled with sawdust. He played three years of college basketball at Murray State, where he was an All-American. After he left college to join the marines, he was stationed in California and played well for the marines basketball team. Like all great players he was discovered. Petey Rosenberg, a former standout for the Philadelphia SPHAS, found him one day playing basketball in San Diego. As Rosenberg recounts the story,

> Nobody'd ever really heard of Fulks when he played in college, but I'd played against him in a service tournament in Hawaii. Fulks was a sub on his team, but when he played, he'd pop the ball into the basket like it had eyes. He could dribble, run fairly well, hit hooks with either hand, and he had a one-handed jump shot that couldn't be defensed. If Fulks couldn't play a lick of defense, well, back in those days, the only guys who did came from the Eastern Seaboard. Anyway, as soon as I could, I wrote a letter to Gotty telling him about Fulks. "If you sign this kid," I wrote, "you could win a championship in any league you could image [sic]." Fortunately, Gotty took my advice to heart.[1]

Gottlieb trusted his former player as he recalled years later,

> I can remember that we brought him in, sight unseen, on the recommendation of Petey Rosenberg, who had seen him play for a service team in the Philippines. I asked Petey if he could help us. He said, "'Get him, and we can win a championship." We got him, and we won.

Ironically, we could have lost him before we ever got him. I wrote him a letter that he never got. Eventually, I learned he was back in college (Murray State, Ky.), and called him. He had no idea who I was, but he knew about our league and was interested in playing. He told me later that Chicago tried to make him a better offer, but that he said he would have to talk to us first.[2]

Fulks signed with Philadelphia and led the Warriors to second place in the Eastern Division with a 35-25 mark, second behind the 49-11 front-runner pace of Washington, a team coached by a young Red Auerbach.

Fulks could score and score, but what made him so successful was his shot and the difficulty in defending him. George Senesky, a standout at St. Joseph's in Philadelphia who was a teammate of Fulks that first year, recalled his impression of Fulks.

He had awkward money shot that nobody could defend. The ball we used was so big and got so heavy with sweat in such a short time that we really had to pound it into the floor to dribble it with some control. To help him keep the ball steady, Joe would start his shot with his left hand underneath it and his right hand in back. He'd wind up shooting his jumper with his right hand but with lots of support from his left hand. And he could get his shot off on the move, while he was twisting in the air and going both left and right. His nickname, "Jumping Joe," came about because of his shot, not because he was a great leaper."[3]

Gottlieb designed the offense around Fulks as Matt Goukas Sr. remembered, "It was understood that Gotty let us pass and cut to our heart's content, as long as the ball eventually wound up in Joe's possession."[4]

With Fulks at the helm the Warriors played steady ball all season. He was also popular with his teammates. Angelo Musi remembered, "That's what made him so easy to be with. None of the publicity he got ever went to his head. We used to kid him about being a hillbilly, and he'd laugh along with the rest of us."[5] As Goukas noted, "I guess I was as friendly with Joe as anyone. If there was one player who revolutionized the game, it was him. He came from the Marines to the big city and became a star. This might've been the first big city he was ever even in. The jump shot was so new . . . and he had a two-handed release from behind his head, a hesitation move, a shot that he would make no matter who was guarding him."[6] "Even though he was in his cups, Fulks was a likeable guy," Petey Rosenberg stated.[7]

From Fulks's perspective his years playing in the military had helped his game considerably: "What did it was playing against a lot of so-called All-Americans overseas. I had read about these guys and don't think I wasn't impressed. But when I got out there and played against them, I knew those press clippings couldn't get those stars a basket or a rebound. I knew I could play in the pro league."[8] "I was 26 years old when I signed with the Warriors. There are some players who think about retiring at that age now."[9] "We had a great team and a great gang of guys. We'd let George Senesky take care of the defensive work. Howie Dallmar and Fred Sheffield liked to pass off, so Angie Musi did the outside shooting and I did it from in close."[10] "However, I tried to make sure three or four of the other guys moved the ball before it came to me. Then nobody would holler if I took a shot."[11]

From the opening tap-off of the new league, Fulks was a sensation, one who surprised everyone and jolted excitement into the game. In his first game, on November 7, 1946, against Pittsburgh, he scored 25 points. In one eight-game stretch he averaged 31 points per game. He set a single-game scoring record with 41 points and a single-season scoring record with 1,611 points. He led the league with a 23.2 points-per-game average. He led the Philadelphia Warriors to the 1947 BAA championship. As Gottlieb summed up after the season, "It was one of the smartest moves I ever made, because a week after I got Joe, Ned Irish told me: 'You've got the best player in the country.'"[12]

The BAA's main competition for talent and exposure was the

National Basketball League, which had existed since 1937. While the BAA had larger arenas in bigger cities, the better basketball players could still be found in the NBL. Over the next three seasons the two leagues coexisted, fighting for the best players, and tepidly attempting to solve their differences and work together.

The 1946–47 NBL campaign witnessed a growth in the number of teams competing. Again the league was divided into an Eastern and a Western Division. The Eastern Division consisted of holdovers: the Fort Wayne Zollner Pistons, the Rochester Royals, and the Youngstown Bears. The Cleveland Allmen Transfers folded. The Eastern Division welcomed the addition of the Syracuse Nationals, the Toledo Jeeps, and the Buffalo Bisons. The four teams who finished the previous season with the Western Division—Oshkosh, Indianapolis, Chicago, and Sheboygan—all joined the league. The Anderson Duffy Packers, who had played in the World Professional Basketball Tournament the previous March, signed on and were joined by the Detroit Gems. With twelve teams this was the best showing for the NBL since its first year, in 1937–38. Rochester and Fort Wayne continued to set the pace in the Eastern Division as Rochester led the pack with a 31-13 record while Fort Wayne was a close second with a 25-19 mark. The other teams in their division were below .500. In the West Oshkosh, Indianapolis, Chicago, Sheboygan, and Anderson all waged a battle for first place, separated by no more than four games in the standings. The Detroit Gems brought up the cellar with a dismal 4-40 mark.

The season witnessed two big developments. The NBL continued to champion the integration of the game; the Tri-Cities Blackhawks integrated with Pop Gates, while Rochester welcomed Dolly King. As Gates remembered,

I was with the Tri-City Blackhawks in their very first year. They started out of Buffalo actually—the Buffalo Bisons—and they moved the franchise during the season to the Tri-City Blackhawks—Moline,

Rock Island and Davenport. Dolly King and myself were recruited up to Rochester. We used to play against Rochester all the time. We used to pick up a team and play throughout that area, so Les Harrison recruited Dolly King and myself to play for the Rochester Seagrams—this would be before 1946. By this time, the National Basketball League was going down and that's when they brought in the Rochester team, which was now called the Rochester Royals. Subsequently they started the Buffalo team, which later became the Tri-City Blackhawks, and I think through the picking of Negro ballplayers at that particular time, Les Harrison recommended me to Leo Ferris or Cliff Ferris of the Buffalo franchise. Dolly went to Rochester and I went to Buffalo, which later went to Tri-City. We started in Buffalo and moved to Tri-Cities after the season started.[13]

After a 5-8 start, Buffalo transferred to Tri-Cities, where the team earned a 14-17 record.

The other development involved George Mikan, who was coming off an MVP performance in the 1946 World Professional Basketball Tournament. Less than a month into the season, Mikan quit the team, contending that the Gears and their financially strapped owner, Maurice White, tried to cut his salary. While Mikan sat at home for six weeks, the team fell in the standings, hovering around .500. Mikan rejoined the team and was joined by player/coach Bobby McDermott. Dropped from the Fort Wayne Zollner Pistons for off-the-court behavior, McDermott brought his outside shooting and fiery temperament to complement Mikan's inside play. The two led a late-season surge into the playoffs. Once the second season began, the Gears proved too strong for the competition and claimed the title over the Rochester Royals, three games to one.

While the NBL and the BAA were competing for talent and exposure, the American Basketball League was slipping into irrelevancy. The ABL assumed a backseat to the BAA league and quickly became a minor league. For the 1946–47 season the league was divided into two divisions. The Northern Division consisted of the Brooklyn Gothams, the Jersey City Atoms, the Troy Celtics, the Paterson Crescents, and the Newark Bobcats. Newark played the season as the Kingston Chiefs and the Yonkers Chiefs. The Southern Division saw the Baltimore Bullets, the Philadelphia SPHAS, the Trenton Tigers, the Elizabeth Braves, and the Wilmington Blue Bombers. Eddie Gottlieb kept the SPHAS playing even as he focused more on the Philadelphia Warriors. The teams played thirty-four or thirty-five games, and the top six teams, based on their records, advanced to the playoffs. Baltimore, jelling as a team since winning the league title the previous year, compiled the best regular season record at 31-3. Although the team won its first-round playoff series, Baltimore bowed out to compete in the World Professional Basketball Tournament. As a result Trenton renewed its city rivalry with the Philadelphia SPHAS and defeated them in three games to win the title.

The ABL as a whole struggled except for the Baltimore Bullets. With a 31-13 record the Bullets withdrew from their league playoffs to compete in the World Professional Basketball Tournament. The ninth annual tournament was set for five days in March at Chicago Stadium. As always the National Basketball League was well represented with eight of the fourteen teams competing. The Fort Wayne Zollner Pistons and the Indianapolis Kautskys were given first-round byes. The other NBL teams included the Oshkosh All-Stars, the Anderson Duffy Packers, the Syracuse Nationals, the Sheboygan Red Skins, the Toledo Jeeps, and the Tri-Cities Blackhawks. The Midland Dows were making their third straight appearance, while the New York Rens were again participating. Incidentally, the Harlem Globetrotters chose not to appear for the second straight year. The East Coast was represented by three teams: the Baltimore Bullets of the American Basketball League, the Herkimer (NY) Mohawk Redskins, and the Pittsburgh Pirates. For the first time in the tournament's history, a team from the West Coast participated, the Portland (OR) Indians. The brackets for the first-round games were arranged so that no NBL team was scheduled to play against another one. That worked to the league's advantage; five of the six opening-round games saw an NBL team win. The lone exception was the Syracuse Nationals, who lost to the Midland Dows. In the quarterfinals seven of the eight teams were NBL squads, which led to an all-NBL semifinal. In the semis Indianapolis defeated Oshkosh, while Toledo defeated Fort Wayne. Indianapolis defeated Toledo for the championship. It marked the fifth time in nine years that an NBL team captured the World Professional Basketball Tournament.

As a whole the 1946–47 professional basketball season was a chaotic affair with a new league, more teams, and plenty of players anxious to play and resume their once-promising careers. Over the next few seasons the landscape would shake out as the BAA and the NBL eventually merged to form the National Basketball Association (NBA) in 1949–50. The Minneapolis Lakers, with George Mikan, would become the NBA's first great dynasty. The NBA would integrate in 1949–50, and by the late 1950s many of the great NBA stars were African American. Scoring continued to increase each year, and by the late 1950s NBA games were televised. During the decade after World War II, the game grew, and that growth was directly related to the how the game had developed during World War II. The war years had a profound and lasting impact on basketball.

APPENDIX A

National Basketball League (NBL) Standings
1941–1942 to 1945–1946

1941–1942

Oshkosh All-Stars	20-4
Akron Goodyear Wingfoots	15-9
Fort Wayne Zollner Pistons	15-9
Indianapolis Kautskys	12-11
Sheboygan Red Skins	10-14
Chicago Bruins	8-15
Toledo Jim White Chevrolets	3-21

Playoffs
Fort Wayne defeated Akron in semifinals 2 games to 1.
Oshkosh defeated Indianapolis in semifinals 2 games to 0.
Oshkosh defeated Fort Wayne in championship 2 games to 1.

1942–1943

Fort Wayne Zollner Pistons	17-6
Sheboygan Red Skins	12-11
Oshkosh All-Stars	11-12
Chicago Studebakers	8-15
Toledo Jim White Chevrolets	0-4

Toledo dropped out.

Playoffs

Sheboygan defeated Oshkosh in semifinals 2 games to 0.

Fort Wayne defeated Chicago in semifinals 2 games to 1.

Sheboygan defeated Fort Wayne in championship 2 games to 1.

1943–1944

Fort Wayne Zollner Pistons	18-4
Sheboygan Red Skins	14-8
Oshkosh All-Stars	7-15
Cleveland Chase Brassmen	3-15

Playoffs

Fort Wayne defeated Cleveland in semifinals 2 games to 0.

Sheboygan defeated Oshkosh in semifinals 2 games to 1.

Fort Wayne defeated Sheboygan in championship 3 games to 0.

1944–1945

Eastern Division	
Fort Wayne Zollner Pistons	25-5
Cleveland Allmen Transfers	13-17
Pittsburgh Raiders	7-23
Western Division	
Sheboygan Red Skins	19-11
Chicago American Gears	14-16
Oshkosh All-Stars	12-18

Playoffs

Sheboygan defeated Chicago in semifinals 2 games to 1.

Fort Wayne defeated Cleveland in semifinals 2 games to 0.

Fort Wayne defeated Sheboygan in championship 3 games to 2.

1945–1946

Eastern Division

Fort Wayne Zollner Pistons	26-8
Rochester Royals	24-10
Youngstown Bears	13-20
Cleveland Allmen Transfers	4-29

Western Division

Sheboygan Red Skins	21-13
Oshkosh All-Stars	19-15
Chicago American Gears	17-17
Indianapolis Kautskys	10-22

Playoffs

Sheboygan defeated Oshkosh in semifinals 3 games to 2.

Rochester defeated Fort Wayne in semifinals 3 games to 1.

Rochester defeated Sheboygan in championship 3 games to 0.

Information for tables taken from Robert Peterson's Cages to Jump Shots *(New York: Oxford University Press, 1990) and Murry Nelson's* The National Basketball League: A History, 1935–1949 *(Jefferson NC: McFarland, 2009).*

APPENDIX B

American Basketball League (ABL) Standings
1941–1942 to 1945–1946

1941–1942

American Basketball League

TEAM	WON	LOST	PCT
First Half			
Wilmington Blue Bombers		3	.769
Philadelphia SPHAS	8	6	.571
Washington Brewers	5	6	.455
Trenton Tigers	5	8	.385
New York Jewels	1	6	.143
Second Half			
Wilmington Blue Bombers	8	4	.667
Trenton Tigers	6	6	.500
Philadelphia SPHAS	5	7	.417
Washington Brewers	5	7	.417

New York Jewels dropped out. Wilmington won both halves of regular season to claim championship.

1942–1943

American Basketball League

TEAM	WON	LOST	PCT
Trenton Tigers	11	2	.846
Philadelphia SPHAS	8	6	.571
Camden/Brooklyn Indians	3	5	.375
Harrisburg Senators	4	8	.333
New York Jewels	1	6	.143

Philadelphia SPHAS defeated Trenton Tigers 4 to 3 to win title. Camden Indians transferred to Brooklyn Indians.

1943–1944

American Basketball League

TEAM	WON	LOST	PCT
First Half			
Wilmington Blue Bombers	12	4	.750
New York Americans	9	6	.600
Trenton Tigers	8	6	.571
Philadelphia SPHAS	4	9	.308
Brooklyn Indians	2	9	.182
Second Half			
Philadelphia SPHAS	8	4	.667
Trenton Tigers	7	5	.583
Wilmington Blue Bombers	5	5	.500
New York Americans	2	8	.200

Wilmington Blue Bombers defeated Philadelphia SPHAS 4 to 3 to win title. Brooklyn dropped out.

1944–1945

American Basketball League

TEAM	WON	LOST	PCT
Philadelphia SPHAS	22	8	.733
Trenton Tigers	21	9	.700

Wilmington Bombers	14	14	.500
Baltimore Bullets	14	16	.467
New York Westchesters/ New York Gothams	11	15	.423
Washington Capitols/ Paterson Crescents	3	23	.115

ABL Playoff

Baltimore defeated Trenton 2 to 1.

Philadelphia defeated Wilmington 2 to 1.

Philadelphia SPHAS defeated Baltimore Bullets 2 to 1 to win title.

New York Westchesters transferred to New York Gothams.

Washington Capitols transferred to Paterson Crescents.

1945–1946

American Basketball League

TEAM	WON	LOST	PCT
Baltimore Bullets	22	13	.629
Philadelphia SPHAS	21	14	.600
New York Gothams	18	16	.529
Wilmington Bombers	15	19	.441
Trenton Tigers	14	20	.412
Paterson Crescents	13	21	.382

ABL Playoff

Baltimore defeated New York 2 to 1.

Philadelphia defeated Wilmington 2 to 0.

Baltimore Bullets defeated Philadelphia SPHAS 3 to 1 to win title.

Information for tables taken from The SPHAS: The Life and Times of Basketball's Greatest Jewish Team *by Douglas Stark (Philadelphia: Temple University Press, 2011).*

APPENDIX C

World Professional Basketball Tournament Results
1941–1942 to 1945–1946

1942 (1941–1942)

Fourth Round

(Chicago) Harlem Globetrotters 40	Hagerstown (MD) Conoco Oilers 33
Sheboygan Red Skins 33	Columbus Bobb Chevrolets 26
Davenport (IA) Rockets 29	Oshkosh All-Stars 44
(Michigan City)Northern Indiana Steelers 37	New York Renaissance (Rens) 55
Detroit Eagles 46	Toledo White Huts 29
Fort Wayne Zollner Pistons 42	Aberdeen (MD) Army Ordinance 56
Chicago Bruins 56	Detroit AAA 46
(Bethpage) Long Island Grumman Flying V's 54	Indianapolis Kautskys 32

Quarterfinals

(Chicago) Harlem Globetrotters 37	Sheboygan Red Skins 32
Oshkosh All-Stars 44	New York Renaissance (Rens) 38
Detroit Eagles 40	Aberdeen (MD) Army Ordnance 34
Chicago Bruins 38	(Bethpage) Long Island Grumman Flying V's 48

Semifinals

(Chicago) Harlem Globetrotters 41	Oshkosh All-Stars 48
Detroit Eagles 44	(Bethpage) Long Island Grumman Flying V's 43

Finals

Oshkosh All-Stars 43	Detroit Eagles 41

Third Place

(Chicago) Harlem Globetrotters 41	(Bethpage) Long Island Grumman Flying V's 43

1943 (1942–1943)

Fourth Round

Akron Collegians 31	Detroit Eagles 36
Indianapolis Pure Oils 52	Fort Wayne Zollner Pistons 56
South Bend Studebaker Champions 44	Minneapolis Rock Spring Sparkles 45
Dayton (OH) Dive Bombers 46	Chicago Ramblers 41

Quarterfinals

Oshkosh All-Stars 65	Detroit Eagles 36
Fort Wayne Zollner Pistons 48	Sheboygan Red Skins 40
Washington DC Bears 40	Minneapolis Rock Spring Sparklers 21
Dayton Dive Bombers 44	(Chicago) Harlem Globetrotters 34

Semifinals

Oshkosh All-Stars 40	Fort Wayne Zollner Pistons 39
Washington DC Bears 38	Dayton Dive Bombers 30

Finals

Oshkosh All-Stars 31	Washington DC Bears 43

Third Place

Fort Wayne Zollner Pistons 58	Dayton Dive Bombers 52

1944 (1943–1944)

Fourth Round

Dayton Acme Bombers 52	Akron Collegians 38
Cleveland Chase Brass 55	Indianapolis Pure Oils 52
New York Renaissance (Rens) 39	Detroit Sufferins 33
Oshkosh All-Stars 51	Rochester Wings 40
(Chicago) Harlem Globetrotters 41	Pittsburgh Sheriffs 40
Brooklyn Eagles 55	Camp Campbell (KY) Tankmen 41

Quarterfinals

Fort Wayne Zollner Pistons 59	Dayton Acme Bombers34
Cleveland Chase Brass 38	New York Renaissance (Rens) 52
Oshkosh All-Stars 31	(Chicago) Harlem Globetrotters 41
Brooklyn Eagles 49	Sheboygan Red Skins 43

Semifinals

Fort Wayne Zollner Pistons 42	New York Renaissance (Rens) 38
(Chicago) Harlem Globetrotters 41	Brooklyn Eagles 63

Finals

Fort Wayne Zollner Pistons 50	Brooklyn Eagles 33

Third Place

New York Renaissance (Rens) 29	(Chicago) Harlem Globetrotters 37

1945 (1944–1945)

Fourth Round

Detroit Mansfields 56	Oshkosh All-Stars 60
Pittsburgh Raiders 53	Newark (NY) C-O 2s 50
New York Renaissance (Rens) 67	Indianapolis Stars 59
Cleveland Allmen Transfers 46	Midland (MI) Dows 61
(Bethpage) Long Island Grumman Hellcats 27	Dayton Acmes 43
Chicago American Gears 58	Hartford (CT) Nutmegs 47

Quarterfinals

Fort Wayne Zollner Pistons 63	Oshkosh All-Stars 52
Pittsburgh Raiders 52	New York Renaissance (Rens) 61
Midland (MI) Dows 50	Dayton Acmes 52
Chicago American Gears 53	(Chicago) Harlem Globetrotters 49

Semifinals

Fort Wayne Zollner Pistons 68	New York Renaissance (Rens) 45
Dayton Acmes 80	Chicago American Gears 51

Finals

Fort Wayne Zollner Pistons 78	Dayton Acmes 52

Third Place

New York Renaissance (Rens) 55	Chicago American Gears 64

1946 (1945–1946)

Fourth Round

Chicago American Gears 69	Pittsburgh Raiders 58
Oshkosh All-Stars 60	Detroit Mansfields 32
Toledo Jeeps 39	New York Renaissance (Rens) 82
Baltimore Bullets 61	Dayton Mickeys 58
Cleveland Allmen Transfers 46	Anderson Chiefs 59
Midland (MI) Dows 72	Indianapolis Kautskys 59

Quarterfinals

Sheboygan Red Skins 51	Chicago American Gears 52
Oshkosh All-Stars 50	New York Renaissance (Rens) 44
Baltimore Bullets 67	Anderson Chiefs 65
Midland (MI) Dows 62	Fort Wayne Zollner Pistons 65

Semifinals

Chicago American Gears 66	Oshkosh All-Stars 72
Baltimore Bullets 49	Fort Wayne Zollner Pistons 50

Finals 2 of 3

Oshkosh All-Stars 61	Fort Wayne Zollner Pistons 59
Oshkosh All-Stars 47	Fort Wayne Zollner Pistons 56
Oshkosh All-Stars 57	Fort Wayne Zollner Pistons 73

Third Place 2 of 3

Chicago American Gears 59	Baltimore Bullets 54
Chicago American Gears 65	Baltimore Bullets 50

Exhibition Game

Anderson Chiefs 55	Sheboygan Red Skins 52

Information for the tables taken from John Schleppi's Chicago's Showcase of Basketball: The World Tournament of Professional Basketball and the College All-Star Game *(Haworth NJ: St. Johann Press, 2008).*

APPENDIX D

Red Cross Charity Matches

During World War II the NCAA and the NIT champions played an annual benefit game at Madison Square Garden in New York to raise money for the Red Cross.

YEAR	WINNER	SCORE	LOSER
1943	Wyoming (NCAA)	52–47	St. John's (NIT)
1944	Utah (NCAA)	43–36	St. John's (NIT)
1945	Oklahoma A&M (NCAA)	52–44	DePaul (NIT)

1943

WYOMING (52)	FG	FT	FTM	PF	TP	ST. JOHN'S (47)	FG	FT	FTM	PF	TP
Kenny Sailors	5	1	2	1	11	Fuzzy Levane	2	1	1	2	5
Jimmie Reese	0	0	0	0	0	Ray Wertis	0	0	0	0	0
Jim Weir	5	3	0	4	13	Lionel Baxter	5	5	1	3	15
Milo Komenich	8	4	0	4	20	Harry Boykoff	6	5	0	2	17
Floyd Volker	3	1	0	2	7	Al Moschetti	4	0	3	3	8
Lew Roney	0	0	0	0	0	Ily Gotkin	1	0	1	1	2
Jim Collins	0	1	3	3	1	Frank Plantamura	0	0	0	0	0
	21	10	5	14	52		18	11	6	11	47

Officials: Pat Kennedy and Joe Burns

1944

UTAH (43)	FG	FT	FTM	PF	TP	ST. JOHN'S (36)	FG	FT	FTM	PF	TP
Arnie Ferrin	6	7	5	2	17	Bill Kotsores	2	3	1	4	5
Dick Smuin	1	0	0	3	2	Ray Wertis	5	2	0	1	10
Fred Sheffield	0	0	0	0	0	Tom Larkin	0	1	1	0	1
Wat Misaka	2	2	1	1	5	Ivy Summer	3	2	1	4	7
Herb Wilkinson	4	4	3	2	11	Norm Mager	0	0	0	0	0
Bob Lewis	4	1	0	4	8	Hy Gotkin	4	4	3	1	11
						Don Wehr	0	1	0	0	0
						Wade Duym	1	0	0	1	2
						Murray Robinson	0	0	0	0	0
	17	14	9	12	43		15	13	6	12	36

Officials: Joe Burns and Hagan Andersen

1945

OKLAHOMA A& M (52)	FG	FTM	TP	DEPAUL (44)	FG	FTM	TP
Cecil Hankins	8	4	20	Gene Stump	5	2	12
Weldon Kern	0	5	5	Nick Comerford	0	0	0
Bob Kurland	4	6	14	Ernie DiBendetto	5	2	12
Joe Halbert	0	0	0	Ted Furman	1	1	3
Blake Williams	0	1	1	George Mikan	2	5	9
Doyle Parrack	3	0	6	Jack Phelan	1	0	2
J. L. Parks	3	0	6	Jack Allen	0	1	1
				Dick Niemiera	0	0	0
				Whitey Kachan	2	0	4
				George Larochelle	0	1	1
				[x] Halloran	0	0	0
	18	16	52		16	12	44

Stats for tables compiled from various newspapers.

APPENDIX E

Service Team Records

This following information is taken from *The Official Basketball Guide* (National Basketball Committee). The results are in alphabetical order.

1942–1943

TEAM	LOCATION	RECORD
Alameda Coast Guard	Governor Island, Alameda CA	25-3
Camp Breckinridge	Morganfield KY	5-6
Camp Campbell	Camp Campbell KY	27-9
Camp Crowder	Neosho MO	7-14
Camp Davis	Wilmington NC	9-0
Camp Edwards	Sandwich MA	17-4
Camp Grant	Rockford IL	31-2
Camp Kohler	Sacramento CA	6-4
Camp Perry	Port Clinton OH	5-10
Camp Pickett	Blackstone VA	23-10
Camp Roberts	Paso Robles CA	10-3
Camp Sibert Replacement Training Center	Attalla AL	6-7
Camp Sibert Stat. Comp	Attalla AL	6-7
Camp Upton	Yaplank NY	22-6-1
Camp Wheeler	Macon GA	19-5
Cherry Point Marines	Havelock NC	8-3

Cochran Air Field	Macon GA	17-8
Corpus Christi Naval Air Station	Corpus Christi TX	23-0
Fort Belvoir	Fort Belvoir VA	17-10
Fort Benjamin Harrison	Lawrence IN	8-3
Fort Dix	Wrightstown NJ	21-12
Fort Eustis	Newport News VA	10-5
Fort Knox	Fort Knox KY	6-13
Fort Lewis	DuPont WA	21-2
Fort Monmouth	Oceanport NJ	25-13
Fort Monroe	Hampton VA	15-6
Fort Story	Virginia Beach VA	30-10
Fort Thomas	Fort Thomas KY	3-4
Fort Totten	Queens NY	12-10
Fort Warren	Cheyenne WY	7-3
Georgia Navy Pre-Flight	Athens GA	7-6
Great Lakes Navy Training Station	North Chicago IL	34-3
Grenier Army Airfield	Manchester NH	9-3
Hammer Field	Fresno CA	27-8
Hill Field	Ogden UT	14-10
Holabird Ordinance Base	Baltimore MD	15-5
Fort Indiantown Gap Military Reservation	Indiantown Gap PA	14-16
Key Field	Meridian MS	19-11
Las Vegas Air Field	Las Vegas NV	7-3
Lawson General Hospital	Atlanta GA	15-10
Lovell General Hospital	Fort Devens MA	13-5
Marianna Air Field	Marianna FL	6-4-1
Mather Field	Rancho Cordova CA	5-11
Memphis Naval Air Technical Training Center	Memphis TN	18-2
Mitchell Field	Garden City NY	21-8
Napier Field	Dothan AL	22-4
Naval Air Station Glenview	Glenview IL	11-6

Naval Air Station Atlanta	Marietta GA	24-3
Naval Air Station Dallas	Dallas TX	9-9
Naval Air Gunnery School	Hollywood FL	28-5
Naval Air Station Pasco	Pasco WA	15-6
Naval Air Station Grosse Ile	Grosse Ile MI	16-6
Naval Auxiliary Air Station Los Alamitos	Los Alamitos CA	25-14
Norfolk Naval Training Station	Norfolk VA	35-1
Olathe Naval Air Station	Gardner KS	13-9
Patterson Field	Dayton OH	12-2
Pendleton Field	Pendleton OR	6-10
Quonset Point Naval Air Station	Quonset Point RI	18-12
St. Mary's Navy Pre-Flight	Moraga CA	10-5
Savanna Ordinance Depot	Proving Ground IL	6-5
Syracuse Air Base	Syracuse NY	11-3
Tuskegee Air Field	Tuskegee AL	13-1
Williams Field	Mesa AZ	20-3

1943–1944

TEAM	LOCATION	Record
Aberdeen Proving Ground	Aberdeen MD	24-10
Alameda Coast Guard	Alameda CA	23-5
Bainbridge Naval Training Station	Bainbridge MD	22-8
Buckley Field Gunners	Aurora CO	19-5
Basic Training Center No. 10 Army Air Force	Greensboro NC	17-1
Camp Cooke	Lompoc CA	31-4
Camp Davis	Holly Ridge NC	6-7
Camp Grant	Rockford IL	27-4
Camp Lee	Camp Lee VA	14-8
Camp Luna	Las Vegas NM	20-8
Naval Construction Training Camp Perry Seabees	Magruder VA	27-8

Camp Shanks	Orangeburg NY	22-9
Camp Myles Standish	Taunton MA	14-16
Camp Thomas	North Kingston RI	15-12
Charleston Coast Guard Base	Charleston SC	25-8
Cherry Point Marines	Havelock NC	21-5
Cornell Navy V-5	Mt. Vernon IA	13-8
De Pauw Naval Pre-Flight	Greencastle IN	18-6
U.S. Coast Guard	Detroit MI	20-12
Ellis Island Coast Guard	New York NY	24-7
Fort Belvoir	Fort Belvoir VA	34-17
Reception Center Service Team	Fayetteville NC	33-16
Fort Harris	Fort Harris IN	19-3
Fort Knox	Fort Knox KY	20-14
Fort Leavenworth	Leavenworth KY	22-6
Fort Stevens	Warrentown OR	11-3
Fort Story	Virginia Beach VA	22–15
Florence Army Airfield	Florence SC	15-10
Georgia Pre-Flight	Athens GA	14-7
Naval Air Station Glenview	Glenview IL	14-9
Mitchell Field	Garden City NY	34-3
Napier Field	Dothan AL	21-4
Great Lakes Naval Training Center	North Chicago IL	32-4
Naval Air Station Grosse Isle	Grosse Ile MI	20-3
Naval Air Station Hutchinson	Yoder KS	16-6
Norfolk Naval Training Station	Norfolk VA	31-2
Kearns Army Air Base	Kearns UT	12-10
Keesler Army Airfield	Biloxi MS	18-5
Kelly Field	San Antonio TX	24-6
Iowa Pre-Flight	Iowa City IA	17-4
Naval Auxiliary Air Station Los Alamitos	Los Alamitos CA	38-4
Lowry Field	Denver CO	14-7
March Field	Riverside CA	20-4

McClellan Field	Sacramento CA	29-7
Mitchell Field	Garden City NY	34-3
Naval Air Station Moffett Field	Sunnyvale CA	12-2
U.S. Naval Receiving Station New Orleans	New Orleans LA	16-15
Naval Aviation Technical Training Center Skyjackets	Norman OK	18-5
U.S. Coast Guard	New York NY	46-9
Naval Air Station	Ottumwa IA	11-6
Parris Island Marines	Parris Island SC	25-6
Randolph Field	San Antonio TX	14-14
Richmond Army Air Force Base	Richmond VA	20-5
Robins Field	Warner Robins GA	9-12
St. Mary's Navy Pre Flight	Moraga CA	15-0
Sampson Naval Training Station	Romulus NY	21-8
Marines Corps Base	San Diego CA	35-0
Savanna Army Ordinance Depot	Savanna IL	10-6
Navy Bluejackets	Shoemaker CA	9-6
Sedalia Army Airfield	Knob Noster MO	20-4
South Plains Army Airfield	Lubbock TX	11-4
Naval Training School	Toledo OH	7-8
Treasure Island Naval Station	San Francisco CA	13-8
Wright Field	Dayton OH	7-9

1944–1945

TEAM	LOCATION	Record
Bainbridge Naval Training Center	Bainbridge MD	28-5
Bergstrom Army Airfield	Austin TX	10-9
Bushnell General Military Hospital	Brigham City UT	23-21
Camp Bradford	Norfolk VA	26-14
Camp Elliott National Construction Training Center	North Kingstown RI	22-5
Camp Lee Travelers	Fort Lee VA	34-11

Camp Lejeune	Jacksonville NC	21-4
Camp Peary	Magruder VA	21-17
Camp Plauche Trojans	New Orleans LA	29-5
Camp Ross	Wilmington CA	25-12
Charleston Coast Guard	Charleston SC	20-5
Cherry Point Marines	Havelock NC	30-4
U.S. Coast Guard Receiving Station	Ellis Island NY	27-7
Alameda Coast Guard	Alameda CA	21-3
Ellington Field	Houston TX	8-13
Camp Shoemaker Fleet City Bluejackets	Shoemaker CA	26-11
Fort Belvoir Engineers	Fort Belvoir VA	29-4
Fort Bragg Personnel Center	Fayetteville NC	29-11
Fort Warren	Cheyenne WY	23-16
Fort Leavenworth Flyers	Leavenworth KS	14-9
Fort Riley Ramblers	Fort Riley KS	18-9
Foster Field	Victoria TX	19-3
Galveston Army Airfield	Galveston TX	20-5
Georgia Pre-Flight	Athens GA	11-7
Great Lakes Naval Training Center	North Chicago IL	32-5
Harlingen Army Airfield	Harlingen TX	20-6
Iowa Pre-Flight	Iowa City IA	17-4
Keesler Army Airfield	Biloxi MS	25-10
Kinston Marines	Kinston Field NC	10-4
Klamath Falls Marines	Klamath Falls OR	19-9
Lee Field	Green Cove Springs FL	20-5
Lincoln Army Air Field	Lincoln NE	30-3
Lubbock Army Air Field	Lubbock TX	16-7
March Field Flyers	Riverside CA	26-3
Maxwell Field	Montgomery AL	18-10
New York District Coast Guard Office	Manhattan Beach (Brooklyn) NY	36-2
Naval Air Station Jacksonville	Jacksonville FL	25-6

Naval Training Center	San Diego CA	27-6
Naval Air Station Olathe	Gardner KS	15-15
Naval Air Station	Isle Grande, Puerto Rico	35-11
Sampson Naval Training Center	Romulus NY	24-2
Norfolk Naval Air Station	Norfolk VA	23-4
Naval Training Center Miami	Miami FL	37-5
Norfolk Naval Training Station	Norfolk VA	26-8
Naval Aviation Technical Training Center Skyjackets	Norman OK	29-5
Naval Air Station	Ottumwa IA	11-10
North Carolina Pre-Flight	Chapel Hill NC	16-6
Perrin Field	Sherman TX	17-14
Richmond AAB	Richmond VA	20-9
Robins Field	Wellston GA	18-12
Roswell Army Air Field	Roswell NM	23-10
St. Mary's Navy Pre-Flight	Moraga CA	12-6
Scott Field Flyers	Belleville IL	26-3
Sedalia Army Airfield	Knob Noster MO	30-5
Valley Forge General Hospital	Phoenixville PA	33-4
Waco Army Airfield	Waco TX	25-1
442d Troop Carrier Group (European Theatre of Operation)		19-7
U.K. 12th Replacement Depot APO 551	(Tidworth, England)	44-3
U.K. 826 Convalescent Center		18-0
U.K. 398th Bomb Group		32-0
U.K. 436 Transport Group		23-1
U.K. General Depot G-25		19-2
U.K. 8th Air Force Service Command		17-1

NOTES

INTRODUCTION

Epigraph: "Dr. Naismith, Who Started Basketball in 1891, Dies," *Philadelphia Inquirer*, November 29, 1939, 30.

1. Thomas J. Deegan, "The Golden Jubilee of Basketball: The Naismith Memorial and Basketball's Hall of Fame," *The Official Basketball Guide 1941–1942* (National Basketball Committee, 1941), 6.

2. Deegan, "Golden Jubilee of Basketball."

3. Deegan, "Golden Jubilee of Basketball."

4. 1942 World Professional Basketball Tournament program. In the possession of the author.

5. James Naismith, *Basketball: Its Origin and Development* (New York NY: Association Press, 1941), 33.

6. J. Naismith, *Basketball*, 33.

7. J. Naismith, *Basketball*, 33.

8. J. Naismith, "Origin of Basket Ball" (presented at Forum, January 5, 1932), Springfield College.

9. J. Naismith, *Basketball*, 35.

10. J. Naismith, *Basketball*, 36.

11. J. Naismith, *Basketball*, 36.

12. J. Naismith, "Origin of Basket Ball."

13. Stuart Naismith with Douglas Stark, "Papa Jimmy: The Grandson of James Naismith Remembers the Game's Inventor as a Delightful and Sweet Man Who Loved to Laugh and Have Fun," *Hall of Fame Tip-Off Program* (Basketball Hall of Fame) November 22, 2000, 45.

14. J. Naismith, *Basketball*, 21.

15. J. Naismith, *Basketball*, 23.

16. S. Naismith and Stark, "Papa Jimmy," 45.

17. J. Naismith, *Basketball*, 23.

18. School for Christian Workers, Springfield, Mass.: Catalogs and Printed Materials, 1885–1890. Springfield College.

19. School for Christian Workers, Springfield, Mass.: Catalogs and Printed Materials, 1885–1890.
20. "Physical Education in the Young Men's Christian Association," Luther Gulick Papers, col. 14, box 5, folder 2, Springfield College, Springfield MA.
21. J. Naismith, *Basketball*, 38.
22. James Naismith, "Basketball—A Game the World Plays," *Rotarian*, January 1939.
23. J. Naismith, *Basketball*, 39.
24. J. Naismith, *Basketball*, 39.
25. J. Naismith, *Basketball*, 39.
26. J. Naismith, *Basketball*, 40.
27. J. Naismith, *Basketball*, 41.
28. J. Naismith, *Basketball*, 43.
29. J. Naismith, *Basketball*, 33.
30. J. Naismith, *Basketball*, 44.
31. J. Naismith, *Basketball*, 46.
32. J. Naismith, *Basketball*, 47.
33. J. Naismith, "Origin of Basket Ball."
34. J. Naismith, *Basketball*, 52–53.
35. J. Naismith, *Basketball*, 56.
36. J. Naismith, *Basketball*, 56.
37. Ernest Hildner interview, Naismith Memorial Basketball Hall of Fame, Springfield MA, hereafter cited as Naismith Memorial Basketball Hall of Fame.
38. "Last of First Basketballers: Rap Freeze, Audiences, Amount of Whistle Tooting," *Philadelphia Inquirer*, December 26, n.d.
39. J. Naismith, "Basketball—A Game the World Plays."
40. "Basket Football Game," *Springfield Republican*, March 12, 1892, 6.
41. "Basket Football Game."
42. "A New Game of Ball," *New York Times*, April 26, 1892, 2.
43. "New Game of Ball."
44. John Devaney, *The Story of Basketball* (New York: Random House, 1976), 15.
45. Robert Peterson, *Cages to Jump Shots: Pro Basketball's Early Years* (New York: Oxford University Press, 1990), 84.
46. "Dr. J. A. Naismith Is Dead in Kansas," *New York Times*, November 28, 1939, 25.
47. S. Naismith and Stark, "Papa Jimmy," 46.
48. "Dr. J. A. Naismith Is Dead in Kansas."
49. "Dr. J. A. Naismith Is Dead in Kansas."

50. "Dr. Naismith, Who Started Basketball in 1891, Dies," *Philadelphia Inquirer*, November 29, 1939, 30.

51. Rob Rains with Helen Carpenter, *James Naismith: The Man Who Invented Basketball* (Philadelphia: Temple University Press, 2009), 88.

52. S. Naismith and Stark, "Papa Jimmy," 46.

53. Milton S. Katz, *Breaking Through: John B. McLendon, Basketball Legend and Civil Rights Pioneer* (Fayetteville: University of Arkansas Press, 2007), 12.

1. AMERICA GOES TO WAR, 1941–1942

Epigraph: 1942 World Professional Basketball Tournament program, in the possession of the author.

1. Ralph Kaplowitz, interview by the author, Queens NY, December 2007.

2. Kaplowitz interview.

3. Kaplowitz interview.

4. Kaplowitz interview.

5. Kaplowitz interview.

6. Kaplowitz interview.

7. James M. Gould, "Bears Open Basket Season with McKendree Tonight," *St. Louis Post-Dispatch*, December 8, 1941, 2B.

8. "LIU Five to Play Lawrence Tech," *New York Daily News*, December 8, 1941, 55.

9. Todd Gould, *Pioneers of the Hardwood: Indiana and the Birth of Professional Basketball* (Bloomington: Indiana University Press, 1998), 102–3.

10. Gould, *Pioneers of the Hardwood*, 103.

11. Gould, *Pioneers of the Hardwood*, 104.

12. Gould, *Pioneers of the Hardwood*, 104.

13. Robert Peterson, *Cages to Jump Shots: Pro Basketball's Early Years* (New York: Oxford University Press, 1990), 111.

14. Gus Alfieri, *Lapchick: The Life of a Legendary Player and Coach in the Glory Days of Basketball* (Guilford CT: Lyons Press, 2006), 55.

15. "NYU Meets Notre Dame Five in Feature of College Double Bill at Garden Tonight," *New York Times*, December 29, 1934, 18.

16. Everett B. Morris, "NYU and St. John's Quintets Meet Out-of-Town Foes Tonight," *New York Herald Tribune*, December 29, 1934, 19.

17. Jimmy Powers, "Notre Dame Bait as Cagers Hit Big Time," *New York Daily News*, December 29, 1934, 28.

18. Stanley Frank, "NYU, Redmen Favored to Pin Back Visiting Quintets' Ears," *New York Post*, December 29, 1934, 17.

19. "NYU Meets Notre Dame Five."

20. Arthur Daley, "NYU Five Downs Notre Dame, 25–18, as 16,000 Look On," *New York Times*, December 30, 1934, Sports 1.

21. Daley, "NYU Five Downs Notre Dame."

22. Daley, "NYU Five Downs Notre Dame."

23. Everett B. Morris, "16,000 Watch NYU Beat Notre Dame Five, 25 to 18," *New York Herald Tribune*, December 30, 1934, sec. 3, p. 1.

24. Fred Wittner, "Basketball Blossoms Out," *Sports Illustrated and The American Golfer*, March 1936, 28.

25. Wittner, "Basketball Blossoms Out," 29.

26. Jim Savage, *The Encyclopedia of the NCAA Tournament: The Complete Independent Guide to College Basketball's Championship Event* (New York: Dell, 1990), 4.

27. Al Corona, "Luisetti: Versatile, Graceful, Unselfish," *San Francisco Examiner* November 9, 1979, 70.

28. Robert Stowe, "A Star in Basketball and in Business: Luisetti Elected to All-Time College Basketball Team," *Hillsborough & Burlingame—Boutique & Villager*, December 19, 1984, in Hank Luisetti clipping file. Naismith Memorial Basketball Hall of Fame.

29. Moe Goldman, interview with Robert Peterson, May 3, 1987, Robert Peterson Collection, Naismith Memorial Basketball Hall of Fame.

30. Anne Byrne Hoffman, *Echoes from the Schoolyard: Informal Portraits of NBA Greats* (New York: Hawthorn, 1977), 9–10.

31. Billy Packer with Roland Lazenby, *Fifty Years of the Final Four* (Dallas: Taylor, 1987), 28.

32. Stowe, "Star in Basketball and in Business."

33. Jon Entine, *Taboo: Why Black Athletes Dominate Sports and Why We're Afraid to Talk about It* (Westport CT: Greenwood, 1994), 200.

34. Jerry Fleishman, telephone interview by the author, September 2006.

35. Sam "Leaden" Bernstein, interview by the author, Philadelphia, summer 2006.

36. Entine, *Taboo*, 200.

37. Ossie Schectman, telephone interview by the author, January 2007.

38. Steve Cohen, "They Took Their Shots: Gil Fitch, a Member of Philadelphia's All-Jewish Basketball Team in the 1930s, Reflects on Violence in Sports," *Naked City*, Philadelphia Citypaper, December 30, 2004–January 5, 2005, available at www.citypaper.net/articles/2004–12–30/naked.shtml.

39. Cohen, "They Took Their Shots."

40. Marty Levin, "Blue Bombers Trounce SPHAS, 40–24, on Armory Court," *Wilmington (DE) Morning News*, December 4, 1941, 22.

41. "Blue Bombers Defeat SPHAS, 48–36, to Take Second Place in Loop," *Wilmington (DE) Morning News*, December 15, 1941, 20.

42. "Blue Bombers Defeat SPHAS, 48–36."
43. Bernie Fliegel, telephone interview by the author, May 2007.
44. Official program, Wilmington Blue Bombers, 1942–1943, in the possession of the author.
45. Fliegel interview.
46. Fliegel interview.
47. Official program, Wilmington Blue Bombers, March 22, 1942, in the possession of the author.
48. Official program, Wilmington Blue Bombers, 1944–45, in the possession of the author.
49. 1942 World Professional Basketball Tournament program.
50. 1942 World Professional Basketball Tournament program.
51. 1943 World Professional Basketball Tournament program, in the possession of the author.
52. Rodger Nelson, *The Zollner Pistons Story* (Fort Wayne IN: Allen County Public Library Foundation, 1995), 136.
53. Gould, *Pioneers of the Hardwood*, 105.
54. Murry R. Nelson. *The National Basketball League: A History, 1935–1949* (Jefferson NC: McFarland, 2009), 95.
55. Gould, *Pioneers of the Hardwood*, 107.
56. Gould, *Pioneers of the Hardwood*, 108.
57. Gould, *Pioneers of the Hardwood*, 108.
58. Gould, *Pioneers of the Hardwood*, 108.
59. Peterson, *Cages to Jump Shots*, 132–33.
60. Peterson, *Cages to Jump Shots*, 133–34.
61. "Playoff Finals Slated for Tonight, Thursday," *Oshkosh Daily Northwestern*, March 4, 1942, 14.
62. "Stars Lose Opener, Must Win at Home Tonight, or Else," *Oshkosh Daily Northwestern*, March 5, 1942, 19.
63. Leo Fischer, "Fort Wayne, Toledo Quints in Title Tourney," *Chicago Herald American*, February 13, 1942, 22.
64. Jerry Rullo, interview by the author, Philadelphia, July 2007.
65. Gould, *Pioneers of the Hardwood*, 109.
66. Gould, *Pioneers of the Hardwood*, 110.
67. Gould, *Pioneers of the Hardwood*, 111.
68. "All-Stars, Zollners Play for Title Tonight," *Oshkosh Daily Northwestern*, March 6, 1942, 12.
69. Leo Fischer, "Oshkosh Enters World's Title Cage Tourney," *Chicago Herald American*, February 20, 1942, 17.
70. Gould, *Pioneers of the Hardwood*, 112.

71. John Schleppi, *Chicago's Showcase of Basketball: The World Tournament of Professional Basketball and the College All-Star Game* (Haworth NJ: St. Johann Press, 2008), 5.

72. Ben Green, *Spinning the Globe: The Rise, Fall, and Return to Greatness of the Harlem Globetrotters* (New York: HarperCollins, 2005), 107.

73. Available at www.aafla.org/SportsLibrary/NASSH_Proceddings/NP1989/NP1989Zd.pdf.

74. 1942 World Professional Basketball Tournament program.

75. "Great Teams Bid for Pro Berths," *Chicago Herald American*, February 8, 1942, pt. 2, p. 4.

76. 1942 World Professional Basketball Tournament program.

77. Leo Fischer, "Greatest Cage Stars to Play in Title Meet," *Chicago Herald American*, February 22, 1942, pt. 2, p. 5.

78. Leo Fischer, "Flyers in Cage Classic," *Chicago Herald American*, February 15, 1942, pt. 2, p. 4.

79. Fay Young, "Globe Trotters Advance in World Pro Tourney," *Chicago Defender*, March 14, 1942, 21.

80. Pop Gates interview, Robert Peterson Collection, Naismith Memorial Basketball Hall of Fame

81. 1942 World Professional Basketball Tournament program.

82. Leo Fischer, "Sixteen Teams Eye World's Cage Laurels," *Chicago Herald American*, March 2, 1942, 18.

83. 1942 World Professional Basketball Tournament program.

84. Leo Fischer, "World's Cage Meet Opens," *Chicago Herald American*, March 7, 1942, pt. 2, p. 14.

85. Peterson, *Cages to Jump Shots*, 113.

86. Peterson, *Cages to Jump Shots*, 113.

87. Leo Fischer, "Deluxe Setting for Cage Classic, *Chicago Herald American*, February 17, 1942, 15.

88. Leo Fischer, "Cage Teams Head Here for World Title Meet," *Chicago Herald American*, March 6, 1942, 21.

89. Fischer, "Cage Teams Head Here," 21–22.

90. Fischer, "Cage Teams Head Here," 22.

91. Leo Fischer, "Sixteen Teams Eye World's Cage Laurels," *Chicago Herald American*, March 2, 1942, 17.

92. Fischer, "Sixteen Teams Eye World's Cage Laurels," 17.

93. Fischer, "Sixteen Teams Eye World's Cage Laurels," 17–18.

94. Fischer, "Sixteen Teams Eye World's Cage Laurels," 18.

95. Fischer, "Sixteen Teams Eye World's Cage Laurels," 18.

96. "Sheboygan Enters World Pro Cage Tourney," *Chicago Herald American*, February 14, 1942, 14.

97. Fischer, "Sixteen Teams Eye World's Cage Laurels," 17.
98. Leo Fischer, "Rens Test Oshkosh Tonight," *Chicago Herald American*, March 9, 1942, 17.
99. "Stars Meet Rens in Pro Cage Contest Tonight," *Oshkosh Daily Northwestern*, March 9, 1942, 12.
100. Harry Wilson, "Oshkosh Victory Cage Stunner," *Chicago Herald American*, March 10, 1942, 14.
101. Wilson, "Oshkosh Victory Cage Stunner," 14.
102. Leo Fischer, "Tonight! Oshkosh vs. Detroit for Title," *Chicago Herald American*, March 11, 1942, 25.
103. Fischer, "Tonight! Oshkosh vs. Detroit for Title."
104. Harry Wilson, "Oshkosh Spirit Key to Victory," *Chicago Herald American*, March 12, 1942, 16.
105. "World's Pro Cage Title Won by Stars in Chicago Tourney," *Oshkosh Daily Northwestern*, March 12, 1942, 19.
106. 1942 World Professional Basketball Tournament program.
107. Harry Wilson, "1942 World's Championship Basketball Tournament," *Converse Basketball Year Book 1941–1942*, 21st annual ed. (Malden MA: Converse Rubber Company, 1942), 33.

2. THE COLOR LINE FALLS, 1942–1943

Epigraph: Robert Peterson, *Cages to Jump Shots: Pro Basketball's Early Years.* (New York: Oxford University Press, 1990), 130.
1. Todd Gould, *Pioneers of the Hardwood: Indiana and the Birth of Professional Basketball.* (Bloomington IN: Indiana University Press, 1998), 104.
2. Gould, *Pioneers of the Hardwood*, 116.
3. Bill Himmelman, interview by the author, Norwood NJ, August 2007.
4. Bill Reynolds, *Rise of a Dynasty: The '57 Celtics, the First Banner, and the Dawning of a New America* (New York: New American Library, 2010), 129–30.
5. Gerry Finn, "Bucky Lew First Negro in Pro Basketball," *Springfield Union*, April 2, 1958, 27.
6. Kay Lazar, "The Fight for Bucky Lew's Name: Lowell Native Broke Pro Basketball Color Barrier, but He's Not Recognized," *Lowell Sun*, Summer 1997, 7.
7. Lazar, "Fight for Bucky Lew's Name."
8. Lazar, "Fight for Bucky Lew's Name."
9. Lazar, "Fight for Bucky Lew's Name."
10. Finn, "Bucky Lew First Negro in Pro Basketball."
11. Lazar, "Fight for Bucky Lew's Name."
12. Caroline Louise Cole, "Recalling How Black Star Broke Barriers in 1902," *Boston Globe*, NorthWest Weekly, February 16, 1997, 6.

13. Cole, "Recalling How Black Star Broke Barriers."
14. Cole, "Recalling How Black Star Broke Barriers."
15. Cole, "Recalling How Black Star Broke Barriers."
16. Cole, "Recalling How Black Star Broke Barriers."
17. Lazar, "Fight for Bucky Lew's Name."
18. Cole, "Recalling How Black Star Broke Barriers."
19. Tatsha Robertson, "Echoes of the Underground Railroad," *Boston Globe*, February 22, 1999, A12.
20. Robertson, "Echoes of the Underground Railroad."
21. Robertson, "Echoes of the Underground Railroad."
22. Douglas Stark, "Paving the Way: The National Basketball League," *Basketball Digest*, February 2001, 75.
23. Michael Funke, "The Chicago Studebakers: How the UAW Helped Integrate Pro Basketball and Reunite Four Players Who Made History," n.d., Naismith Memorial Basketball Hall of Fame.
24. David S. Neft, Roland T. Johnson, Richard M. Cohen, and Jordan A. Deutsch, eds. *The Sports Encyclopedia: Pro Basketball*. (New York: Grosset and Dunlap, 1975), 36.
25. 1943 World Professional Basketball Tournament program, in the possession of the author.
26. "Invaders to Give Team Real Fight," *Sheboygan Press*, November 24, 1942, 12.
27. "Redskins Open League Season Tonight: New Team Has Lots of Class," *Sheboygan Press*, November 25, 1942, 18.
28. "Redskins Drub Chicago, 53 to 45," *Sheboygan Press*, November 27, 1942, 10.
29. "Oshkosh Wins over Chicago by One Point," *Sheboygan Press*, November 30, 1942, 12; "Stars Gain League Victory in Closing Minutes," *Oshkosh Daily Northwestern*, November 30, 1942, 13.
30. Peterson, *Cages to Jump Shots*, 131.
31. Funke, "Chicago Studebakers."
32. "Chicago Studebakers Oppose Pistons in Opening Contest," *Fort Wayne News-Sentinel*, December 1, 1942, 11.
33. "Chicago Studebakers Oppose Pistons."
34. "Chicago Studebakers Oppose Pistons."
35. Ben Tenny, "Pistons, Beaten in Home Opener, Go on Road Trip," *Fort Wayne News-Sentinel*, December 2, 1942, 22.
36. Gould, *Pioneers of the Hardwood*, 117.
37. Funke, "Chicago Studebakers."
38. Funke, "Chicago Studebakers."
39. Peterson, *Cages to Jump Shots*, 131.
40. Peterson, *Cages to Jump Shots*, 131.

41. Funke, "Chicago Studebakers."

42. Peterson, *Cages to Jump Shots*, 129.

43. "Zollner Piston-Toledo Clash Is Postponed until Wednesday," *Fort Wayne News-Sentinel*, December 8, 1942, 21.

44. "Studebaker Pro Quintet to Face Toledo Tonight," *Chicago Tribune*, December 11, 1942, 34.

45. "Redskins Face Heavy Basketball Week-End," *Sheboygan Press*, December 10, 1942, 27; "Redskins Drub Rens, 65–47," *Sheboygan Press*, December 12, 1942, 10.

46. "Gerber, Chuckovitz to Be Here with Toledo," *Oshkosh Daily Northwestern*, December 11, 1942, 15.

47. "Gerber, Chuckovitz to Be Here."

48. Stark, "Paving the Way," 76.

49. "Studebakers Turn Toledo Back, 42–30," *Chicago Defender*, December 19, 1942, 21.

50. Murry R. Nelson, *The National Basketball League: A History, 1935–1949.* (Jefferson NC: MacFarland, 2009), 117.

51. "Studebakers Turn Toledo Back."

52. Peterson, *Cages to Jump Shots*, 130.

53. "Redskins Drub Rens."

54. Peterson, *Cages to Jump Shots*, 130.

55. Sid Goldberg interview, Robert Peterson Collection, Naismith Memorial Basketball Hall of Fame.

56. Goldberg interview.

57. "Toledo Out of Pro Loop," *Toledo Blade*. December 23, 1942, 19.

58. "Toledo Leaves League," *Sheboygan Press*, December 23, 1942, 12.

59. "Toledo Five 70–51 Victim of Zollners," *Fort Wayne News-Sentinel*, December 10, 1942, 32.

60. Stark, "Paving the Way," 77.

61. "National League Suspends Toledo Franchise," *Oshkosh Daily Northwestern*, December 22, 1942, 17.

62. "Redskins Beat Fort Wayne 55 to 50," *Sheboygan Press*, March 2, 1943, 8.

63. "Redskins Win Championship," *Sheboygan Press*, March 10, 1943, 7.

64. Gould, *Pioneers of the Hardwood*, 119.

65. "Redskins to Be Honored at Banquet Here on Thursday," *Sheboygan Press*, March 12, 1943, 11.

66. Minutes of Meeting, December 4, 1942, ABL Collection, Naismith Memorial Basketball Hall of Fame.

67. Minutes of Meeting, December 4, 1942.

68. Minutes of Meeting, December 4, 1942.

69. Minutes of Meeting, December 4, 1942.

70. Minutes of Meeting, December 4, 1942.

71. Minutes of Meeting, December 4, 1942.

72. Minutes of Meeting, December 4, 1942.

73. William J. Scheffer, "Trenton Beats SPHAS, 36 to 27," *Philadelphia Inquirer*, March 7, 1943, S3.

74. William J. Scheffer, "SPHAS Triumph to Take Crown," *Philadelphia Inquirer*, April 4, 1943: S1.

75. Scheffer, "SPHAS Triumph to Take Crown."

76. Scheffer, "SPHAS Triumph to Take Crown."

77. Jimmy Corcoran, "Cork Tips: Greatest Basketball Treat of Season on Tap for Next Week, Irony Present in Case of St. Patrick's Day Final without Celts," *Chicago Herald American*, March 7, 1943, pt. 2, p. 2.

78. Leo Fischer, "Sidelines," *Chicago Herald American*, February 24, 1943, 21.

79. 1943 World Professional Basketball Tournament program.

80. Pop Gates interview, Robert Peterson Collection, Naismith Memorial Basketball Hall of Fame.

81. James Enright, "Basketball's Best: '39 Cage Champs Back, but As Bears,'" *Chicago Herald American*, March 10, 1943, 24.

82. Leo Fischer, "World Champs in Title Cage Tourney," *Chicago Herald American*, February 18, 1943, 19.

83. Leo Fischer, "Army 'Jive Squad' Cage Feature," *Chicago Herald American*, March 9, 1943, 18.

84. James Enright, "Firing Starts for Cage Title," *Chicago Herald American*, March 14, 1943, pt. 2, p. 3.

85. Leo Fischer, "Trotters, Dayton Top Cage Tonight," *Chicago Herald American*, March 15, 1943, 19.

86. Fischer, "Trotters, Dayton Top Cage Tonight," 21.

87. "Studebakers Out of Pro Cage Meet," *Chicago Defender*, March 20, 1943, 21.

88. Fischer, "Trotters, Dayton Top Cage Tonight," 21.

89. "Bears Pro Basketball Champions," *Call*, March 26, 1943, 10.

90. "Bears Pro Basketball Champions."

91. 1943 World Professional Basketball Tournament program.

3. WARTIME BASKETBALL, 1943–1944

Epigraph: Lieutenant Commander Frank H. Wickhorst, "Basketball, a Naval Training Device," *The Official Basketball Guide 1941–1942* (New York: A. S. Barnes, 1941), 17.

1. Bill Himmelman, interview by the author, Norwood NJ, August 2007.

2. "Special Services Division" handbook, February 15, 1944, RG 160, Records of Headquarters Special Services Division General Records, 1941–45; RG

353.8, Research File—Sports (box number not recorded), National Archives and Records Administration II, College Park MD.

3. "Great Lakes, a Commanding Force in the Athletic World," *Chicago Stadium Review*, 1942–43, 3, in the possession of the author.

4. "Great Lakes, a Commanding Force in the Athletic World," 3.

5. "Great Lakes, a Commanding Force in the Athletic World," 21.

6. Lieutenant Commander J. Russell Cook, "Basketball at Great Lakes," *Converse Basketball Year Book 1941–1942*, 21st annual ed. (Malden MA: Converse Rubber Company, 1942), 27.

7. "Rival Coaches Bring Great Cage Records," *Chicago Stadium Review*, 1942–1943, 16, in the possession of the author.

8. "Rival Coaches Bring Great Cage Records."

9. Cook, "Basketball at Great Lakes."

10. Cook, "Basketball at Great Lakes."

11. "1,000 Teams to Play in Basketball Program Here," *Great Lakes Bulletin* (United States Naval Training Station, Great Lakes IL) 17, no. 46 (November 13, 1942): 7.

12. "1,000 Teams to Play."

13. Cook, "Basketball At Great Lakes."

14. Lieutenant Joseph G. Daher, "Wartime Conditioning through Basketball," *Converse Basketball Year Book 1943–1944*, 23rd annual ed. (Malden MA: Converse Rubber Company, 1944), 10.

15. "Great Lakes Five Spanks Northwest'n, 47–38," *Great Lakes Bulletin* (United States Naval Training Station, Great Lakes IL) 17, no. 3 (January 17, 1942): 3.

16. "Great Lakes Five Spanks Northwest'n, 47–38."

17. "Incidentally . . . ," *Great Lakes Bulletin* (United States Naval Training Station, Great Lakes IL) 17, no. 12 (March 21, 1942): 3.

18. "Station's Sport Stars Carry On 1918 Tradition," *Great Lakes Bulletin* (United States Naval Training Station, Great Lakes IL) 17, no. 52 (December 25, 1942): 7.

19. Seymour Smith, Jack Rimer, and Dick Triptow, *A Tribute to Armed Forces Basketball 1941–1969* (Lake Bluff IL: self-published, 2003), 126.

20. "Midwest's Top College Quintets to Perform Here," *Great Lakes Bulletin* (United States Naval Training Station, Great Lakes IL) 17, no. 45 (November 6, 1942): 7.

21. "Midwest's Top College Quintets."

22. "Midwest's Top College Quintets."

23. "Short Shots," *Chicago Stadium Review*, January 17, 1943, 28, in the possession of the author.

24. "Short Shots."

25. "Great Lakes Wins Third Straight Championship," *Great Lakes Bulletin*, March 10, 1944, 7.

26. Bruce Jenkins, *A Good Man: The Pete Newell Story* (Lincoln: University of Nebraska Press, 1999), 22.

27. Jenkins, *Good Man*, 23.

28. Jenkins, *Good Man*, 24.

29. Ned Irish, "Basketball's Third War Season," *National Basketball Committee Official Basketball Guide 1944–45* (New York: A .S. Barnes, 1945), 15.

30. *Converse Basketball Year Book 1943–1944*, 21.

31. *Converse Basketball Year Book 1943–1944*, 25.

32. Randy Roberts, *A Team for America: The Army-Navy Game That Rallied a Nation at War* (Boston: Mariner Books, 2012), 61–62.

33. Wickhorst, "Basketball, a Navy Training Device," 20.

34. Roberts, *Team for America*, 87–88.

35. Al Del Greco, "For the Record: Ben's Impossible Dream," Ben Carnevale Hall of Famer File, Naismith Memorial Basketball Hall of Fame.

36. Del Greco, "For the Record."

37. Jerry Radding, "Two Elected to Cage Hall of Fame," *Springfield (MA) Republican*, January 25, 1970, 57.

38. Bernie Fliegel, telephone interview by the author, May 2007.

39. Ken Shouler, Bob Ryan, Sam Smith, Leonard Koppett, and Bob Bellotti, *Total Basketball: The Ultimate Basketball Encyclopedia* (Wilmington DE: Sport Classic Press, 2003), 672.

40. Vadal Peterson, "Skyline Basketball," *National Basketball Committee Official Basketball Guide 1944–45* (New York: A. S. Barnes, 1945), 16.

41. Peterson, "Skyline Basketball," 16.

42. Louis Effrat, "Kentucky and Oklahoma Aggies Triumph in Invitation Tourney before 16,273," *New York Times*, March 21, 1944, 22.

43. Louis Effrat, "Utah Upsets Dartmouth in Extra Period to Take N.C.A.A. Basketball Title," *New York Times*, March 19, 1944, 16.

44. Effrat, "Utah Upsets Dartmouth."

45. Effrat, "Utah Upsets Dartmouth."

46. George L. Sheibler, "Utah Comes Thru in Red Cross Classic," *National Basketball Committee Official Basketball Guide 1944–45* (New York: A. S. Barnes, 1945), 28.

47. Sheibler, "Utah Comes Thru."

48. Douglas Stark, "Wat Misaka: An Asian Basketball Pioneer," *Basketball Digest*, February 2002, 51–52.

49. Stark, "Wat Misaka," 51–52.

50. Stark, "Wat Misaka," 51–52.

51. Leo Fischer, "Jeannette in 4th World Cage Meet," *Chicago Herald American*, March 7, 1944, 14.

52. Robert Peterson, *Cages to Jump Shots: Pro Basketball's Early Years.* (New York: Oxford University Press, 1990), 128.

53. Peterson, *Cages to Jump Shots*, 134.

54. Peterson, *Cages to Jump Shots*, 136.

55. Rodger Nelson, *The Zollner Pistons Story.* (Nappanee IN: Evangel Press, 1996), 128.

56. "Zollner Pistons' Home, League Road Schedules Are Completed," *Fort Wayne News-Sentinel*, October 27, 1943, 19.

57. Robert Peterson, *Cages to Jump Shots*, 141.

58. Todd Gould, *Pioneers of the Hardwood: Indiana and the Birth of Professional Basketball.* (Bloomington: Indiana University Press, 1998), 110–11.

59. Gould, *Pioneers of the Hardwood*, 111.

60. Jerry Fleishman, telephone interview by the author, September 2006.

61. Shikey Gotthoffer, interview by Robert Peterson, May 1987, Robert Peterson Collection, Naismith Memorial Basketball Hall of Fame.

62. Sam "Leaden" Bernstein, interview by the author, Philadelphia, summer 2006.

63. Gotthoffer interview.

64. "Wilmington Passers Meet SPHAS Tonight on Latter's Court," *Wilmington (DE) Morning News*, February 19, 1944, 9.

65. Ossie Schectman, telephone interview by the author, January 2007.

66. John J. Brady, "SPHAS Beat Bombers, 42–35—Keglers Tie for Top Prize," *Wilmington (DE) Morning News*, March 6, 1944, 12.

67. Brady, "SPHAS Beat Bombers, 42–35."

68. "Bob Dorn Signed by Bombers—Savold Beats Baski," *Wilmington (DE) Morning News*, March 11, 1944: 12.

69. "Bombers Add Fitzgerald—Wilmington Park Mud Doomed," *Wilmington (DE) Morning News*, March 18, 1944, 12.

70. John J. Brady, "Bombers Win 1933–44 American Basketball League Title," *Wilmington (DE) Morning News*, March 29, 1944, 12.

71. Official Program. Wilmington Blue Bombers, 1944–45, in the possession of the author.

72. Harry D. Wilson, "1944 World's Championship Tournament," *Converse Basketball Year Book 1943–1944*, 23rd annual edition (Malden MA: Converse Rubber Company, 1944), 45.

73. Harry Wilson, "World Cage Briefs: Picks Rens for Title," *Chicago Herald American*, March 11, 1944, 12.

74. Harry Wilson, "Sheboygan in World Cage Meet," *Chicago Herald American*, February 23, 1944, 18.

75. Leo Fischer, "Oshkosh 13th Bidder for World Cage Title," *Chicago Herald American*, March 3, 1944, 22.

76. Leo Fischer, "Cleveland Five in World Cage Play," *Chicago Herald American*, February 28, 1944, 14.

77. "Trotters Take Rens, 37–29, for 3rd Place as Zollners Top Pro Cagers, *Chicago Defender*, April 1, 1944, 9.

78. Harry Wilson, "World Cage Briefs: Best of the Trotters," *Chicago Herald American*, March 8, 1944: 18.

79. "Rens, Zollners, Eagles, Trotters in Cage Race," *Chicago Herald American*, March 23, 1944, 18.

80. "Rens, Zollners, Eagles, Trotters."

81. "Rens, Zollners, Eagles, Trotters."

82. "Trotters Take Rens, 37–29, for 3rd Place as Zollners Top Pro Cagers," *Chicago Defender*, April 1, 1944, 9.

83. "Trotters Take Rens, 37–29."

84. "Trotters Take Rens, 37–29."

85. Leo Fischer, "Ex-Champs in Cage Bid," *Chicago Herald American*, March 6, 1944, 14.

86. Harry Wilson, "Army Five Bids for World's Title, *Chicago Herald American*, February 14, 1944,14.

87. Harry Wilson, "World Cage Briefs: Meehan Courts Magic," *Chicago Herald American*, March 14, 1944, 14.

88. Harry Wilson, "World Cage Briefs: Sheriffs; Stars Shine," *Chicago Herald American*, March 3, 1944, 23.

89. Jack "Dutch" Garfinkel, telephone interview by the author, October 2006.

90. Alex Zirin, "Chuckovitz Lines Up Strong Quintet," *Cleveland Plain Dealer*, March 8, 1942, C-2.

91. Stan Friedland, *Play It Again Sam: The Sam Schoenfeld Story* (Xilibris Corporation, 2004), 154.

92. Garfinkel interview.

93. Garfinkel interview.

94. Leo Fischer, "Brooklyn, Dayton, Rens Win Openers," *Chicago Herald American*, March 21, 1944, 14.

95. Leo Fischer, "World Cage Meet Brews 'Civil War,'" *Chicago Herald American*, March 16, 1944, 18.

96. Fischer, "Brooklyn, Dayton, Rens Win Openers."

97. Leo Fischer, "Fort Wayne Wins Cage Title, Flays Eagles, 50–33," *Chicago Herald American*, March 26, 1944, pt. 2, p. 1.

98. Fischer, "Fort Wayne Wins Cage Title."

99. Fischer, "Fort Wayne Wins Cage Title."

100. James Enright, "Zollners Hold Up Name; Perform like Pistons," *Chicago Herald American*, March 26, 1944, pt. 2, p. 1.
101. Ben Tenny, "Pistons Rule Professional Basketball Realm for 1944," *Fort Wayne News-Sentinel*, March 27, 1944, 9.
102. Gould, *Pioneers of the Hardwood*, 113.
103. Gould, *Pioneers of the Hardwood*, 113.
104. Gould, *Pioneers of the Hardwood*, 114.
105. Gould, *Pioneers of the Hardwood*, 114.
106. Gould, *Pioneers of the Hardwood*, 115.
107. Gould, *Pioneers of the Hardwood*, 114.
108. Gould, *Pioneers of the Hardwood*, 102.

4. THE BIG MAN COMETH, 1944–1945

Epigraph: Ken Shouler, Bob Ryan, Sam Smith, Leonard Koppett, and Bob Bellotti. *Total Basketball: The Ultimate Basketball Encyclopedia* (Wilmington DE: Sport Classic Press, 2003), 673.

1. William D. Richardson, "Giant Centers Top Court Bill Tonight," *New York Times*, March 29, 1945, 27.
2. Michael Schumacher, *Mr. Basketball: George Mikan, the Minneapolis Lakers, and the Birth of the NBA* (New York NY: Bloomsbury USA, 2007), 31–32.
3. Charles Salzberg, *From Set Shot to Slam Dunk: The Glory Days of Basketball in the Words of Those Who Played It* (Lincoln: University of Nebraska Press, 1987), 9.
4. George L. Mikan and Joseph Oberle, *Unstoppable: The Story of George Mikan, the First NBA Superstar* (Indianapolis: Masters Press, 1997), 41.
5. Schumacher, *Mr. Basketball*, 31.
6. Schumacher, *Mr. Basketball*, 31.
7. Shouler, Ryan, Smith, Koppett, and Bellotti, *Total Basketball*, 674.
8. Mikan and Oberle, *Unstoppable*, 44.
9. Schumacher, *Mr. Basketball*, 32.
10. George Mikan as told to Bill Carlson, *Mr. Basketball: George Mikan's Own Story* (New York: Greenberg, 1951), 41–42.
11. Richardson, "Giant Centers Top Court Bill Tonight."
12. Richardson, "Giant Centers Top Court Bill Tonight."
13. Mikan and Oberle, *Unstoppable*, 57.
14. Schumacher, *Mr. Basketball*, 47.
15. Schumacher, *Mr. Basketball*, 48.
16. Louis Effrat, "Oklahoma Aggies Top De Paul, 52–44," *New York Times*, March 30, 1945, 20.
17. Mikan as told to Carlson, *Mr. Basketball*, 41–42.

18. Ray Meyer with Ray Sons, *Coach* (Chicago: Contemporary Books, 1987), 55.

19. Mikan and Oberle, *Unstoppable*, 59.

20. Robert Peterson, *Cages to Jump Shots: Pro Basketball's Early Years* (New York: Oxford University Press, 1990), 149.

21. Richard F. Triptow, *The Dynasty That Never Was: Chicago's First Professional Basketball Champions, the American Gears* (Lake Bluff IL: R. F. Triptow, 1996), 1–2.

22. Triptow, *Dynasty That Never Was*, 160.

23. Triptow, *Dynasty That Never Was*, 156.

24. "Brevities," *SPHAS Sparks* 7, no. 3 (November 11, 1944): 2, in the possession of the author.

25. Todd Gould, *Pioneers of the Hardwood: Indiana and the Birth of Professional Basketball* (Bloomington: Indiana University Press, 1998), 124.

26. "Fort Wayne, Cleveland Fives Start Playoff Series," *Fort Wayne News-Sentinel*, March 6, 1945, 8.

27. Ben Tenny, "Pistons Shoot, Play Well to Hand Cleveland Quintet 78–50 Trimming," *Fort Wayne News-Sentinel*, March 7, 1945, 10.

28. Ben Tenny, "Pistons Enter Final Series against Sheboygan," *Fort Wayne News-Sentinel*, March 9, 1945, 11.

29. Ben Tenny, "Sheboygan Five Backs Pistons to Wall," *Fort Wayne News-Sentinel*, March 13, 1945, 8.

30. Tenny, "Sheboygan Five Backs Pistons."

31. Gould, *Pioneers of the Hardwood*, 125.

32. ABL Minutes October 20, 1944, Naismith Memorial Basketball Hall of Fame collection.

33. ABL Minutes December 23, 1944, Naismith Memorial Basketball Hall of Fame collection.

34. Official Program, Wilmington Blue Bombers, 1944–45, in the possession of the author.

35. "SPHAS Beat Bombers, 49–44, in Opener of Court Series," *Wilmington (DE) Morning News*, March 19, 1945, 13.

36. William J. Scheffer, "SPHAS Triumph in Playoff Game," *Philadelphia Inquirer*, March 18, 1945, 1S.

37. "SPHAS Beat Bombers, 49–44."

38. Scheffer, "SPHAS Triumph in Playoff Game," 4S.

39. Jack Gibbons, "Bombers Trounce SPHAS, 48 to 29, to Even Playoff," *Wilmington (DE) Morning News*, March 22, 1945, 8.

40. "Wilmington Beats SPHAS; Evens League Playoffs," *Philadelphia Inquirer*, March 22, 1945, 23.

41. William J. Scheffer, "SPHAS Victors: Reaches Finals," *Philadelphia Inquirer*, April 1, 1945, 2S.

42. Robert Elmer, "Bullets Face SPHAS Tonight," *Baltimore Sun*, April 5, 1945, 16.

43. Elmer, "Bullets Face SPHAS Tonight."

44. "SPHAS Defeat Bullet Five in Playoffs," *Philadelphia Inquirer*, April 6, 1945, 25.

45. "SPHAS Defeat Bullet Five in Playoffs."

46. William J. Scheffer, "Baltimore Beats SPHAS, Tie Series," *Philadelphia Inquirer*, April 8, 1945, 2S.

47. "Bullets Nip SPHAS, 47–46," *Baltimore Sun*, April 8, 1945, 18.

48. "SPHAS Defeat Bullets, 46–40," *Baltimore Sun*, April 15, 1945, 23.

49. William J. Scheffer, "SPHAS Capture 7th Title, 46–40," *Philadelphia Inquirer*, April 15, 1945, 2S.

50. Harry Wilson, "Stadium Scene of World Cage," *Chicago Herald American*, February 1, 1945, 16.

51. Wilson, "Stadium Scene of World Cage."

52. Wilson, "Stadium Scene of World Cage."

53. Harry Wilson, "Ticket Sales under Way for World Cage Meet," *Chicago Herald American*, February 5, 1945, 12.

54. Keith Brehm, "Cleveland Second World Cage Entrant," *Chicago Herald American*, February 19, 1945, 12.

55. Triptow, *Dynasty That Never Was*, 228.

56. Keith Brehm, "Dow Chemicals to Bid for World Cage Title," *Chicago Herald American*, February 26, 1945, 12.

57. Brehm, "Dow Chemicals to Bid for World Cage Title."

58. Brehm, "Dow Chemicals to Bid for World Cage Title."

59. Keith Brehm, "4 Battles Tonight on World Cage Card," *Chicago Herald American*, March 21, 1945, 22.

60. "Grumman Five Is Returning to Pro Picture," *Long Island Daily Press*, December 1, 1944, 20.

61. Harry Wilson, "Grumman Returned for World Cage Try," *Chicago Herald American*, February 27, 1945, 12.

62. Keith Brehm, "Zollners, Gears, Rens, Acmes Advance," *Chicago Herald American*, March 22, 1945, 18.

63. Brehm, "Zollners, Gears, Rens, Acmes Advance."

64. Keith Brehm, "Chicago Gets First World Cage Meet Bid," *Chicago Herald American*, February 18, 1945, 21.

65. Brehm, "Chicago Gets First World Cage Meet Bid."

66. Keith Brehm, "Hartford, Dayton Fill World Cage Field," *Chicago Herald American*, March 3, 1945, 14.

67. Keith Brehm, "Gears, Stags, Rens Win in World Cage," *Chicago Herald American*, March 20, 1945, 12.

68. Triptow, *Dynasty That Never Was*, 17.

69. Keith Brehm, "Globe Trotters Bid for World Cage Role," *Chicago Herald American*, March 2, 1945, 26.

70. Brehm, "Zollners, Gears, Rens, Acmes Advance."

71. Brehm, "Zollners, Gears, Rens, Acmes Advance."

72. Triptow, *Dynasty That Never Was*, 17.

73. Keith Brehm, "World Cage Semifinals Slated Tonight," *Chicago Herald American*, March 23, 1945, 22.

74. Brehm, "World Cage Semifinals Slated Tonight."

75. Brehm, "World Cage Semifinals Slated Tonight."

76. Keith Brehm, "Zollners, Acmes Meet for World Title," *Chicago Herald American*, March 24, 1945, 18.

77. Brehm, "Zollners, Acmes Meet for World Title."

78. Harry Wilson, "Famous Rens Third to Enter World Cage," *Chicago Herald American*, February 20, 1945, 12.

79. Keith Brehm, "Indianapolis Fives Join for World Cage," *Chicago Herald American*, March 1, 1945, 18.

80. Brehm, "Gears, Stags, Rens Win in World Cage."

81. Keith Brehm, "Newark Five Seeks World Cage Crown," *Chicago Herald American*, February 23, 1945, 18.

82. Keith Brehm, "4 Battles Tonight on World Cage Card," *Chicago Herald American*, March 21, 1945, 22.

83. Keith Brehm, "Detroit Eagles Earn World Cage Perch," *Chicago Herald American*, February 21, 1945: 20.

84. Brehm, "Zollners, Gears, Rens, Acmes Advance."

85. Brehm, "Zollners, Gears, Rens, Acmes Advance."

86. Ben Tenny, "Pistons Face Rens Friday in Semi-Finals of Pro Cage Meet," *Fort Wayne News-Sentinel*, March 22, 1945, 15.

87. Brehm, "Zollners, Acmes Meet for World Title."

88. Brehm, "Zollners, Acmes Meet for World Title."

89. Leo Fischer, "15,119 See Ft. Wayne Keep Pro Title," *Chicago Herald American*, March 25, 1945, 25.

90. Ben Tenny, "Pistons Are First Repeaters in World's Pro Hardwood Tournament," *Fort Wayne News-Sentinel*, March 26, 1945, 11.

91. Gould, *Pioneers of the Hardwood*, 126.

92. John Schleppi, *Chicago's Showcase of Basketball: The World Tournament of Professional Basketball and the College All-Star Game* (Haworth NJ: St. Johann Press, 2008), 74.

5. LOOKING TOWARD THE FUTURE, 1945–1946

Epigraph: Red Holzman and Harvey Frommer, *Red on Red* (New York: Bantam Books, 1987), 16.

1. "122. Radio Address to the American People after the Signing of the Terms of Unconditional Surrender by Japan," Public Papers of the Presidents Harry S. Truman 1945–1953, Harry S. Truman Library and Museum, Independence MO.
2. 1945–1946 Rochester Royals Program, copy in the possession of the author.
3. Robert Peterson, *Cages to Jump Shots: Pro Basketball's Early Years* (New York: Oxford University Press, 1990), 138.
4. 1945–1946 Rochester Royals Program.
5. 1945–1946 Rochester Royals Program.
6. Peterson, *Cages to Jump Shots*, 138.
7. Murry R. Nelson, *The National Basketball League: A History, 1935–1949* (Jefferson NC: McFarland, 2009), 144.
8. 1945–1946 Rochester Royals Program.
9. "A Special Tribute to Al Cervi in Recognition of His Election to the Naismith Memorial Basketball Hall of Fame," Al Cervi Files, Naismith Memorial Basketball Hall of Fame.
10. "Special Tribute to Al Cervi."
11. Nelson, *National Basketball League*, 143.
12. "Special Tribute to Al Cervi."
13. "Special Tribute to Al Cervi."
14. Nelson, *National Basketball League*, 147.
15. Holzman and Frommer, *Red on Red*, 14.
16. Richard F. Triptow, *The Dynasty That Never Was: Chicago's First Professional Basketball Champions, the American Gears* (Lake Bluff IL: R. F. Triptow, 1996), 229.
17. Leo Fischer, "Youngstown Sixth Team in World Cage," *Chicago Herald American*, March 8, 1946, 26.
18. Triptow, *Dynasty That Never Was*, 232.
19. Richard Triptow, *Dynasty That Never Was*, 228.
20. Todd Gould, *Pioneers of the Hardwood: Indiana and the Birth of Professional Basketball* (Bloomington: Indiana University Press, 1998), 130.
21. "Harrison Sees Royals in Top Form," *Rochester Democrat and Chronicle*, March 6, 1946, 20.
22. 1945–1946 Rochester Royals Program.
23. Leo Fischer, "Sheboygan Tenth World Cage Entry," *Chicago Herald American*, March 12, 1946, 14.
24. Triptow, *Dynasty That Never Was*, 147.
25. Triptow, *Dynasty That Never Was*, 227.
26. Gould, *Pioneers of the Hardwood*, 127.
27. Gould, *Pioneers of the Hardwood*, 128.
28. Elliot Cushing, "Fort Wayne Clips Royals in Opener, 54–44," *Rochester Democrat and Chronicle*, March 13, 1946, 20.

29. Ben Tenny, "Can Pistons Take Two-Tilt Series Lead? Learn Answer Tonight?" *Fort Wayne News-Sentinel*, March 13, 1946, 11.

30. Elliot Cushing, "Royals Whip Zollners to Even Series, 58–52," *Rochester Democrat and Chronicle*, March 14, 1946, 22.

31. Cushing, "Royals Whip Zollners to Even Series."

32. Cushing, "Royals Whip Zollners to Even Series."

33. Elliott Cushing, "Royals Defeat Ft. Wayne for 2–1 Lead, 58–52," *Rochester Democrat and Chronicle*, March 16, 1946, 16.

34. Cushing, "Royals Defeat Ft. Wayne for 2–1 Lead."

35. Cushing, "Royals Defeat Ft. Wayne for 2–1 Lead."

36. Elliot Cushing, "Royals Win, 70–54; Gain Playoff Final," *Rochester Democrat and Chronicle*, March 17, 1946, 1C.

37. "Pistons Eye Pro Tourney as Their Comeback Chance," *Fort Wayne News-Sentinel*, March 18, 1946, 7.

38. Elliot Cushing, "Royals Humble Sheboygan in Opener, 60–50," *Rochester Democrat and Chronicle*, March 20, 1946, 20.

39. Nelson, *National Basketball League*, 144.

40. Elliot Cushing, "Royals Clip Sheboygan, 61–54, for 2–0 Lead," *Rochester Democrat and Chronicle*, March 22, 1946, 28.

41. Elliot Cushing, "Royals Rip 'Skins for League Title," *Rochester Democrat and Chronicle*, March 24, 1946, 19.

42. Elliot Cushing, "Royals Speed Lauded," *Rochester Democrat and Chronicle*, March 25, 1946, 20.

43. Cushing, "Royals Speed Lauded."

44. Ralph Kaplowitz, interview by the author, Queens NY, December 2007.

45. Kaplowitz interview.

46. Kaplowitz interview.

47. Robert Elmer, "SPHAS Whip Bullets, 70–46, to Force Playoff for Pro Cage Loop Title," *Baltimore Sun*, March 14, 1946, 15.

48. Robert Elmer, "Bullets Rally to Defeat SPHAS for Pro Basketball Tournament Title," *Baltimore Sun*, March 7, 1946, 18.

49. Robert Elmer, "Bullets and SPHAS Score Victories in Professional Basket Tourney," *Baltimore Sun*, March 6, 1946, 15

50. Elmer, "Bullets and SPHAS Score Victories in Professional Basket Tourney."

51. Robert Elmer, "Bullets Rally to Defeat SPHAS for Pro Basketball Tournament Title," *Baltimore Sun*, March 7, 1946, 18.

52. Robert Elmer, "Bullets Seek Title Tonight," *Baltimore Sun*, March 13, 1946, 14.

53. "Bullets Top SPHAS, 63–61, to Win Pro Cage Title," *Baltimore Sun*, March 17, 1946, Sports 1.

54. "Bullets Top SPHAS, 63–61."

55. "Bullets Top SPHAS, 63–61."

56. William J. Scheffer, "SPHAS Beat Bombers, 75–72, Gain Finals with Balti-more," *Philadelphia Inquirer*, April 24, 1946, 1S.

57. "Bullets Lose Playoff Game," *Baltimore Sun*, March 31, 1946, Sports, 1.

58. "Bullets Lose Playoff Game."

59. Robert Elmer, "Bullets Subdue SPHAS to Even Professional Basketball Playoff Series," *Baltimore Sun*, April 1, 1946, 14.

60. Elmer, "Bullets Subdue SPHAS."

61. "Baltimore Wins to Even Series," *Philadelphia Inquirer*, April 1, 1946, 25.

62. "Bullets Drub SPHAS, 68–45," *Baltimore Sun*, April 14, 1946, Sports 1.

63. William J. Scheffer, "Bullets Beat SPHAS, 68–45; Lead Playoff," *Philadelphia Inquirer*, April 14, 1946, 1S.

64. Robert Elmer, "Bullets Beat SPHAS, 54–39, for Pro Cage League Playoff Championship," *Baltimore Sun*, April 15, 1946, 16.

65. Letter from John J. O'Brien, February 27, 1945, ABL collection, Naismith Memorial Basketball Hall of Fame.

66. "World Cage 'Ceiling' Set," *Chicago Herald American*, February 3, 1946, 27.

67. Keith Brehm, "Announce World Cage Schedule," *Chicago Herald American*, March 13, 1946, 23.

68. "World Cage 'Ceiling' Set."

69. Keith Brehm, "World Cage Teams Bolstered by Vets," *Chicago Herald American*, March 18, 1946, 15.

70. Brehm, "World Cage Teams Bolstered by Vets."

71. Brehm, "World Cage Teams Bolstered by Vets."

72. Keith Brehm, "Pittsburgh, Cleveland in World Cage," *Chicago Herald American*, March 11, 1946, 14.

73. Keith Brehm, "Mikan Turns Pro: To Play in World Cage," *Chicago Herald American*, March 16, 1946, 14.

74. Triptow, *Dynasty That Never Was*, 47–48.

75. Triptow, *Dynasty That Never Was*, 150.

76. Triptow, *Dynasty That Never Was*, 40–41.

77. Brehm, "Mikan Turns Pro."

78. Brehm, "Mikan Turns Pro."

79. Keith Brehm, "'60-Grand' Mikan Set for World Cage Play," *Chicago Herald American*, March 17, 1946, 30.

80. Brehm, "'60-Grand' Mikan."

81. Brehm, "'60-Grand' Mikan."

82. Brehm, "Mikan Turns Pro."

83. George L. Mikan and Joseph Oberle, *Unstoppable: The Story of George Mikan, the First NBA Superstar* (Indianapolis IN: Masters Press, 1997), 68.

84. "Mikan—and the Rest!," *Chicago Herald American*, March 23, 1946, 14.

85. Keith Brehm, "World Cage Meet Opens Tomorrow," *Chicago Herald American*, March 24, 1946, 31.

86. Leo Fischer, "Gears, Dows, Chiefs Win World Cage," *Chicago Herald American*, March 26, 1946, 14.

87. Leo Fischer, "Sheboygan Tenth World Cage Entry," *Chicago Herald American*, March 12, 1946, 14.

88. Fischer, "Sheboygan Tenth World Cage Entry."

89. Fischer, "Sheboygan Tenth World Cage Entry."

90. Leo Fischer, "16,951 Cheer Gears in Cage Triumph," *Chicago Herald American*, March 30, 1946, 14.

91. Fischer, "16,951 Cheer Gears in Cage Triumph."

92. Leo Fischer, "Mikan Turns to Play in World Cage," *Chicago Herald American*, March 16, 1946, 14.

93. Keith Brehm, "Powerful Oshkosh Team in Cage Meet," *Chicago Herald American*, March 14, 1946, 20.

94. Leo Fischer, "Rens Enter World Cage," *Chicago Herald American*, March 3, 1946, 27.

95. Keith Brehm, "Resume Cage Tomorrow," *Chicago Herald American*, March 26, 1946, 14.

96. Leo Fischer, "H-A Classic Provides Many Thrills," *Chicago Herald American*, March 23, 1946, 14.

97. Cliff Jaffe, "Battle of Scorers Marks World Cage," *Chicago Herald American*, March 24, 1946, 22.

98. Leo Fischer, "Baltimore in Cage Meet," *Chicago Herald American*, March 10, 1946, 23.

99. Leo Fischer, "Dayton Bombers to Try Again for World Cage Title," *Chicago Herald American*, March 15, 1946, 15.

100. Leo Fischer, "Rens, Baltimore, Oshkosh Cage Victors," *Chicago Herald American*, March 28, 1946, 28.

101. Gould, *Pioneers of the Hardwood*, 133.

102. Gould, *Pioneers of the Hardwood*, 134.

103. Gould, *Pioneers of the Hardwood*, 134.

104. Gould, *Pioneers of the Hardwood*, 133.

105. Keith Brehm, "Of World Cage Play," *Chicago Herald American*, March 23, 1946, 23.

106. Fischer, "Gears, Dows, Chiefs Win in World Cage."

107. Fischer, "16,951 Cheer Gears in Cage Triumph."

108. Gould, *Pioneers of the Hardwood*, 134.

109. Gould, *Pioneers of the Hardwood*, 135.

110. Keith Brehm, "Dow Chemicals Out for World Cage Title Again," *Chicago Herald American*, March 7, 1946, 21.

111. Fischer, "Gears, Dows, Chiefs Win in World Cage."

112. Fischer, "16,951 Cheer Gears in Cage Triumph."

113. Mikan and Oberle, *Unstoppable*, 68–70.

114. Leo Fischer, "Fort Wayne, Oshkosh in World Cage Finals," *Chicago Herald American*, April 4, 1946, 20.

115. Michael Schumacher, *Mr. Basketball: George Mikan, the Minneapolis Lakers, and the Birth of the NBA* (New York: Bloomsbury, 2007), 70.

116. "It's Pistons vs. Oshkosh in Pro Finals," *Fort Wayne News-Sentinel*, April 4, 1946, 14.

117. "It's Pistons vs. Oshkosh in Pro Finals."

118. Leo Fischer, "Oshkosh near World Cage Title," *Chicago Herald American*, April 5, 1946, 15.

119. Ben Tenny, "Pistons Start Final Bid for Another Pro Net Crown Tonight," *Fort Wayne News-Sentinel*, April 5, 1946, 12.

120. Ben Tenny, "Pistons to Bid for World's Pro Net Championship," *Fort Wayne News-Sentinel*, April 8, 1946, 8.

121. Ben Tenny, "Zollner Pistons Retain World's Pro Basketball Championship," *Fort Wayne News-Sentinel*, April 9, 1946, 11.

122. Keith Brehm, "Fort Wayne, Ind., Zollner Pistons: World Professional Basketball Champions," *Chicago Stadium Review Eighth Annual World's Championship Basketball Tournament Official Program*, 6.

EPILOGUE

1. Charley Rosen, *The First Tip-Off: The Incredible Birth of the NBA* (New York: McGraw Hill, 2009), 182.

2. Phil Jasner, "Joe Fulks: NBA's 1st Superstar," *Philadelphia Daily News*, March 22, 1976, 61.

3. Rosen, *First Tip-Off*, 183.

4. Rosen, *First Tip-Off*, 184.

5. Rosen, *First Tip-Off*, 182.

6. Jasner, "Joe Fulks."

7. Rosen, *First Tip-Off*, 182.

8. Ray Kelly, "Jumping Joe Tells of Greatest Game as a Pro," n.d., clipping files, Naismith Memorial Basketball Hall of Fame.

9. Kelly, "Jumping Joe Tells of Greatest Game."

10. Kelly, "Jumping Joe Tells of Greatest Game."

11. Kelly, "Jumping Joe Tells of Greatest Game."

12. Kelly, "Jumping Joe Tells of Greatest Game."

13. Pop Gates interview, Robert Peterson Collection, Naismith Memorial Basketball Hall of Fame.

INDEX